HARNESS
the
DARKNESS

KATIA CHRISTIANA

Trilogy Christian Publishers
A Wholly Owned Subsidiary of Trinity Broadcasting Network
2442 Michelle Drive
Tustin, CA 92780

For information, address Trilogy Christian Publishing
Rights Department, 2442 Michelle Drive, Tustin, Ca 92780.
Trilogy Christian Publishing/ TBN and colophon are trademarks of Trinity Broadcasting Network.

For information about special discounts for bulk purchases, please contact Trilogy Christian Publishing.

Manufactured in the United States of America

10 9 8 7 6 5 4 3 2 1

Library of Congress Cataloging-in-Publication Data is available.

ISBN 978-1-64088-551-6 (Print Book)
ISBN 978-1-64088-552-3 (ebook)

DEDICATION

*M*ore than anything, I want this story to encourage all of the wounded spirits and shattered hearts, desperate for total acceptance. Our Heavenly Father wants to wholly heal and lavishly love you!

The Lord wanted His people to see
How great and glorious His law is,
He wanted to show them
That He always does what is right
Enemies have carried off everything…
They own
All of my people are trapped
In pits or hidden away
In prisons
They themselves have become like stolen
Goods
No one can save them
They have been carried off…and
There is no one who will say,
Send them back. (Isaiah 42:21–22)

CONTENTS

Chapter 1 7
Chapter 2 27
Chapter 3 47
Chapter 4 54
Chapter 5 67
Chapter 6 84
Chapter 7 89
Chapter 8 97
Chapter 9 114
Chapter 10 123
Chapter 11 133
Chapter 12 148
Chapter 13 153
Chapter 14 160
Chapter 15 167
Chapter 16 176
Chapter 17 185
Chapter 18 189
Chapter 19 204
Chapter 20 223
Chapter 21 239
Chapter 22 258
Chapter 23 271
Chapter 24 285

Acknowledgements 311
Works Cited 315

CHAPTER 1

Fearfully and wonderfully made
—Psalm 139:14

MY STORY

*T*his life for me... Well, let's put it this way: Do you remember the reaction of the woman professor of parapsychology in the movie *Poltergeist*? She and Carrie Ann's mom opened the door to her daughter's room to see the lamp and all the toys spinning and turning upside down.

The next scenes were shot in Robbie's room, with the lightning and thunder scaring the daylights out of the poor little guy.

Oh my gosh... Then there appeared that horrible, crazy-faced clown, smiling, with the music intensity screeching louder and louder as he appeared and disappeared and reappeared with that frightening and bizarre smile.

Then there was the long expanding hallway where Carrie Ann's mother walked faster and faster, not getting anywhere, running in place, desperately trying to get to her baby girl who was held hostage by the tyrannical entity.

But Carrie Ann's mom refused to give up, using all her strength after crying out, "God help me!" to crash through the door to come face to face with the monster creature, the Beast!

This life, for me, could be filmed symbolically as the movie *Poltergeist*. After I realized that my very own life had all the bizarre roller-coaster dips, climbs, herky-jerky twists, one-hundred-eighty-degree turns... I knew. Similarly, my journey has been chock-full of the riveting events that, at the very least, keep life from being boring... I knew. And because of my deep love for my real Heavenly Father... I knew. I knew I had to tell my unvarnished truth. It took some tough years, but eventually, I came into the light.

On several occasions, friends and family have encouraged me to put my story on paper, and up until now, I declined for a couple of reasons. My wavering self-esteem whispered to me, "You, Katia (Kah-tee-uh), are not skilled to take on something so challenging." In the back of my mind, I always wondered if I measured up... "*Who* do you think you are?" True, I have had quite a struggle with some things, but it isn't *who* I am, it's *whose* I am. Over my lifetime, I always ran to My Almighty Authority for *everything*. I have discovered, through my many trials and errors, that I have a rare opportunity to help all my brothers and sisters who have gone past or are right in the middle of similar catastrophic events. My decision was sealed in blood to tell of the betrayal, debauchery, adultery, rape, titillating occurrences, sacrilegious happenings, and finally the near death or final demise of loved ones.

So I have accepted the daunting task and therapeutic release to let you all into my twisted trilogy that almost took me down and the freaky environmental illness which just about sent me into the celestial cyberspace.

What you are about to embark upon is not for the judgmental or squeamish…but feel free to read on anyway. Most importantly, I know there would be no story, no life, no me without our Awesome Heavenly Father's divine intervention. I would not be holding this pen, breathing, or have a heartbeat had He not touched me. I found He keeps His promises and that we *are* "Fearfully and wonderfully made." His work is never shoddy (Psalm 139).

WILDFLOWER YEARS

The little cottage that I came home to fifty-something years ago was all white with cute gray shutters and a white wrought-iron fence in the front and neatly trimmed evergreen bushes around. It was serenely set on a side street with the kindest of neighbors. My dad kept up with any repairs on the house, and the grass was manicured regularly. Dad was a maintenance supervisor for the telephone company and knew how to fix anything. At the beginning of my life, I'd say both of my parents were pretty normal. Mom was seven years younger than Dad, but she managed to be a good little mom to both myself and my brother Skip, who was older by three years.

To me, my dad was the best "daddy" ever! Every time he came into my room after work, he'd scoop me up in his big arms, and I knew that nothing could hurt me. He was my protector, he was my playmate, and he was my daddy. We would cuddle. I could be sitting on my blanket on the floor playing, and if my daddy walked in the room and gave me his big loving smile, I'd crinkle up my little nose and grin with my big blue eyes shining like two blue diamonds. He was my daddy and I was his "*Wildflower*." He made up a song about wildflowers and sang it to me in tender moments. Shortly then, he'd take my arms and spin me around while picking me up and up onto the top of his comfy shoulders. We'd bounce all over the house like I was saddled on a pony. Mom and Dad got Skip and me our own hobby horses, and some family members told us that my dad helped to make them.

A couple of other wonderful memories of my baby years, now a toddler, were of Dad bringing out his old "Handy Andy Kit" from when he was a little guy. He'd let me carry it all over the house as he repaired things. Skip did not care to fix anything except cars. He was obsessed with cars! For Christmas, he received a big wheel that he could sit in and drive, and we have many pictures of him always in or around his big car. They became his biggest hobby later in life too. Jaguars were his all-time favorite vehicles.

I loved cats. We always had a few, and the mommas with their babies were my passion. Mom and Dad both preferred cats over dogs. Dad grew up on a huge farm with several barns, and out there were many cats with kittens. Needless to say, with my extreme love for all cats any size and any color, I was always more than ready to jump in Dad's car and go out to Grandma and Grandpa's fantastic farm! This wonderland place not only had several cats and twenty -plus kittens, but it also had two of the biggest, nicest plow horses to help plant and cut the hay. There were apple groves, peach trees, and my favorite, walnut trees. In the woods grew hundreds of rows of blackberries along with gorgeous sunflowers, buttercups, bluebells, and marigolds, which made the hillside look like a beautiful kaleidoscope.

The whole family, except for my mother, loved the farm. The most fun for me was gathering the eggs and then going right next to the barn to gather me up an armful of kittens!

My grandpa always said, "If you see the baby, she'll have an armful of kittens."

Dad would smile really big and comment, "That's my Wildflower." My dad always beamed when people would say I looked just like him. Mom had Italian and German blood in her, but most of her sisters and brothers looked more Italian than anything. I got the name Katia, and my brother was named Maxim Junior.

Conversely, Dad's parents were both German and Scandinavian. I got the blonde hair, light blue eyes, and very pale skin, just like my cousins on my dad's side. I look nothing like my mom at all. Skip and I resembled each other when we were babies. In fact, on our baby pictures, if you didn't see the clothing we were wearing, you could mistake him for me and vice-versa. One thing over the years that stayed the same was we kept the same smile. Mom was named Jezabella, and Dad and Skip had the same first name, Maxim. Skip's name was the same, thus resulting in the nickname. My name with Dad was always "Wildflower;" in fact, it was "*my* Wildflower." Both sides of our family were great!

To put it another way, the first three and a half years of my life with Dad and his side of the family were the best years a toddler could ever imagine! At the farm, Dad would plunk me on horses, which were my second favorite animals. Those marvelous, beautiful, and hard-working girls would carry my brother and me all over the fields. When I rode Molly, I looked like a peanut on top of a black mountain. I loved feeding Molly apples that Dad would lift me up to pick straight off of the tree. Molly was so sweet natured, and she'd wait to see me running to bring her an apple for that visit. She always seemed happy to see me coming. Molly would look down and lower her big strong head to my level as I'd be on my tip toes, arm outstretched, with her red juicy treat just under her nose. After she finished her apple, she got many gentle pats and strokes of love from me and she loved it. Grandpa Max, most of the time, would give me a sugar cube or two to hand her flat handed, and she would show us her approval by opening her lips wide enough that we'd see her teeth as if she were smiling back at me. To show that she liked all her treats, Molly nodded her head up and down as if to say, "Yes, this was good."

My mother and I started having problems. Well, maybe they were not problems for her; however, I had issues with mom. First of all, she hated the rural life and only felt comfortable in the city. Dad loved the country and wanted us all to move out by his brother and family on a few of Grandpa's acres near them. Mom's one older sister had a restaurant and saloon out by my grandparents, so we all tried to convince my mother to please move out to the beautiful and calm countryside. Besides all the topography, my cousins, two girls, were out there too. We all loved romping together with the baby calves and goats all over Grandpa's one hundred and fifteen acres! But my mother's feet were in cement, and she wasn't budging anywhere unless it was another place in the silly city. So with this wedge now between Mom, Dad, and me, she took a job at the school up the street to help make some money because she loved to buy clothes and knick-knacks and such. The church, nearby, also had a small school as part of the compound, and Mom secured a position as a kindergarten teacher. Now I was a bit younger than K-1, but the priest who was in charge allowed Mom to have me enter school early so she didn't have to get a babysitter. I wish she had sent me to Grandma, who had volunteered to keep me until Mom was out of school. Rats!

Unfortunately for me, the decision was made that I would be in my mother's K-1 class. The first couple of weeks of school weren't so bad. Mostly we drew things since art was one of my mother's favorite things to do. Nevertheless, something changed with my mom. She and Dad were starting to disagree a lot, and sadly, those arguments took place in front of Skip and me. Dad always loved a beer or two at night, but now, it seemed that he was getting more than usual out of the refrigerator. In the meantime, Mom and I rode to school together, and every day in her class was becoming harder and harder to bear. For example, I was talking to one of the other little gals behind me, but she was really doing all the talking. Of course, Mother saw this differently, and I was the one that she pulled up by my hand and marched off to be closed in the storage closet where the class sharpened their pencils. The strong, horrible smell of that sharpener about did me in! She left me in there for twenty minutes or so. I remember I had to gently tap my foot against the door so she would not forget to let me out. The worst part is it was very tiny and dark; I could not reach the light switch, so in the dark, claustrophobic environment, I cried quietly until my foot taps got her to open the door and let me out. Mom also made me sit high up on a stool with a clown hat if I chewed gum or something silly like that. The class would laugh and point at me, and my mother did nothing about it.

Remember the clown in the *Poltergeist* movie? Well, my mother collected clowns. I hated clowns! Still do. In our bedroom, Skip and I never remember having stuffed animals like other kids had; our mother bought us *clowns*. Did I tell you I hate clowns? I don't care if they are baby clowns or clowns that have cat heads, they are creepy and not cute to me! Since Mom and Dad were already at odds with one another, I kept what my mom did to me to myself until years later. My five-year-old mind wondered if Mom was mad at me because I was "Daddy's little girl." That year, Dad started drinking a bit more than usual, and my parents were at each other's throats over the smallest thing. I remember a couple of times when they were really yelling, Skip would run over to me holding his fingers in my ears and then back to his own ears. The hollering and cussing were really affecting him. On the other hand, I'd go outside and pick up my cats. With my blanket laid in the front grass, my cats and I would snuggle up until the noises in the house died down. Skip, being older, went a couple of doors down and played with the neighbor kids.

Some of the men from Dad's work would often come over to visit. Some were buddies from Dad's World War II or high school days, and many times, they would bring their kids over to play with Skip and me. Two of the families were Jewish, and Dad's favorite army buddy and his family were black. It didn't matter, we liked all races. I was raised attending church and always had the Holy Trinity teachings in school from the first grade on. Speaking of church stuff, my mom's boss got a huge job offer. He was to become the CEO of the only retreat center camp within one hundred fifty miles in any direction. He needed a secretary, so he offered *my mother* the job, but we all had to move on the other side of the river in a completely different county. Now Skip and I don't remember Mom and Dad *talking* specifically about this, but there was a lot of arguing about something, and then all of a sudden, the announcement was made. "We're moving!"

During the last couple of weeks at our old home I had to visit all my furry friends that lived in the neighborhood and, oh yeah, the families too. Sparky was Mrs. Englehart's part-Pitbull dog, and he was my buddy as long as I didn't have any kitties with me. I had many visits sitting in Mrs. Englehart's front lawn with Sparky licking all over my face. I was such a big animal lover, and animals seemed to know it. Case in point; everybody in the neighborhood exclaimed about how vicious Sparky was. In fact, he was known by every service person and had bitten the milkman, mailman, gas and electric man, etc. etc. Mrs. Englehart had been asked to remove him from her home. But any time Sparky saw me coming, he'd wag his tail wildly and whine like a puppy until I got through the fence to pet him and love him up. One particular day, my mother reminded me about when she could not find me and went around yelling, "Where's my little girl? Has anybody seen my baby?" Mind you, this dangerous dog had a reputation of being a Tasmanian devil! A couple of hours before Dad got home, Mom squealed, "Oh my God, she's in the yard with that beast!" There was Sparky growling at Mom to not come an inch closer while he kept licking my face. Mom said she "couldn't believe her eyes!" She said she could not get to me until she went all the way back home to call Mrs. Englehart to bring Sparky into her house. Then Mom was able to get me out of the yard. I noticed something though; my mom always seemed to lose track of me.

My parents purchased a new home in a completely different county when my mom took the job as a secretary with Father Quinton from my old school. I was enrolled with my brother in the parochial school system, and then Dad drove us all down the most beautiful street I had ever seen in my life. Suddenly, my eyes caught sight of a *golden palace* on a perfect lot of lush green grass lined with the same types of flowers that were up on Grandpa's farm. We pulled in the driveway, and I knew that I was at last home. What a house! It was tan brick with the biggest front porch I had ever seen in my life! The house faced a lovely wooded lot, and no other houses were on that side of the street; the privacy meshed with beauty impressed all four of us. Starting first grade was quite an experience for me.

The first morning of school was quite a traumatic memory for me and, I'm sure, for my mother also. The reason being, once again, she could not find me to drive me to the school. This was one of the worst days of my young life, because I found out how mean my mom could get. I'm sure my running down in the basement to hide behind the furnace, where dirt and cobwebs were, would have made any mother angry, no doubt. However, I discovered my mother had quite a list of curse words that I had never heard before this! I mean she was "livid" (one of the frequently used words she used to describe her feelings about my dad). She wailed on and screamed at me while she grabbed me by the top of my arm and roughly escorted me back up the steps. I almost fell several times, and she ended up dragging me because I wasn't going fast enough. It was the first devastating time I was called "no good." I missed the school bus and waited while I watched her angrily throw stuff around as she got ready to take me to school herself. She practically threw me in the car followed by my books and my lunch box. I think I was too shocked to cry, but the sad part is I wanted to get away from my mother and run to school, far away from her! Mom never said another word to me the whole way. Upon arrival, she only opened my door and just pointed the way. Happily, my elementary day went fine; however, a few of the nuns who taught me were old and cranky sometimes. A good thing is schools were no longer allowed to spank children; conversely, being forced to walk right past the principal's office every morning was a wakeup call. Most every day, some kid or two or three, were sitting in there, crying their eyes out. I really didn't want to know the reason why, but I sure as heck didn't want to be caught by Sister Attila the Hun (that was her nickname!) Need you ask why she was given that title? Her real name was Sister Aquila Hunter. No matter, either name, I did not want to ever end up in her dark and spooky office where the biggest scariest picture of a crucified person was on the wall... And it wasn't Jesus!

Meanwhile, back at home, neither my mother nor my father ever apologized for anything at any time—not to each other, not to Skip, and not to me. Mom and Dad would do something nice for you like make you a bologna-and-onion-roll sandwich. The only communication Skip and I can remember out of either parent was when they were mad at each other. There were no family meetings, no husband-and-wife discussions, and no kind conversations. Everyone just went through the motions with the same routine *until* I turned seven years old. This is when my dad started drinking more beer, because he and Mom were arguing. They had issues when Mom took the teaching job. Those days were very noisy with their bickering back and forth, and now it had started up again. Skip was really upset whenever Dad got on Mom, but worse to me was when Mom would scream back at Dad and would throw something to try to hit him! Dad and I did great in our new neighborhood together; we tossed balls, played basketball with Skip and, of course, the best game was "horse." All four of us would sit in the wonderful side yard and sunbathe, and on Sundays, we'd all get dressed up and go to church. Coming home, Dad would cook Sunday breakfast after we stopped to pick up a cherry meringue coffee cake to go along with the country sausage and sunny side up eggs. I never liked the taste of coffee—still don't. Another thing I don't like the taste of is beer; however, Skip did like it. Dad always gave me two drinks of his when we were on the porch after supper. I never refused Dad simply because he was Dad and I wanted to please him; we were still buddies. Without delay, when Dad called, "Wildflower, let's go" I'd flip my baseball cap backward, in my blue jeans wearing one of his big shirts, roll up my sleeves, toss a wad of gum in my mouth, and away we'd go. If I delayed in some way again, I would hear, "*Wildflower!*" and then he'd snap his fingers and start singing the wildflower song. My response would be to hurry and gallop like a pony toward him and end up with one big leap in his waiting arms.

My brother didn't appreciate sports the way I did… I loved to challenge the boys in our neighborhood with the good skills my dad taught me. There were a dozen boys my age and only two girls besides myself. Neither one of them was any good at sports, but I also loved to roller-skate. The two girls and I would take off at the top of the street next to us and skate from the top all the way to the bottom. Now, this road was so steep that people had to put some vehicles in four-wheel drive to get up it in the winter. Mary Jo, Patty, and I would take off all at the same time and coast down, zigzagging side by side to the bottom.

Life was good, and for several months, it seemed they had a truce between them. They even sat in the same rooms together and read the newspaper or would sit out on the front porch. Dad's favorite subject was baseball. He even used baseball terminology when he described someone's success. For instance, if they did well he would say, "They hit a homerun." Sometimes, he might talk like someone "struck out" or they hit a "foul ball." Mom hated sports; in fact, I can't think of one thing either one of them had in common. Mom's boss increased her hours. This did not make my father very happy because Skip and I would be alone two hours after school. I could not put my finger on it, but there was a rumbling current of stormy clouds creeping in over all of us. In my eighth year of life, Father Quinton, Mom's boss, was really irritating my father. Dad was barely handling my mom working at all, and now this! Thus, the bigger arguments started up *all over again*—our home was no longer a home of any peace. Dad started drinking heavily now, and the yelling and the shoving of each other was frightening Skip and me. It was especially nerve-racking to Skip. Even though he was a good-sized guy, he was very gentle in nature and known to be easy going. For this reason, my brother signed up for every club and after-school activity there was. He was voted class vice president, he was a cub scout, and he even went to Mom to see if there was some job he could do at the camp where Mom was a secretary. Skip was now eleven years old, so Father Quinton said that he could become a stable boy and help with the horses the camp had for riding the trails. For some reason, this too made my dad very angry. I didn't understand why Dad was constantly getting upset...but I know this—I hated it!

MORE PET NAMES

My grandpa Maxim and Dad were named the same. However, Mom did not want a third generation "Maxim." She skipped it, thus my brother was given his nickname, "Skip." He was never called anything else. I think he even put "Skip" on his driver license.

My name Katia was changed too. My nickname became "Kitt" because I love cats so much. As a toddler on, my family always had a minimum of three cats. Usually, they were not spayed females, so we always had six or seven kittens beside that. I just *love kittens*, they are the most adorable "baby creatures" that were ever created. The entire family knew that, if you saw little me, I always had at least one kitten, usually two, wrapped in my arms, so I inherited the name Kitt. My friends also knew of my love for felines too. I especially loved the big cats out in wildlife and, of course, their "Kitts." Leopards fascinated me, and tigers are awesome! Lisa Bevere loved the *big* cats too; you need to read her book, *Lioness*; it is excellent.

MERRYLAND

Mom was told that not only could Skip work at the camp and earn some money, but I was allowed to ride with Mom in the summer when school was out and play on the camp playground. This made me very happy; I loved Camp Merryland! Skip and I both loved retro stuff. My hobby was watching old Disney movies. One of my favorite actresses was Haley Mills; I dearly loved all her films. Skip watched her too. I think he had a crush on her, but he always said I acted like Haley when I would crinkle up my nose and use my finger to push up the heavy, too-big glasses that I loved to wear.

Skip left home to move out to the camp all summer long with the horse crew. I still had to come home afternoons with Mom to an angry father who drank too many beers. I determined that my brother was the "lucky" one. I went to my mother to see if she would ask Father Quinton if there was any job he could give to me too. Father Quinton said that I could help make copies of the camp brochures that they mailed out to all the businesses, churches, and schools to advertise for the camping season. At the ripe age of nine, I made fifty dollars per week working in the camp copy and mail room. Other family on Mom's side had positions working at various areas all over the camp and retreat lodge. There were a hundred apartments at the retreat center, and my grandma, who was Mom's mother, cleaned rooms and made beds. My grandpa worked with Father Quinton and Dad on the shrubs and bushes and became a gardener and groundskeeper. My uncle Gino got a job heading the maintenance crew. Aunt Louise had two jobs. First, she sold religious items in the shop. Aunt Louise's other position was the best, and I was going to receive a promotion that enabled me to work with her in the neatest place of all—the grill! The grill had every kind of candy bar, snack chips, hot fudge sundaes, malts, ice cream cones and, later, even had hot dogs, hamburgers, and cotton candy. I got to meet every person involved.

The grill also had soft drinks, chocolate milk, popcorn, and nachos! Now this was a *job*. I loved coming to work and fixing all the stuff and punching the campers and counselors' canteen cards. There was only one drawback… Aunt Louise was Mom's older sister. Like my mom, she had an attitude. In fact, with her long face and never-ending nose that could easily have a wart at the end of it, she pointed her spider-like fingers here, there, and everywhere to get me hopping and keep me jumping at her commands. Even my mother told me she tried to boss her all around most of her life.

Skip took care of the horses with Uncle Cory. Despite Aunt Louise always getting on to any of us who worked for her, still, I had a great time for three summers serving all my friends at the Canteen N' Grill.

On the negative side at home with my parents, things were not going well at all. In fact, do you remember when I talked about the clouds becoming darker? Well, at this point, darkness was hovering like a gray tarp over our house. Mom and Dad could hardly be in the same room without one of them starting a fight. With Skip and I both working at the camp, Mom decided to invite Father Quinton down to our house for supper one night a week. The problem was that she left work early those days to go shop and prepare gourmet meals for Father Quinton, and we all noticed she never did anything this extravagant for us. Dad was the one who noticed it first. Mom was a good cook; however, she picked up Rock Cornish game and Lobster Newberg to cook, plus she spent hours preparing it all for Father Quinton. I never thought a thing about it, but Skip ate fast and excused himself, and so did my father. He went in to read the paper in his favorite lazy boy. During the school year, Skip and I did have to do our homework; however, why didn't Dad stay and talk at the table with Mom and Father Quinton after the meal? Father Quinton was our boss, so where did Skip and Dad go and why? I stayed with them for a while, and later, they asked me to accompany them to go to the movies. Over time, Father Quinton took us to see *The Ten Commandments*, *The Song of Bernadette*, and *The Greatest Story Ever Told*. They were mostly religious films at first; at the crucifixion scene, I threw up all over the theater...

After a supper night with Father Quinton, Mom and Dad would get into the worst arguments. These battles were not just verbal: very quickly, they had resorted to slapping at each other. There was always tension between the two of them ever since Mom worked out of the home. I just couldn't see why, because Father Quinton was always so nice to all of us. He had a gift for all of us when he came too. I thought he was a very good priest and he helped out my relatives and gave them all jobs.

The nights we all had supper together, Dad drank a lot more too, and then he'd excuse himself from the table and go up to bed. Father Quinton would leave after Mom made sure he took all the extra food she made with him. This was the same routine, including the drinking and the fights, for three years. Skip was never home. Between school, extracurricular activities, and camp work, he was rarely ever home.

By the time that I was seven, Dad was belligerent, drinking, and just plain mean to all of us. However, right after work, he and I many times went outdoors to play horse or toss, but nothing was really like it used to be. Father Quinton loved dogs, and he wanted us to take one that a friend of his was giving away. Father Quinton said the dog was very special. We had to wait a few months as the man had some plans that he had to firm up first. Skip and I begged Dad to let us have the dog, and he agreed, but not before letting me know I was too rambunctious and that I would never let up. These things seemed to irritate him.

Merryland was where I could run and play to get my high-spirited energy released. What a great escape routine! Regularly, from age three on, another escape plan was intact. Dad still had Skip come home Saturdays so we all could spend the day at Grandpa's farm. We didn't know it, but apparently, there was no love lost between Grandma and Mom. So many times I remember Mom came up with some excuse not to go to the farm with us, and sometimes, it was just Skip, Dad, and me. After we spent the whole day helping Grandpa feed the chickens and after Grandma and I had gathered eggs, Dad took me to the barn, and I got to milk the cows and play with the young calves. That was fifty times better than playing with dumb ol' dolls. The adventuresome routine was a great escape from the turbulent storms at home; Mom and Dad were not on the same property. So there was peace, fun, and animals. Dad was very different at the farm

Of course, Molly was always there, and brushing her and feeding her treats was the highlight of my day. Dad, until I got old enough to mount up on her myself, would hoist me up and plop me on top of her back. Grandpa didn't have saddles because Pat and Molly were work horses, so I learned to ride bareback. Do you know, because Grandpa Max took such good care of both of them, the girls lived to be thirty years old! Grandma always had cold meals with lunch meat and salads. However, at night, we'd all gather around the dining room table, and Grandma brought out a treat. First of all, they made their own homemade ice cream, which was fabulous! Then Grandma had these big soda-fountain-type glasses, and they were huge parfait crystal goblets. She then plopped three delicious scoops of ice cream half of the way up and then poured an icy cold Coca-Cola over the glass of ice cream. These scrumptious concoctions were called "black cows." I've eaten potato chips all my life, but Grandma's always were so fresh and crisp. We all just loved the combination of the night "special." For thirty years, I remember the same cozy and welcoming routine. Later in life, when we had our own families, we would continue the family tradition with all of our loved ones also. Right now, I smile and tear up thinking about these untouchable times. Nothing compared.

My mother had her own agenda brewing on the home front. Father Quinton started bringing us all very expensive items. He left no one out with the large appliances—new couch, big screen TV, and new side-by-side refrigerator. Father Quinton, a priest, got good deals with all the business merchants who may have wanted to take their families camping. Father Quinton was known to wheel and deal with the best of them. He never missed any occasion to give us presents on birthdays or Christmas. We, in turn, would do the same for him. Even Dad was fine with the gifts and kindness. The presents we received were name brands too, which my brother and I both loved. Dad even hung around a little after the meals. Father Quinton also took the whole family on trips for vacation. With him, we got to see the mountains, the beaches, places like Florida, The Smoky Mountains, lovely rivers, ghost towns, monuments, and historical landmark cities and towns. Father Quinton opened up a whole new world to all of us, and I enjoyed it immensely. My mother got the travel bug, and this was to become a source of problems between Mom and Dad again, because it involved her job and Father Quinton.

Out at the camp, Skip was experiencing all kinds of exciting adventures, and Father Quinton was his coach and teacher. Skip's extreme love of, and interest in horses, landed Skip a promotion to be a horseback riding instructor. I was so proud of him; I knew he had wanted to secure that job for the longest time. Skip also became Father Quinton's errand boy, though Father Quinton had to do the driving; after all, Skip was only fourteen years old.

Father Quinton taught Skip and me how to swim, boat, ride horses with saddles, trap animals safely, drive a car, and shoot a rifle at skeets. I'd never shoot an animal; however, both Skip and I could shoot with just about any firearm and could do so like a marksman. Skip was also a part-time boy's camp counselor after he gave riding lessons. I, on the other hand, was still working under the tyrannical service of Aunt Louise, and she was forty-six and pregnant! Father Quinton gave me some wonderful news also... I was going to be in charge of feeding and taking care of the new wildlife center, where campers would learn about animals indigenous to our area. He knew how much I loved all of God's creatures!

Our great big backyard was a perfect place to fence in a really nice dog run for our new puppy. Skip and I loved our backyard best of all, with its rolling gentle hills spotted with large and lush oak and elm trees. One of the strong branches was the home for our huge tire swing that Dad put up for us. The very terrific thing for me was that, at the end of our property, down at the bottom of the last hill, bubbled the prettiest stream full of minnows, salamanders, and crawdads. For a tomboy like me, that was better than the beach! I spent many happy and fun-filled days down at the creek with my shoes off, wading in the clear and welcoming brook. Sometimes, after a big fight between Mom and Dad, I'd run down the hill full speed to calm my confused mind. I am one who believes that getting back to nature is what we are supposed to do. Escaping from the turmoil and yelling out the windows was my crucial quiet space. Seemingly, many times, just sitting on a big rock and listening to the water gently bubble and flow was very comforting and soothing.

CHAPTER 2

Yet man is born unto trouble.

—Job 5:7

NOT SO MERRYLAND

*A*round the age of eight for me and eleven for Skip, all hell broke loose! Skip's escape and comfort obviously was Camp Merryland...and I think I was a bit jealous that he got to live there and I couldn't! Nevertheless, since I adored my older brother, I was happy that at least one of us escaped the noise pollution of the battles at home. Ever since Father Quinton came to dinner, my dad became meaner to my brother and me. I sure hoped he wouldn't change his mind and not allow us to get the Irish-Setter pup. Dad had not started the fence yet; still, Father Quinton volunteered to help him build it. With Dad's sour attitude toward Father Quinton, I was worried that he'd pull the rug out from underneath the whole new dog notion. The next night that Father Quinton came to dinner, Dad did his famous disappearing act after he ate his last morsel. Right after Father Quinton left, Dad went in where Mom was putting dishes in the dishwasher, and I heard him say, "I don't want your boss to come to *my* home for supper anymore." Mom screamed back at Dad with rage that he had no right telling her who she could and couldn't have at *her* house for *any* reason. She further retorted that it was none of his business, because Dad did not pay for the food. Well, one thing led to another, and before long, Dad slapped Mom, and she jumped right back in front of Dad and clawed his arms with her nails; she had drawn blood! Skip, conveniently, was gone, and *I didn't know what to do!* That was all it took. Dad took hold of her, and I couldn't handle the sounds of the repeated slaps that Mom withstood… It was horrible! Then Dad's arms had streaks of blood streaming down them… Oh gosh, it was awful! I wanted to call somebody, but there was no time, so I tried to block Mom from being hit, and I hopped on Dad's back all the while crying and begging for them to "please stop it!"

Finally, I clasped my hands together to pray and pleaded with my daddy to leave Mom alone! Mom was only five feet, one inch, stout, and not very agile, so of course I didn't want Dad to harm her. Similarly, I did not want my mom to draw blood on my dad either. It was such a mess! After what seemed like hours, they shoved each other one last time, and Dad went upstairs to the bathroom to wash off his arms and spray Bactine on his wounds. Meanwhile, I followed Mom down to the basement because she said there was wash to be done. Mom would very seldom cry after these fights. Her face would be blood red, and her eye, or both eyes, swollen, and she just stayed angry, even with me. After she put the wash in, Mom sat in semi-darkness near a little phone and table by the pillar in the corner, almost completely hidden. She'd always call Father Quinton and whispered while she spoke very quickly. *Click* went the receiver, and she came over to the washer and spoke to me as if what I had just horrifyingly witnessed never happened! Astonishingly, instead of either one of them sleeping on the couch, Mom would trudge up with an armful of clothes that she had washed and vanish into the master bedroom. Mom and Dad never ever closed their door… I know because my bedroom was directly across the hall maybe nine feet from theirs. Anyone could look in and see that they always slept back to back but in the same regular-size bed. As I said, Mom was little, but Dad was six-foot-four and two hundred twenty pounds. Skip and I would have to cover our eyes when we had to use the bathroom. Sometimes Dad would be stark naked coming out to walk to their bedroom after a shower. We only had one tub and shower on the second floor until Skip turned sixteen! Father Quinton, please forget the fluff stuff—get Mom a second bathroom!

Besides all the animals which lived in the woods that we humanely trapped to put in the wildlife center, Father Quinton went out and purchased a miniature monkey, a baby deer that turned out to be blind and adorable, de-scented skunks, two snakes, five guinea pigs, three baby goats, a black lamb, two peacocks, and two Shetland ponies. All in all, I took care of thirty-eight different animals. Within a couple of camp seasons, we expanded to a petting zoo also. Merryland became my home just like it did for my brother. It always seemed that the sun shined much brighter when we were out at Merryland! Father Quinton wanted to advertise for Camp Merryland, and he had the idea to put me on the front page of the state newspaper. He asked Mom and she said okay. I was photographed feeding a baby deer with a baby bottle. The rest of my family members were pictured at various activities they did too. Skip was shot riding a horse, Uncle Gino was filmed on a bulldozer, etc. Father Quinton even had Mom and Dad both sitting in redwood deck chairs close to the lake.

Father Quinton took Skip and me under his wing and wanted us to try all kinds of things to see what interests we had and where our true talents were. He was quickly becoming like a second father to us. From the time Skip was seven and I was four, he showed us adventure and excitement. I especially liked many of the daredevil stunts that Father Quinton enjoyed. He loved the water so he water skied, jumped horses over barrels, raced speed boats, bobsledded, ice skated, drove cattle by horseback, maneuvered heavy equipment like bulldozers, bush hogs and steam rollers... Come to think of it, he'd try anything. He even talked about skydiving, but my mom pitched a fit about that one, so he declined when the time came to sign up for it.

As has been noted, my dad had problems with Father Quinton and his heavy involvement with Mom. Now, Dad was starting to have issues with Skip and my absence at the house and our lack of help with the chores. This was another bone of contention with Dad against us. Mom stuck up for us and got into an argument to push for Skip and me to live out at the camp at least during the summers. We worked a compromise that we would take turns coming home every other weekend to help with household jobs.

What was really amazing about both of our parents was that they would get into terrible knock-down-drag-out fights, but the next morning at breakfast, you'd never know that there had even been a disagreement! It was as if you stepped into "the outer limits," where the atmosphere was polar opposite of what occurred the night before. If an outsider walked into our kitchen, they would observe Mom scurrying to make sure we all had what we needed to eat for breakfast while she was singing some romantic love movie score and Dad hummed or whistled aloud with her... Eerie.

Similarly, in *Poltergeist*, the in-between scenes were calm and serene...

BIG RED

The day finally came when Father Quinton brought the puppy we all talked about a couple of months prior. He was such a large reddish pup that I wanted to call him Big Red. Everybody liked it, so that was it. He was four months old, and he looked like he was full grown. For me, it was love at first lick. Big Red followed Skip and me everywhere, and now I didn't want to go back to Merryland as much. I asked if I could go part-time because Red came to us during the school year. Each morning, as I got ready for school, Red was always by my side. Mom would watch as Red walked me to the bus stop, and when she saw the bus coming up the hill, she'd call Big Red back in the house. By the way, Dad liked Red so much that he allowed him to stay right in the house with us! We got Red while I was six years old, and we had him about five years. He loved to play ball, so when I went a few doors down to play softball with all the neighbor kids, Red followed. We were constantly together.

Dad loved him so much that, with company, Big Red laid right by Dad. My dad had his same old army buddies come to visit him. Whenever they came they all drink beer, but Dad always got wasted and had to go to bed early. My dad and at least two of the other men were in the battle at Normandy Beach. Mom found out somehow why my dad drank more when these guys all got together but refused to tell anyone in her family. After so much heartache and pain suffered at Dad's hands, one of the men took Mom aside and told her what job Dad had in the Battle of the Bulge. My father and another man had to drive behind the ambulances and pick up the remains of the body parts that had been blown off the dead soldiers! So my poor dad suffered from Post-Traumatic Stress Disorder; no wonder my dad was irritable and drank all the time. However; why didn't my mom tell anybody to get him help? I always wondered if she told Father Quinton. Probably not; my mom was secretive about lots of stuff. Under all those circumstances though, life was really difficult, and you never knew what to expect. The only consistent thing was Mom and Dad fought at least two to three times a week, maybe more, during most of my childhood.

An extremely sorrow-filled happening occurred that involved Big Red. One fall morning, he was by my side as we were walking across the street. Instantly, I looked up and saw my school bus barreling up the street, and Red ran fast to chase a squirrel, and the stupid bus driver ran into him! The big powerful bus knocked my big beautiful dog up into the air, and he landed hard on the blacktop. My heart sank. I went spastic and went after that idiot bus driver... How could he not see Red? The jerk, I hated him! I was crying so hard, my mom running toward me could not contain me. I pulled away and tried to help Red, who was half yelping and half whining so horribly... Red was dying, and there was nothing I could do. I screamed for Mom to call Father Quinton... She must have, because while I tugged at Red to drag him on my lap, Mom's boss and my friend drove screeching up. He flew out of his car and tried to cradle both me and Red in his arms... I wouldn't let go of Big Red. He was my best buddy, my companion, and I needed him. Father Quinton tenderly picked up my big, beautiful, bloody puppy with me, still holding on to his fur, and he was placed on the back seat on a blanket Father Quinton had already prepared for him. Red stayed alive for a few minutes, and I let out a wailing scream. "Oh, Big Red, please don't die!" Within a few minutes, Red took one deep final breath and then expired. Part of me died with him too. I lay in my front grass and sobbed and sobbed. Mom was on the school bus helping to keep the other kids calm. Father Quinton found out by getting next to the bus driver that he had been drinking... He said he smelled of alcohol. There was no comforting me, and I sure wasn't going to go on that terrible bus with that drunken killer bus driver either!

Father Quinton promised he'd bury Big Red out on his land not far from Merryland. Placing Red at Merryland itself may not have been good, because I didn't want sadness out there. Merryland was the only place that I felt good all the time. Having my dead dog with us would be far too sad. So Father Quinton buried Red on his own personal farm. Now I wanted to spend time out at Merryland. Father Quinton said that Skip and I were welcome anytime for as long as we wanted to stay there. On Christmas break, I went out with Mom and ice skated on the frozen lake. My cousin Buck had his pony, Little Charlie, at the horse stables. Skip took care of him along with several others that didn't get boarded to families to care for them and ride them until spring. Little Charlie was harnessed up to a sleigh he pulled, and I rode in it all over the campgrounds. Cats and other animals have always been a comfort to me when I was hurting. Since Big Red's tragic death, I have needed my cats and other animals around for solace. Red was my first experience of loss.

I grieved for months, but a few months later, Father Quinton came to the house for his usual weekly gourmet banquet. He showed up a lot earlier to announce that he had a pair of the most lovable Basset Hounds. They were also four months old and they needed a good home. Father

Quinton wanted Dad to help him build a dog run to get ready for the puppies.

OTTO AND OLLIE

It was very strange for Father Quinton and Dad to work side by side. Even though we all knew that Dad really had a problem with his influence over mother, they'd stay nice and friendly doing projects together. Father Quinton liked all animals and made sure they were well taken care of; Dad too was practical about pets. I, on the other hand, got gushy over cats and puppies! I was really looking forward to these new little Basset Hounds coming here. Mom was the one who made the comment that she loved their sad eyes and droopy ears. So Father Quinton found just what Mom wanted. Mom was also given the task of naming the pups. She named the girl Ollie and the boy Otto. Arrival day was exciting; the dog pen was huge, and they had lots of lush green grass to roll in. Rather than make the run square, Dad made it long and halfway down to the stream in the backyard. The season was fall; in fact, they came to us right around my birthday. All three of us had birthdays in fall or winter. Skip was still out at camp during part of the school year. However, he did come home to greet the dogs…and just like the rest of us, he loved them… They were so cute! Their ears, when they were standing, almost touched the ground; their beautiful, shining coats were tri-colored and healthy looking. Ollie barely had teeth an inch long yet, and their big feet were adorable. Father Quinton did well. The whole family came together to play with them and to buy them toys, balls, blankets, and give them love.

No Way Max

Our mother could be very nasty. Remember, Aunt Louise was her sister! The animosity between Mom and Dad was still very obvious; the truth was they did not agree on anything. Their fights escalated and, even when they weren't physically attacking one another, the tension was like a thick dark blanket over the atmosphere. Dad and I had a huge falling out when I was about twelve years old. This involved our two dogs that were now kept outdoors most of the time. My father said that Basset Hounds are just a little different than Beagles or hunting dogs, so outside was just fine for them. I took them on walks all the time, and therefore, I know they got plenty of exercise. On the flip side, winter was another story, and this was the first winter the pups were to be out in the cold and snow. Needless to say, me being the major animal lover that I was (and still am!), I protested very strongly against this injustice! Winter can be pretty brutal in the north. The next step was to catch Dad in a good mood, which was getting less and less possible. The day came when I asked him. Dad had this mentality of saying "yes" or "no" depending on whether Skip or I had gotten into any trouble or had been disobedient throughout the week. The stance would be yes if our records were clean only. If you didn't break any rules, your week could go well; on the other hand, you could feel you walked through hell! Dad's decision was thumbs down. I must have messed up somewhere. Well, I had made up my mind that my pups were not going to suffer out in the cold night. Dad's last comment was that he put extra hay in their dog houses, but they probably would huddle together in one anyway. *Probably* was not good enough for me though. The news and weather channel predicted twenty degrees with sleet...so no way I was going to allow my dogs to be subjected to those kinds of conditions. There was no "perfect behavior" gauge that was to determine Otto and Ollie's fate!

The cold winds were howling... I was gearing up to rescue my dogs without Dad finding out. I waited until both parents were in bed. I checked where he was when I activated my plan to get a flashlight and head down the hill to leash up those sweet babies. It was really pretty easy to go out in the cold because, all of our lives, Skip and I were told to go outside in the sub twenty-degree temps and stay outside until we had rosy cheeks. It was more army junk. Dad said we'd stay healthy and keep our resistance up, whatever that meant. To launch my maneuvers, I bundled up and grabbed the pup's leashes, and down I went with my flashlight lighting the way to the dog pen. When I got there, sadly, they were shivering, so I put on their leashes, and together, we trudged back up the hill. The ice had not hit yet, thank goodness! We got to the huge non-electric garage door that I had left unlocked after supper. The door weighed at least fifty pounds, and I pulled and kept pulling and finally managed to push it all the way up. Both dogs had their tails wagging when they felt the warmth of the inside. I tugged over an old quilt from the wash pile on the floor and bedded down the dogs by the furnace. They would be nice and toasty there. As I was taking off their leashes, I was suddenly startled when I heard *click!* Instantly, the basement bulb lit up! Oh no! Dad! Yikes! I slowly brought my head up to see his bigger-than-usual figure looming at the top of the steps, and there was rage in his eyes. He made some mumbled comment about those "damn dogs" and "pushy priest," and he quickly walked down the steps. I stood without budging with my arms crossed, shielding the two shaking pups. I was angry and ready to protect my puppies. At the last step, he tried to reach and slap me in my face, so I quickly ducked, and all of a sudden, he slipped off the landing and went tumbling off the three last steps! He went face down! Oh dear God, of course I ran over to see if he was all right. As I tried to help him get back up, he looked up from the floor and whispered with his chin and nose slightly bleeding, "What the hell, Wildflower?" He had been drinking, and between that and the wind being knocked out of him, he simply worked at trying to raise himself and turned around without another word and found his way upstairs. I went over to the pups (who were being very good), rolling as if to say, "Rub our bellies and stay with us for a while," which I did. After that night, my dad never had a problem with me bringing those dogs, nor any other pets we had, into the garage when it got below fifty degrees! I never told anyone what happened that night, and I wouldn't doubt Dad did the same. He and I both knew that someone was watching over the pups and me that night! My father never gave me another problem on comforting our pets.

FATHER QUINTON IS EVERYWHERE

Father Quinton, on the other hand, was quickly becoming the most prosperous and popular priest in the area. Father Quinton was making hand over fist money for the church, and they were extremely pleased with his continued success. He was photographed constantly in all the business magazines, and story after story was being printed about him. He was a mover and a shaker, and nothing was going to stop this advertisement for the retreat compound and Camp Merryland. People were flocking to both facilities, and Father Quinton just kept raking in the money and donations for the church. Local businesses were very generous when tax season came around; many of the furniture, appliances, and electronic stores donated free stuff to both places too.

Further, since Father Quinton was my whole family's boss, he was invited to all of our family holidays, picnics, reunions, wedding, and funerals. Mom not only had him over once a week for dinner, but she also made him meals to take home. Mom was always cooking on the weekends for Father Quinton. She wanted him to have three to four meals of hers, especially in the winter, when the cooking staff was away. The camp was closed for fall and winter. Unless Father Quinton could scarf up something, he had to pick up a carry out or eat a TV dinner, which was popular back then.

Father Quinton and Mom started to invite me to go to lunch with them at some really nice public community restaurants. Dad found out that I was going with Father Quinton and Mom, which did not make him happy. However, Father Quinton had been nothing but kind and respectful to my brother and me; he had become very close to us. In fact, I was driving the camp vehicle at age fourteen and I crashed into the Merryland entrance pillar. I did not go to my dad; I went straight to Father Quinton. He just laughed and said, "We'll fix it." Skip was hardly ever home. Father Quinton had given him all kinds of extra jobs and personal errands to do for him.

CAMP VS. HOME

At the camp, Father Quinton had all kinds of improvements planned. He purchased another hundred acres from the neighboring farm and was opening the camp to all denominations. It was not just boys and girls camp, it had become a family camp, and the groups of relatives loved this too! Seven more log cabins were built, with the two lakes in the middle. More activities came about such as ping pong, shuffleboard, an Indian village, counselor stunt programs, a cinema, big bonfire, camper stunt night, and the big Olympic-sized pool that had lifeguards giving professional swimming and diving lessons. Here's where I came in. I had gotten my junior lifesaving certificate after attending swimming lessons at my high school. Father Quinton made me a junior lifeguard at the age of fourteen, and this is one job I absolutely loved! The guys and gals that were the really "cool counselors" were the senior guards…and I got to be right in there with them every morning and every night because the pool had gorgeous underwater lighting. I finally got to put that white sunscreen on my nose and sit high up on the platform in the lifeguard chair like all the big guys did. So cool!

Uncle Gino was hired to bring his band out and play music. The families loved him, and Aunt Bev could come and listen too. The boys were always out at the camp now all summer. They always wanted to hang out with me, especially now that I had the neatest job up at the pool. Uncle Gino got roped into playing music for the square dances where, quite honestly, I had a blast!

In the meantime, Dad was not happy at all on the home front. All this hoopla about Father Quinton was really getting him down. Father Quinton was still coming one afternoon a week for supper, usually Saturday night, and by now, he brought along company. I guess he was of the mindset that there was power in numbers, so he brought another priest friend from the church with him. Of course, Mom was in her glory flitting around with hors d'oeuvres and fancy tiny plates with tiny forks with designs on the handles and those cute napkins… These were my father's thoughts after everyone left. I kind of felt sorry for him, but I still didn't understand why he was angry every time Father Quinton and his guests would leave. One thing that was crystal clear: there was always an argument and a big fight with lots of screaming and threats on both sides! Please, God, let me live at Merryland all year round... I can't take the battles! Father Quinton was invited to more weddings, funerals, picnics, and family reunions, parties, Christmas, and more... Dad drank heavily!

Father Quinton did not seem to pay any attention to Dad's disdain for him. Many times, I was the only one left at the house to reap Dad's unending wrath! Mom and Father Quinton were out of town even more now; my mother was given the title of "executive secretary." Mom was given a large clothing allowance to go out and buy even more expensive garments to wear on her trips with the group. Mom was really enjoying all the fuss; she was always into excitement and glory, so this was right up her alley.

Regarding alleys, from the age of eight to eighteen years old, I would have been better off with the boogie man in a dark alley rather than the way my father was tormenting me now. I no longer felt safe around him, and sleeping in my own bed was very uncomfortable to me... Not because it wasn't soft, but because my father was lurking outside my door. Skip literally made himself more than scarce. I was still under driving age, so I was at the mercy of my father's moods. When Mom was away and Skip was gone, I almost panicked! I tried to keep out of Dad's way, but it always seemed the more I tried that... Dad wanted to talk or do projects together. Five years ago, I would have jumped at the chance to spend time with my dad. Not anymore; he was someone I didn't recognize as my dad. Coming in my bedroom and invading my privacy did it in for me... I was finished! All I wanted was to go to Merryland to be with

Aunt Bev, Mack, Sam, and Byron; I missed them and all the years of fun. The school year sucked with Mom gallivanting all over who knows where, Skip running away from the turmoil…and stuck me with Dad sucked again.

Just being at home with him was unnerving. I had to take the school bus to class, and even during the winter, I brought my swimming suit for indoor lifesaving lessons in fourth period. I liked school very much, simply because the extracurricular activities were awesome. After lunch, we could bowl at the bowling alley right next to the lunchroom. I learned that English, specifically literature, was my all-time favorite class! I always got straight As in that, and I loved being able to get lost in the wonderful stories and biographies. Skip had to come home sometime, and I always felt so much better when he was around. We'd eat supper, and I'd usually do the dishes. No dishwasher working; I had to do them in the sink. Skip's job was to always feed the dogs. He would sneak and use the *electric* can opener that Mom said to keep for *people food only*. I never said a word. Skip was always such a character. Everybody loved him, and he was known as a class clown, but he still was voted to class vice president and most popular guy. Let's face it, my brother was a fantastic person, and I loved him dearly. On dish-dog food night, we played a game of "sting" with the dish towel. He was so much better than me with the towel, and unfortunately my bare legs, when in shorts, were stung several times versus the one or two time I got him, and he only wore jeans. Anyway, if I could get my brother to be home, it was a welcome notion with me—even if I had to endure the pain of the dish towel. I adored my big brother. At Merryland, we'd saddle up our horses and ride all over the camp and the woods together, and for that stint of time, we forgot all the trouble at home. Skip never talked badly about Mom or Dad; in fact, Skip would not gossip nor listen to any, and truthfully, neither would I. Presently though, and unfortunately for me, I was Dad's *main target,* and my heart ached as to why? What happened for him to dislike me...even hate me? Why was my father being so mean? He now threw me into the enemy mix with Father Quinton and Mom. He barked orders at me as if he was still in the army. When Skip and I were in school, Dad would put his hands to his lips as if to blow a trumpet and pretend to play reverie until we woke up and he would yell, "Roll out," and expect us downstairs at zero whatever hundred hours! That was creepy too, but Skip and I went along with it, not to make waves.

It sure seemed like Mom and Dad were becoming more and more estranged from one another. When he got back home from work, Dad would get wasted on booze just about every night. When Skip was home, Dad would go after him for the tiniest thing. Our dad was turning into a monster with his watching everything we did and would not let us have anything to drink with our meals. I hated that my food would get stuck in my throat; it was awful. He just wanted to let each of us know he did not like what we all were doing with Father Quinton. I recall always being afraid of a cold, desolate, and icy dark place called Siberia. That is where my dad said, if I befriended Father Quinton, that I was going to "end up and in an igloo!"

We both had stomach issues all the time, and Skip had nose bleeds at sixteen because of high blood pressure. No one in Mom's family would say a negative word about either man. First of all, Father Quinton was big boss to at least eight of them, and more joined the force at Camp Merryland as my cousins got older. If Dad wanted to alienate Mom's whole family and possibly have the whole town on him because of their fondness for Father Quinton and all his accomplishments… Dad drank.

Skip did his usual disappearing act and would head to camp even during the school year because he drove now. What freedom!

From age eight to eighteen, I was stuck at home with my father. I did not feel like calling him Dad. Suffice it to say, Father Quinton was becoming, and probably always has been, a better father to both Skip and me. Mom was thrilled that we loved her boss so much. Eventually, rather than receiving cash bonuses, Mom received gifts from Father Quinton. Another thing that happened was Mom started adding to her collection of clowns. Did I tell you I *hate clowns!* And she was given one of the ugly things for any occasion… They were everywhere in the house again, even in our bathroom. It was another thing that I just couldn't get used to that my dad seemed to turn on me too. Not only did he hit me if I did some small infraction, he began coming in my bedroom in the night hours when he got drunk! Mom was travelling for the national business on the weekends, and Skip was out at the camp on the weekends. The first couple of times, I pretended I was sleeping. He just looked around—really, I should say stumbled through—and made his way back to his room. At that time, my young mind thought at eight years old, *Oh, Dad can't find his own room.* However, sadly it was not that, because the next time he entered falling all over, he was heavy, and since it was fall, I had a thick quilt on me, so he could do no real damage. I begged Mom not to go out of town or leave since I now had an uneasy fear of my father seeing him in action with Skip. One time, I caught him clobbering my brother pretty good, and Skip tried to block the many blows with his arms. I grabbed a broom and backed my father off of hurting Skip. Again, *Mom* was nowhere around. I really did not know this enraged madman who had a grudge against the U.S. Army and now an obvious huge problem with a Catholic priest!

The retreat center and camp were in constant public view. In the same realm, Father Quinton used Skip and me for much of the advertising, and our pictures were in many of the same publications. Skip was photographed with kids, families, and horses, showing the color topography of Merryland. I, on the other hand, was filmed in a bathing suit up at the swimming pool with the other lifeguards. Father Quinton had pictures taken of Aunt Bev and Uncle Gino as they were a very good-looking couple. Skip was told he looked like a lighter haired Wayne Newton, the Las Vegas crooner. Thinking back on it, he did look like him!

THE TARNISHED GOLD PALACE

Up to the present time, my dad, to outsiders, would be an abuser, an alcoholic, a victim of PTSD, and a terrible father, true, but what was over the edge for me was his nighttime uninvited visits to my bedroom. This was intolerable, and if no one else was going to help, and I was terrified to tell on my father because of what he was capable of doing to me... I had to come up with a plan to hide. He was *huge* and very intimidating. He was trying to fondle me, but in his drunkenness, he was too clumsy. I piled so many quilts on me now, even in warm weather, he couldn't get to me if he wanted to. But again, something rose up in me and said that this was not going to happen on my watch... What I possessed was the neatest closet within a big closet. There was a "cubby hole," and when I was hiding in there or just wanted to get away from noise, my cats and me could climb in there. Once you were inside, you could stand all the way up because the cupboard was all the way up to the roof inside. It was perfect…so the next time my dad tried to come in my room, I got extra pillows and put them under my quilts as if someone was sleeping there, and I escaped to my cubby hole inside my closet. It was pitch black in there, so I did make sure I had a flashlight with extra batteries. Merryland was my sanctuary, and I longed for summer to come. Since my father went after me more when Mom and Skip were away, that did leave many chances for my father to come into my room. Remember, this guy was six-foot-four and pushed two hundred and forty pounds now. My attempts to *yell him out* of my room were *iffy*, even though I did that a couple of times. The best strategy was for me to make haste and sleep in my cubby hole with my cats. These years reminded me of the stuff in *Poltergeist*—twisted and totally not normal. Coupled with this, Mom's clowns were about to come up missing… Maybe they juggled their way out the backdoor. I sure hope so!

So on the nights of his attempts, I learned to scream my head off. He instantly seemed to become coherent and he let out a howl, "Wildflower… I'm so…" and he never finished his sentence, because he seemed to have caught himself and backed away and ran up the steps. I buried my head in my pillow, and I remember I sobbed what seemed like all night. I felt safer downstairs with him now back upstairs. The next morning, I had gotten out of the house to stay overnight with Aunt Bev; I called her and asked her to come down and pick me up. I think Aunt Bev liked Dad better than she did Mom, so I didn't want to ruin Dad for her. I again decided to keep my mouth shut.

My mom was due to get home the next day, so I decided to tell Mom about Dad. She looked at me with a questioning expression and one that said, "Are you sure about this?" Well, that ticked me off, but I kept firm and unflinching and repeated what had happened again. This time, she flippantly asked, "Are you having nightmares about your father?"

I quickly retorted, "No, ma'am, I wish I were!"

With a continued puzzled look, she said she'd see about this, but it was said with a questioning attitude of me. She even had the nerve to say that she, Dad, and I were having problems with each other, so maybe I was getting mixed up and getting the wrong signals. Oh my God! *There were no mix ups, there were no wrong signals.* The only thing wrong is that he was trying to *bed down* in the wrong room! It was no use; she wasn't going to accept it. Later on, when I relayed my facts to a good friend and psychologist that I knew, the response was… "It sure sounds like Mamma did not want to believe it because *she didn't want the guilt* of what *could* have happened." That day, I realized that I was on my own and if I was going to survive physically and emotionally, my *mother was no comfort whatsoever.*

CHAPTER 3

Eat, Drink, and be Merryland

MY SANCTUARY

$\mathcal{S}$omething crucial I discovered was that, even though at the time I never knew it, God had His hand on me all my life. Many years it didn't come into view, but in retrospect, this fact is crystal clear to me. Each and every time in my cries for help, my Heavenly Father was listening, from the smallest insult to the largest assault, I know He never left me nor forsook me.

Moreover, the best gift He gave me to escape my father's unprovoked wrath was *my hiding place* within my closet. I leapt for joy because, just like God gave David caves to be safe from his enemies, He gave me my "secret places" too to protect me when Dad was the enemy in my own home. King David was hidden out many times by God (Psalms). My hiding place was my *cozy cubby closet.*

Merryland was Skip's and my escape to a non-threatening beautiful and mystical place. It was the complete opposite of the spectrum from our turmoil and upheaval at our house. Where we grew up was not our home, Merryland was. Skip and I happily bounced up and down in the back seat with Dad to Grandpa's farm, another runaway place.

Since I was five years old, I watched Disneyland on our one big TV. When I did have to be at home during the school years, my favorite shows were on the Disney channel. As I mentioned, I loved Hayley Mills and became addicted to watching everything she ever starred in. Dad, when he was nice to me, used to say that I was just like her, getting into messes and still landing on my feet.

Hayley also loved other kids and pets. In her famous movie, *That Darn Cat*, like her, I loved the Siamese cat. I was rambunctious like Hayley.

That was another thing; Dad would always call me in to watch Walt Disney and the news with him. I felt as if I was a yo-yo—really! That's why, at the start, I talked about the *Poltergeist* connection. The startling changes and spinning and climbing and up and down, toys turning around and around—these were my childhood years. There was no consistency in the behavior that could be counted on. The only stable thing that you could count on was chaos! One day, Dad was nice, and it didn't even have to take until the next morning for him to turn like a clock hand for him to be unbearable. Where did my *dad* go? Though I see him he's not really himself. God, I need your safe place.

By this time, I let it out to my mother what Dad was trying on me when she was away. I told her that Dad was being weird—worse than ever. She spun around and darted a glare as if to say I don't want to hear this. Without flinching, I repeated what I had said with emphasis on *when she wasn't around.* Mom came back with, "I know you *hate* your father, but really, come on." That "come on" was her hallmark statement of her accusatory doubt. I turned on my heel and slowly walked away from her; for some reason, she didn't believe me! After that, our very few moments together were fewer and short, as if she now was avoiding me. I didn't know where to turn. I knew that both Aunt Bev and Aunt Dory loved me. Aunt Dory begged for me to live with her all the time, but as much as I loved to visit her, I did not want to live above a restaurant and tavern that she owned. But Aunt Dory knew how to love kids. Did you teach her that? She never talked about you much. I'm so sorry, God.

I Need You, Father God

Oh my God, why is this man bothering me now again? Where is Mom? Why is she *always gone* when I need her the most? For weeks, Dad came in at night, and each time, he was wasted on beer-I was so scared. I was frozen stiff at first when he attempted to molest me. So far, it had only been attempts, thank goodness! At this point, I had only been afraid of his punishments, but now, I was deathly afraid of him. I remember as I lay tucked under my quilts and talked to a higher power to make him not touch me or find me. I really learned to put layers of clothes onto my two quilts. Dad never came in until the wee hours…so I tried to sleep some other places in the house first. I got to where I would go down to the first floor and sleep on the couch. My brother had moved permanently out to Merryland except for two days a week. So I played musical beds to *outfox the wolf.*

Even though Skip and I were very close, I could not bring myself to divulge to him what Dad was trying with me.

When it came to Dad, Skip did not want to hear anything about him at all. Skip lived in a total escape world and that included not wanting to see or hear any evil. Merryland was Skip's real home.

SUPPORT ME, HOLIEST FATHER

Father Quinton still wanted me to go to restaurants and movie cinemas with them. Usually, Father Quinton was taking us to religious movies, but now, he was taking Mom and me to more secular movies and ones Dad would never allow me to see. I remember Mom expected me to get ready for Father Quinton to pick us both up, and I put my ten-year-old foot down and cried, "No, I'm not going anymore."

My mother did not do anything or push me now for some odd reason. I didn't care why not; I just was fed up! I remember every time I rode out to Merryland, I dreamed of living there—the scenery, lakes, woods, activities, counselors, campers, Aunt Bev and her brood; I loved it all!

My Italian family—even though half of them worked for Father Quinton—had begun to start nasty rumors about my mom and Father Quinton. The boys were the ones who started it. Not Aunt Bev's boys, the others there, Tyler's boys. They were saying that Mom and Father Quinton were "more than boss and secretary." I turned on them for saying this! But is this true, Father? Tyler was Father Quinton's nephew...and a jerk.

My extended family—Aunt Bev, my mom's sister-in-law, along with my mother—were always saying how cute I dressed; they loved my honey-colored hair, blue eyes, and pug nose. They were very complimentary on some things about me. They thought I got the best looks of both parents.

Some of the girl counselors were really knock out beautiful, true. But Aunt Bev was adorable. She was petite and more than pixie cute and very loving. She had no competition for Uncle Gino's affection, though she never believed it.

Aunt Bev had nothing to worry about; Uncle Gino had eyes only for her and his work. I loved Uncle Gino too; he was a character and told great stories. My brother Skip was a great storyteller too, many people claimed he'd make a great comedian. Little did they know that the "life of the party" was falling apart on the inside. The fights between Mom and Dad were more than he could handle. He always sided with Dad, I think more out of fear though. Skip was actually punched in the stomach a couple of times! I hated Dad for that! Skip had a very weak stomach anyway, and Mom took him to the doctor who diagnosed that he could have an ulcer! It seemed like I was living with the poltergeist beast that had Carrie Ann imprisoned! This was Skip's and my lot in life also.

I was fourteen, and I did not want to sleep in our family house anymore. *I wanted away* from my lecherous, drinking, abusive father! So I asked Aunt Bev if I could stay with them. They had three boys in a three-bedroom house, so we had to fix the sleeping arrangements. Aunt Bev and Uncle Gino agreed that it was okay for me to stay there. Thank God, another escape, and next to my other favorite place—Camp Merryland!

I packed up all of my good belongings and moved in with my favorite family. We had so much fun! Right from the start, my life went from chaos to calm. I was so happy now. It was less and less, but at home, when I'd visit back and forth, Dad would have those moments when we were watching TV together where he would say very kind things. Things like, "You know, Wildflower, you do look like that cute Hayley

Mills and sure act like her." I relished in the good comments even from him. He used to be nice!

Besides our outside dogs, we had at least two cats in and around us all the time. The cats were always with me, on my bed or in my arms, while I laid on the big front porch with them in my lap. The other favorite place for my cats, Spunky and Princess, was in my hide-away cubby hole right in the wall of my closet. There's a sweet song in *Cinderella*, the newer movie, where she sings about her own little corner in her own little chair… I can identify with her because I had my own little closet inside my big closet where I felt safe and happy. It was so comfy; I was piled high with quilts and blankets and some clothes stored too. The cats, my two spayed females, would fall asleep with me many hours. It was a terrific hiding place from Dad also. Thanks for my safe place, Lord.

HOME IS WHERE MY HEART IS

Between lifeguarding at Camp Merryland and now being allowed to live with Aunt Bev and her great family, what a treat! Father Quinton wanted all of us to have our pictures taken again for the camping season. We were all going to be in several pictures in the newspaper, and it was going to be on the front page. Aunt Bev and her three boys were playing in the pool, and I was life-guarding them plus seven other kids. Father Quinton had an assistant running the advertising, and she told me to stand up next to the lifeguard chair and diving board. This time, our picture took over the whole front page. Aunt Bev was thrilled, because now, her boys became local stars.

I had a blast every day and night! Uncle Gino's wife and the three boys made me happy. I lived with them, ate with them, and taught the boys all kinds of camping skills. They all became talented at baseball, football, ping pong, and horseback riding. My brother, being a riding instructor, taught me. My brother was taught by Father Quinton, who was self-taught. As I stated, he was an excellent equestrian rider.

Now, the one thing that all the boys were terrific at was swimming and diving. I taught them well. They always came up to the pool where I was lifeguarding, and when there weren't many counselors or campers in the pool, I'd work with them. I was more like a big sister to them and lived it to the second I left! All three boys told me later, when I moved away, that they didn't have as much fun anymore, but while I was with them, I too was happier. I always tried to have a place to swim everywhere I moved.

For the first time in my life, I felt free and peaceful! What a joy it was to have been with a good family. My uncle would raise his voice at the boys and my Aunt Bev, but it was nothing like what I went through with my dad. This was a nice home with my Aunt Bev, Uncle Gino, and my *other* brothers, Matt, Sam, and Byron. I felt very much at home again *maybe for the first time!* I do not ever remember a storm at Merryland or at Aunt Bev's; it always seemed bright and sunny.

CHAPTER 4

SWEET SIXTEEN

During this time, Father Quinton and I became close again. He even tried to get closer to my uncle Gino, who was the maintenance and grounds manager for the retreat compound and camp. My aunt always wanted a job at the camp too, but her husband didn't want her to work at the time. Aunt Bev was very easygoing and wanted to make Uncle Gino happy, so she agreed not to work for a while. But that did not keep her away from bringing snacks to him and the three boys who eventually worked for Uncle Gino's work crew. Speaking of Uncle Gino's guys that worked for him; I want to set the record straight. Yes, two or three flirted big time with me, but they were five to eight years older than me! I knew the rules!

Now, Father Quinton knew that I was sixteen and driving—that I wanted to make more money. Camp work never paid much, but it was a fun job, so nobody seemed to mind. He knew of my extreme love for animals and found out that his veterinarian, where he took his dogs, was in need of an assistant. His previous one was his daughter, but she was getting married. She was leaving within three months. I watched her and did all the things she told me to. She was very kind and patient with me. She told me she saw the newspaper with my picture at the pool; swimming laps was her hobby.

I took the job, and until she left, his daughter trained me. All was well the first year I was there. By now, after working with animals and being able to help them, I loved my job! I got two raises, and Father Quinton was regularly involved in my success out in the working world; he cheered me on. It was just Dr. C. and me for two years, we did fine. The clients were so nice, and I got to know many of them and their pets. Dr. C. was an older man and seemed kindly.

But trouble loomed over the horizon. All was going the same—same routine, same bookkeeping, helping hold the pets, assisting with surgeries, and more. But slowly, things were getting a bit uncomfortable for me. I noticed my boss was watching me, not just with the work, but just watching me. He was as old as my uncle. Dr. C. was married with four kids. However, one day, he disclosed to me he was not getting along with his wife and may not make it as a couple. He was normally not very talkative but, for some reason, wanted me to know that they may separate. I thought his wife was cute. But their relationship was none of my business, so I wondered why he was telling me that. I loved my job, it meant a lot to me, and so him being my boss, I just pretended to listen. Dr. C. made working for him comfortable and pleasant *until now*. What was this new approach? And what could I do about his problem with his wife? So again, darkness hovered, I hate that part of my life; there always comes, "but then" and "however," and I despised darkness, dark nights, souls, and people. This job was beginning to register atmospheric pressure.

My first good outside job, was about to be ruined. I could sense a glitch in my happy world. Thunder clouds were approaching. God, I hate grey winds of turmoil! I dreaded going to work there; it's so unfair, but I really liked being with all the pets.

Along with working my job, just out of high school, I took some night classes at a Catholic college. With all the events at work that made me uneasy, I decided to skip a night and stay with my aunt Bev. She was never judgmental. We rode around a while and talked. When we spied on Uncle Gino, Aunt Bev liked me with her as I worked at the camp and it wouldn't look suspicious for us both to visit the camp together.

After we rode out to the camp and surveilled the work site and saw no women around Uncle Gino, Aunt Bev picked up a pizza for all of us. Aunt Bev knew by now about my father's sexual perversions and the abuse inflicted upon my mom, Skip, and me. My aunt Bev and Uncle Gino were about fifteen years younger than my mom, so they were the young and "with it" aunt and uncle; Aunt Bev and I had a lot in common. I loved her so much, and for many years, we always sat together at any family event; she even invited me to sit with her side of the family during large family gatherings. Aunt Bev and I would work the festival booths together. I hated to leave them; I forever knew a big piece of my heart would be with all of them. I've always had to be with authority that pulled me away from what I like. I was still underage, so I had to comply, but I didn't like it!

Sadly, so sadly, after three years of *bliss*, I moved back with my mom and dad as arguments between them settled down. Mom and Father Quinton *finally* believed my story from years before. Father Quinton believed about Dad's drinking, coming into my room at night, and his exhibitionism. Somehow, they got him to stop it all, at least for a while. Mom and Dad were happy to see me making money, and they said they'd even help me buy a car of my own! Back then, Father Quinton had a hook with a car dealership, a Chevy-owned one, and I was allowed to pick my car within a certain price range. I kept away from my father now. There was no talk at all. I did not disclose anything other than surface talk with Mom and Father Quinton either. They had all betrayed me in some way. Nevertheless, I picked a sea frost green Chevy Camaro. It was beautiful, new, and mine. I drove it into work, the pet clinic, and everywhere else. At work, it wasn't unusual for me to get purebred kittens for free, as the vet was the animal doctor for several pure breeds. I loved when his clients brought in their show cats. I especially got excited when the precious kittens were brought in litters! Is there anything cuter then a kitten? These smaller ones would be the "runts," and they were my favorites! On several occasions, these weaker, tiny ones grew into the most healthy, gorgeous cats of them all. That reminds me of the parable of the tiny mustard seed in the Bible. It was so teeny when planted, but it germinated and grew to become a lush, healthy, huge tree! God takes care of His nature, but many times, human beings are the trouble. Sometimes, the owner breeders would suggest having the "unfit" kittens put to sleep; to them, they weren't show quality. I always would ask if I could take them. I enjoyed the runts most of all. I knew my family on both sides loved cats! I never had a problem giving the spared cutie pies to one of my aunts, cousins, or friends. The whole three years I worked at the animal clinic, neither a cat nor dog were put to sleep; unless they were terminal, I took them all.

CAT HUNT

Now, I personally was on the lookout for a young female Persian, not spayed. I wanted to breed her one time with a breeder friend's stud male. I called the ads and got directions to buy another female. Meanwhile, at home, to my surprise, my big beautiful "rescued" Persian we already had was overtaken by my dad at home. He named him "Cameron." Even though he treated Cam like any other alley cat, that cat loved him. During the winter, as Dad shoveled the snow, Cameron would be outside with him, jumping up and riding on Dad's snow shovel. It was a game; Dad would gently toss Cameron on a high snow pile. Cameron seemed to really enjoy it; he'd run back for more. Dad miraculously had Cam for many years. Maxim was becoming softer. He loved and cared for his cat.

With the Persian hunt on, the newspaper ad in hand, I called the woman, "Donna," about the Persian cat for sale. I then drove to her house to see the cat. Within one hour of talking to the woman, I knew all about her husband and four kids! She was also ironing and muttering about all the work she did. One of her sons happened to be the same age as me, just a month apart, she eagerly informed me. The father came in for a moment to just say hello and then quickly exited out of the door and headed down the street. He was a lot older than she was. But I peeped out the window and noticed a distinct spring in his steps as he almost ran down the street and disappeared around the corner.

The next family member I got to see and introduce myself to would be their youngest daughter, Donna Jr., and she was very pretty and quite sweet. She leaned over and whispered to me that "the cat was not all Persian." The mother was still talking and ironing. I tried to listen to be polite or at least look like it. She loved to talk. The daughter suddenly left; one could tell she was annoyed by her mother. I was beginning to wonder if this was a good idea. I should have gone to my psych night class. I said to myself, *No cat? I should go!*

On the other hand, the father promptly came back in the room, but this time, he had his son, Lance, with him. He was my age. Wow! I thought he was awfully cute. He resembled greatly a television actor who is now very popular with the young high school and college girls, "Axel Heck" from *The Middle* on TV now. Lance even had the same curly hair. Needless to say, I stayed put for a while.

His mother introduced him, and we both greeted each other. On the sly, he told me to ignore his mother's ad; like his sister, he confirmed it wasn't a genuine Persian, plus, it (he) was a male! The mother just wanted the kitten to find a good home; she was only asking ten dollars for it. When I saw the ad asking for such a low price, I should have known it wasn't a genuine Persian, but I had nothing better to do. Besides, their mom was sincere to help her cat, how could I be bothered by that? And now, that night was evolving into a very enjoyable visit.

THE TRIP

Father Quinton had just booked my mother and me on a tour of Europe! The idea of going to Europe was both good and bad for the two of us. Father Quinton paid for it all, including the plane and hotel stays. I was to go with my mom and Aunt Katia on this trip. The news didn't make Lance very happy at all. And for me, something I looked forward to, the trip became very sad, because I just met a guy I really liked! I now hated the idea of going and was trying desperately to get out of it. Note though, my mother, when ticked off, *had the most evil glare* that would send shivers down your spine. She was doing *this* the day I tried to get out of "her" trip!

59

Of course, my new "let's stay at home" attitude was greatly upsetting my mother. She yelled at me for being an ungrateful brat and I better not do this to her. But really, I had received so many threats from my father like, "If you tell anything, I'll make your life miserable." I knew what "miserable" was; I didn't want to lose the first good thing that happened to me—meeting Lance. I cried, begged, and yelled back, but nothing. My mother was not going to give in to me... A quick *hot* slap let me know who was going to get their way.

She barked, "Get busy, young lady, and start packing."

I tried everything I could to get out of the trip. But they even had my dad convince me to go on the trip. Staying alone with him was *not* an option! Aunt Katia said she would not go if I didn't. I knew how much she wanted to go, and I loved her; she was my namesake. So I finally agreed to go because Father Quinton said he would marry Lance and me after we waited a year when we got back from Europe. He'd even talk both of my parents into really liking and being nice to Lance. Many promises were made, but we'd see. Skip was gone and newly married at the time. I really missed my big brother, but I wanted him to be happy. Caroline seemed to make him delighted, so I was all for that. Skip and she had been dating one year and fiancées another year. Caroline thought Skip was ready. Me next to marry. Hmmm...

Coming from Father Quinton, I tried to believe it. Lance was with me, and I had been dating every other night for six months. I was so upset that Mother was forcing this on me and manipulating everyone to convince me to go. But he left it up to me, so I said I'd go but not to expect me to be cheerful about it! See, it dawned on me later that Mom wanted Aunt Katia and me to go on the trip so it wouldn't look suspicious with just her and Father Quinton. Now,

Lance, being a born investigator and Scorpio, pegged Mom and Father Quinton the second time he was with them. Just about everybody who rumored it, even our family, suspected "foul play." Mom's family knew it too, but nobody dared not speak aloud about it. Most of me knew it too, but a part of me did *not* that Mom and Father Quinton were intimately involved. But the triangle caused a lot of trouble in the family; Lance said it was unfair to the kids—us.

I hated the trip now, and to show it, because I was forced into it, I stuck to my aunt like glue, so *I didn't have Mom in my face*. She knew, and so did Father Quinton, that I wrote to Lance every day. Father Quinton would always help me find a mailbox in Europe. I even used the money I had for the trip to buy my boyfriend a beautiful cinnamon-colored cashmere sweater from Piccadilly Circus.

AUNT KATIA, MY NAMESAKE

I was happy to be able to see all the famous sites that everyone talked about, and much of the food was delicious. Venice and Saint Mark's square were my favorite visits! We even got to be on a set for a James Bond movie up in the mountains of Switzerland. All of the little villages smelled like sweet coco. The movie staff was polite, and they were not filming that day, but they were still in town. The trip was memorable in many ways. I guess everyone should go to Europe at least once in their life!

Aunt Bev and Aunt Katia were my closest aunts. Aunt Katia, to me, was like a reserved princess who was demure and gentle. She was strikingly exotic in facial features. Aunt Katia was a truly Italian-looking woman. She had jet black shiny ringlets that glistened when she perspired in her home in Florida. Every summer and Christmas, she and Uncle Felix would grace Grandma and Grandpa Ciro's home for visits. I absolutely adored Aunt Katia. I was her namesake, of course, and she was my godmother. She was also very bright and up on all the latest medical stuff, politics, and glamour.

Aunt Katia, though having very pointed features, was extremely feminine in dress and adornment. She loved Chinese silk clothing and jewelry, and her home was decorated art deco style combined with Chinese figurines in each room.

Aunt Katia's alternate attire would be a Hawaiian moo-moo look that hid her lovely but childless figure. I remember how she'd look at me with her dazzling smile and beautiful black piercing yet friendly eyes. She told everybody in the family that I was her favorite. Mom, Father Quinton, and I were the only ones who would travel to Florida to visit her and Uncle Felix. I loved going!

Father Quinton was very adventurous, and so marlin fishing over the cobalt blue ocean was one of his favorite things to do. My thing was staring out, trance like, and walking into the gorgeous white caps while they lapped against the beach.

Whenever I visit the beach or drive up to the mountains, God's awesomeness sings out. Can you imagine how powerful He is that He can speak a thing of such magnitude and force to simply appear?

I had discovered a whole new part of the world. Since Aunt Katia was with me, I thought the European trip was not miserable after all. It was great!

Rubbing Shoulders With...

In Mom's many national and worldly travels with Father Quinton, she went to every state and just about every country. She met a lot of semi-famous people and a few famous people. She met three popes. In England, she sat at a banquet with the Queen of England and her family, she met Ethel Kennedy; Mom even bought some of her clothes at a consignment shop in Hainesport, saw Rose Kennedy, and many more. Mom bought all the Hollywood magazines, yellow journals, and detective magazines. She loved the gory mysteries of brutality and rape, but I was the exact opposite. That stuff was too violent and perverted for me.

Oh my goodness, how I hated those detective stories! Mom used to lie across her bed at night. During the summers, she'd have her windows open and the fan at full blast on the table next to her. She'd ask me to climb in bed with her, we'd talk, and she'd read her terrible murder and rape mysteries to me. Even though it was a bit strange, I still had my alone time with her, no Dad and no Father Quinton around.

I can't even remember Mom sitting with me to have girl talk. I had those with my friends. Some things never change. On our visits back home for the holidays, the same magazine rack full of hundreds of detective magazines was still next to Mom's lazy boy, and woe, more and more of those dreadful, ugly clowns from every country she visited. They wore the cultural clothing for that area. She loved them all!

All of her worldly travels were educational and enlightening to be sure. She has been to Italy, Spain, Greece, Russia, Africa, South America, Japan, China, Alaska, Canada, the Netherlands, Newfoundland, Switzerland, Germany,

Scotland, and many more. And, yes, she had a *clown* from every country she visited.

To our dismay, Father Quinton had taken any free time that my mother should have had to spend with her children away from us. Anytime Mom wasn't doing anything, Quinton was sniffing around her. Even though we occasionally saw Mother, there was absolutely no time for her to read to us, bake cookies, help with our homework, or take us trick-or-treating as children should. Every once in a while, we would go shopping together. Since Skip married Caroline, he never did anything with Mom if Quinton was around. She minced no words about my mother's love triangle. She wanted no part of my mom unless she was accompanied by our dad, and of course, Skip agreed with her. They dropped the "father" with Quinton now too. However, I remained in denial about my mom and him for the longest time.

BYE-BYE, MOM, DAD, AND FATHER QUINTON

My brother Skip was married two years; his wife, Caroline, got along with Dad better than anyone. Ironically, Skip and Caroline met at a retreat in winter for college students. She attended the same all-girls Catholic high school that I did. She was the senior president of the class and cute, model-like, and she was as tall as my six-foot-tall brother.

Dad was almost six-foot-five and weighed two hundred and forty pounds. He was huge, unlike my five feet, one inch mother, heavy set with a huge top. Skip looked more like Mom, chubby cheeks like her own and a little on the plump side. Mom had auburn hair with grey-blue eyes. She really did, in her younger years, look like Elizabeth Taylor. Grandpa (her dad) was 100 percent Italian, but Mom's mother was all

German. I mentioned previously that Grandpa Ciro was a great Italian cook, and Grandma was too! We visited them most Friday nights. All of us enjoyed a huge pot of spaghetti and a loaf of Italian bread.

My dad was handsome, and everyone said I looked more like Dad. I'm five-foot-five, fair complexation, with long honey-colored hair and blue eyes. My aunts, uncles, and cousins compared me to one of David Copperfield's ex-girl-friends. I don't know, but it was sweet that they thought that. Aunt Bev always said the nicest things about me.

Everybody always got along so well with my brother's wife. She was a welcomed gift. I liked her right from the start. Caroline and Skip both had Jaguars, and hers was a convert-ible! How neat. Caroline's family came from "old money."

My brother and sister-in-law were going to buy my parents' house. Mom and Dad were moving to a really nice English country home on the lake. Father Quinton took care of everybody. He hired an architect from our area to design the house along with Mom. She loved it!

There was another Merryland photoshoot planned and this was to take place at the brand-new boat marina at Merryland! I lived in my bathing suit and was always out there. I loved to swim and be with all of my cousins and Aunt Bev in the boats or at the pool. Lance loved most of my family. Dad commented that "My Wildflower is a water dog!" He taught me how to swim, throwing me off the dock at three years old. I immediately started paddling the doggy paddle; now, I was swimming up a new river.

Lance and I were planning to get married, but we were just figuring out the details when something occurred at my work. I didn't know it, but my boss had a big crush on me; he, by now, flirted, saying he had a "model" for an assistant and made sure our hands touched. This happened about six months before I even married Lance. Dr. C. said he saw me in a whole "new light" in the newspaper display for the camp.

In the same realm, I found out, from his mother and sisters, what a "jealous maniac" Lance's father was as well as his dad's four brothers! It set off a red light to not let him find out about my boss and his advances! The mother of Lance and Donna Jr. said that, several times, the men in the family would punch another guy who they perceived as flirting with their women… Yikes! There goes my job! So unfair. I really adored all the pets that came in! With all I had been through with my own father, I sure didn't need this controversy to *raise its big ugly head!* And Lance was built strong; he could do some real damage to a skinny, ugly veterinarian. I could handle my boss. I acted like the flirting never happened. I convinced myself, so I told no one anything. Rule number one, let someone you trust know; it could be very bad if you don't. There could come "tempestuous peril," as T.D. Jakes declared in his book about time speeding and trouble brewing. My boss became obsessed with the newspaper camp advertisement. He had a copy in his desk; it was becoming creepy.

CHAPTER 5

Perverted men will have their place in The Lake of Fire
—Revelation 21:8

EVIL LURKED... THE FORECAST
WAS FOR PARTLY CLOUDY SKIES
AND POP-UP SHOWERS...

*T*he really bad part was my boss's advances *did* keep me worried. I was working and, like always, planned to meet my aunt Bev with my cousins; we were to go swimming at the camp. So this particular day, I brought my bathing suit to work. It was a Thursday, my boss's day off, and I was the only one at the vet hospital. He always played golf. I fed and bedded down all the surgery pets and borders. I went up the carpeted steps to the room where I changed my clothes for swimming at Merryland, which was five minutes away. When it came time to clock out, I went into the room next to the bathroom to change into my bathing suit. There were no people or staff around anywhere.

Getting ready to meet Aunt Bev and the guys, I locked the doors and scurried up the steps to the room with the radio. I had my tote bag and laid it on the chair in the corner of the room. I turned on the radio, and while the music was blaring, I proceeded to get undressed to change into my two-pieced suit bottoms. I had everything off, and as I walked over to the chair to get my tote, I saw what I thought was a shadow. I spun around to dart a look. Startled, I focused… Oh my God, Oh my God! It was my boss! And he was openly staring with a wide smile right at all of me! My scream shocked him! I quickly and clumsily covered myself with my hands and ran toward my tote, screaming louder. I was a wreck fumbling for my stuff. I dropped my tote down low to cover me up me. Gulp! He was right in the doorway—the only exit! Hyperventilating, I said, "Please get out of my way now!"

He whispered weirdly, "You are so beautiful…"

What he did next caused me to let out the most blood-curdling scream I could muster. Appallingly, he unzipped and pulled out his private parts. "Oh Jesus! Oh God help me!" I refused to look. By now, I had scrambled to find a small towel, and I aggressively jolted toward the door.

He said, "Come touch me"

I jumped back and took a leap, I slapped my hands over my eyes, and he blocked the door. Well, something rose up inside me and boldly proceeded to quickly charge with a running start and another running start, and just that fast, I grabbed my stuff and rammed right into him, bouncing against the half-opened door and the frame with my shoulder! Screaming, "Let me through!" I jammed my shoulder blade but kept going through the hall, down the steps.

At the top, he yelled, "You look like a model!"

Oh God. "You creep! You are so sick!" I screamed freaked out and almost in shock. Hysterically, I flew out to my car. Now, the perverse storm was upon me. I got in and drove away, my car squealing all the way up the long driveway. I was still pulling out my clothes from the tote while I was driving and trying to dress! That is next to impossible! I managed to put my cover up over me at least. I got away, and it down poured a deluge.

I headed straight out to Father Quinton. He'd know what to do, or so I thought! Screaming still the whole drive, I'm sure other drivers thought I was nuts! I know I ran a few stop signs, and maybe even a red light, I don't recall it at all. I just needed to get to Merryland. I was still screaming, "Oh God, Oh God," when I banged on Father Quinton's door. He was there, but I pushed right past him and threw myself on his couch! I was so hoarse from yelling and screaming I couldn't even get any words out!

He said, "Are you okay?"

And I let out one long scream, "Nooo, I'm not!" It was so traumatic! I felt like a mad scientist observed me as his lab specimen. It felt so weird and intrusive.

What a hideous sight I witnessed! I dropped my head in my hands and sobbed. As always, Father Quinton would hug Mom or me, but when he tried, I put my hands up and said, "Don't! Not now!"

He did as I asked. I proceeded to try to tell him what happened; I was wringing my hands, and now I got up and nervously paced and tried to spill what happened. As I spoke, I remember I pulled my hood to my swimming robe up over my head. Then as I told him step by step what occurred, I pulled and tugged my robe tighter and tighter to where I wrapped myself around like a mummy! I was such a nervous embarrassed wreck! How could I tell this to a man, even Father Quinton?

Dear God... Why are Old Men such Perverts?

While I was wrapping my robe and jabbering, not really making sense, his expression was one of a puzzled look and a bit of worry. He had that typical worried brow look like he did when he pulled his back out. I, then, out of nowhere, slapped my hands to my face and cried out, "How could this happen?"

My screams startled poor Father Quinton. He jumped and looked frightened at me! Then he'd say, "It's okay, everything will be all right."

No, Father Quinton, you don't understand, this is *the* worst thing, worse than Dad, worse than pets dying. Oh my God! He walked toward me to put his arms around me again. As he reached, I flinched and yelled, "No, No, No! No one will ever touch me again! In fact, I will never take anything off to even bathe!"

Father Quinton could tell this was not the usual—this was a true disaster! I thought back to all the other times he had helped me, like when he rescued me and kept it from Mom and Dad, or the time I was fourteen and practiced driving his old station wagon and I accidentally ran into the parking sign at the retreat house and took out the front headlight. Then, when I was fifteen and playing in the camp Jeep, Father Quinton had to run after me racing down the hill; he jumped in and scooted me over just in the nick of time to put on the emergency brakes before we plummeted over the embankment right into the deepest part of Merryland Lake!

Then, of course, when Big Red got hit and killed by that stupid drunken bus driver. *God, why do men have to drink?* They do the worst of things and cause destructive damage when they do! That's it; maybe my boss was drunk... No, no, no, I'm not giving that jerk an out. What do I care? It's just a job to me. Oh, I'll never get over this… Why did I leave Merryland?!?

Woe this vet boss thing, this was so horrible! How am I going to get that out of my mind? Father Quinton, I thought *you* were the one who said, "*Try my wings!*" My private most intimate parts of me exposed to a pervert employer! I felt violated, angry, hurt, embarrassed, I never will go back there again, ever! I don't care what I left there.

And then Father Quinton said something so strange. He said, "Now, don't be so hasty." Father Quinton excused himself and told me to rest. He'd make sure nobody bothered me. He said he'd call Aunt Bev but not tell her *why* I didn't make it. He came back after what seemed like an eternity. I asked him what I should do now. My father was just waiting for my job to fail, I needed money; Mom and Dad charged me rent ever since I turned fourteen.

My mind was swarming with questions. Are all men the same? What do I tell Lance? His mom said his father was very jealous and Lance was the same… Yikes! Oh dear God, how can I deal with this? Lance will kill him!

Father Quinton informed me that he had called Aunt Bev. Still shaking, I thanked him. Then he said he spoke to Dr. C. and then shocked me again with his next comment! "Well, I think things will be fine *if you want to keep your job.*"

"What?! What did you say?" I retorted tensely.

He said, in essence, he had smoothed it all over. Then Father Quinton told me what the vet told him. He said he was drinking, stopped at the clinic to go to the bathroom, forgot to close the bathroom door! I happened to walk by and see him. "It was embarrassing for both of us!" Oh my God, is he kidding? Is he nuts!? What a big slimy liar!

Father Quinton shook his head and shrugged his shoulders and said, "That's what his story is."

"Give me a break. Oh dear Lord, I can't take it," I exclaimed with intensity now. My mind did flip flops. This was Father Quinton? Oh, dear God, why would he believe this idiot over me. Or does he? Why would he be saying this? Ooh, that vet's weird and bizarre smile. So eerie and sick! Like the strange dark man at the door in *Poltergeist* who kept wanting to come in.

Then Father Quinton said, "Either way, he's learned his lesson and now you've told me, so we leave it to God now."

Oh, now *God* comes into it huh? I thought *not* to be disrespectful, but Father Quinton (I wanted to cup my hands over my mouth like a megaphone and yell), "Are you insane?!" Picture the bizarre, ugly clown appearing and then disappearing in *Poltergeist*. Do you see him? Now the chairs insanely pile up, and then the parapsychologist looking in the mirror losing his face? Now you're getting it. I know you're intelligent. Visualize the scene. All of them clumped together into one. Are you getting the confusion, distrust, and horror?? And finally, but not the ending—the evil. Did Father Quinton make some kind of deal with the... employer? He's always wheelin' and dealin'. But why would he *sell me out?* I thought he cared about Skip and me. Too many mixed thoughts. Father Quinton seemed to have very clouded judgement here, and I had to get out of there fast! Maybe I needed to get out of the whole town! *My urgent need to leave superseded everything*! I wanted to crawl in my cubbyhole! Why didn't I see what happened? I should have confronted him about his touchy, patting ways. Why am I always so *afraid* of men to speak up?

My psychologist friend Lydia again came through with the answers. In plain language, both my father and my mother blew it when it came to teachings about do's and don'ts, as neither one of them at any time, even between themselves, *honored boundaries*, so how could I learn at home? Then writer and the wife of a pastor, Paula Sanford said in her terrific book, *Healing Victims of Sexual Abuse*, Parents definitely send mixed signals which have caused a base of confusion and fear for little ones early in life. Who can be trusted if Mom and Dad cannot be trusted? What about bad advice from a priest? Strike three and we're out!

Then Paula again comments, "Children need affirmation and love. Exploitation and terror should *never* be in any child's life. Saying "No" to Mom, Dad or a Boss in the real world could bring consequences," See the confusion?

The real confusion comes into the picture when the daddy that called me to him to swoop me up in his arms and cover me with kisses and love, now, five years later, I have to run away from him to keep him from hurting me or attacking me. This is a complete 180-degree turnaround and could and did make me feel like *my private world was crazy!*

Just as *my boss* had changed drastically from the first year doing everything just fine to this... a complete 180-degree turnaround after simply seeing me in a bathing suit other than a work uniform. Satan was doing his usual tempting the flesh and giving pleasure to the senses. I wanted no part of it—of any of it. I was out of there!

ENTER THE TEMPTER

The devil tried to tempt Jesus with pleasures also. A devil or demon spirit opposes God 100 percent. They can tempt humans to do evil, and men continue to walk in this sinful path unless God is brought in to cast out the darkness.

First temptation (with Mom) that should have been avoided was the first appointment to go to a priest whom my mom knew she had a crush on. The sin cycle started at the point where they snuck behind my father's back to be *together alone*. The "tempter" starts all the trouble first, and then the flesh or "carnal" side of man agrees with the sin path and the two, the tempter and the flesh, rule. Not God's spirit. With this vet, it was not his spirit side in control, obviously.

I did not understand about Satan and the sneaky manner he used to lead all four—Mom, Dad, Father Quinton and my boss—of these self-driven souls to perversion. I only knew that I had finally "had it!" It was as if the enemy was using all of them to make me have a nervous breakdown or worse, end it all. My mother and her dubious questions of my intentions, my father with his sex-starved ways and PTSD, Father Quinton protecting his reputation and misleading advice, and now this veterinarian jerk with his way-out-of-line behavior confused me. I should have gone to the police about all of this.

The intimate relationship between my mother and Father Quinton, no matter what, could *never* become a blessed union. The Bible is very clear about adultery. "For the lips of an adulteress drip honey and smoother oil in her speech, but in the end, she is bitter as a worm weed, sharp as a two-edged sword, her feet go to death, her steps lay hold on hell" (Proverbs 5:3–5).

Father Quinton stayed a priest. Many family stated that both Mom and Father Quinton "wanted their cake and to eat it too." It seemed that Quinton needed to read Matthew 15:8. "These people honor me with their lips, but their hearts are far from me." As a daughter, I did not judge them. God is the only righteous judge. I simply discerned that my whole family was insane!

OUT WITH THE OLD

Back in my hometown, when I was about the age of eight to fourteen, we all went to an amusement park. There was a very different and erratic type of roller coaster they called the "Mad Hatter." Now, this roller coaster kept passengers unnerved from the time they got in the carts to the very last jerk to stop the dizzy, crazy, and scary ride. The quick stops, the jolting starts, the squeaks of the cart, the high climbs plummeting at warp speed down the dips kept hearts racing and long hair in a tangled mess! Every passenger who descended the exit ramps was shaking their heads and visibly wobbling. This was what the family in *Poltergeist* experienced in that house with the entity.

This describes my childhood and most of my entire life quite adequately—chaos, constant turmoil, and upheaval. I had to find Jesus, the Prince of Peace. God always had been with me though. I didn't acknowledge Jesus until much later. I now had a permanent outlet where I could dismiss the negative thoughts and scenes that were used to play over in my mind.

STARK CHANGES

Do you remember, in *Poltergeist,* the scene that showed all the chairs stripped from the table and clumsily stacked on top of each other? Now you're getting the picture of my screwed-up surroundings. Each and every time Carrie Ann's family came upon another frightening and startling occurrence, I've had equally the number though I was forced to deal with them on my own. *That's* how I know that I was *not* alone. Really, my Heavenly Father was protecting me all along. It took me all these years to realize why He seemed to let me get to the eleventh hour. Although it has to do with "what doesn't kill you makes you stronger" and "When I am weakest I am strongest." It is *Him*, never me.

As I disclosed the whole graphic story to you all on the sexual harassment for these reasons:

1) Don't stuff down bad things that have happened, find someone trustworthy to tell like a family member, a pastor, a counselor—someone, so it doesn't stay ugly and hidden.

2) Sadly a few relatives of mine have conjured up their own lies about me. They were not there, but they decided to try to ruin my reputation rather than accept the facts about the incident. I forgive them.

Speaking for myself, I told you all what happened for another reason: Those of us who have been tormented by authority figures from a young age do not have the correct thinking processes formed. Children who are treated with respect are valued and know they are loved can learn limits when to give back love and receive it. Anything goes for we who are passed over by a father passed out from booze and spilling over with anger. The facts of life don't come from a mother who has a double life and is too busy sowing her own middle-aged oats! You're just thrown out into the treacherous world with no teeth or claws because they were amputated at home.

If our mother and father, with their volatile never-ending fights, constantly invade our boundaries and quiet spaces, why wouldn't the outside world? What my boss did about what he saw in the newspaper and *dreamed up* about him and me was in his fractured, sick mind.

God's Word states emphatically about those who are guilty of the abuse of children, "It would be better if a millstone was hung around his/her neck and they were drowned in the depths of the sea." And this is in red letters in the King James Bible (Matthew 18:6). Many are falling into this category. Maybe Father Quinton himself.

Also, he actually said I should reconsider and go back? Give me a break. What benefit would that be to him? Why would Father Quinton want me to return to that *snake pit?!* And with a man who is obsessed with me now? *Another* authority figure bites the earthly dust.

OH COMFORTING SPIRIT

> My bed is soaked with my many tears. I'm growing weary from living. Take me out of here, show me the way, my path is slippery and scary. There are leeches on every side. Depart from me all you workers of iniquity: for the Lord had heard the voice of my weeping... Let all my enemies be confused, sore, vexed and ashamed. Please Lord, My God in you I put my trust, save me from all them that persecuted me and deliver me... O let the wickedness of the wicked come to an end... You are my defense...Who save the upright in heart. Especially Lord, *You* have seen it all... Thou behold the mischief and spite, to requite it in your hand, the needy commits to you, *You* are the helper of the fatherless. Break out and

comfort me, seek out the wickedness till
you find none. O my Father, You have
heard the desire of your humbled (me)
and will cause your ear to hear…to judge
the fatherless and the oppressed that
the man of Earth may no more oppress.
(Psalm 10)

Then specifically against the vet, I prayed further.
"Father, watch the evil man. He was lurking, waiting in secret,
his eyes set privy against the innocent. The wicked lie in wait,
secretly, as a lion in his den. He does this to catch the weak,
he draws (her) into his net, he crouches, so that the weak may
fall by his strength… He (the wicked) has forgotten God…
He says God will not see… *Arise, O God.* Lord, lift up your
hand and forget me not… The humbled… Thank you so
much, Father."

Living now all year at Merryland, I arose and saddled
up my handsome boy "Pal" and rode like the stormy winds,
fast and furious as if someone was chasing me! Morning after
morning, I had to let out the extreme anger and shameful
feelings. Pal seemed to know I was hurting.

Eventually, Father Quinton told me to quit my job *but
never tell anyone* what happened. He said, "You've confessed
it to me. Leave him to God now. *He will judge Him.*" He
even asked to *keep that incident between us.* Still thinking as
a priest, he had some answers; I thought it over and then
agreed. But in my heart, I was reluctant. And sadly, I felt
dirty and "no good," as Mom said when I was hiding behind
our furnace. I hated the idea of anybody touching me. My
father, and now this creep, violated me and my spirit! I closed
myself off for a while. I had almost no trust of men—any
men. I just wanted to dwell in my cubby hole, my secret

place. Instead, I went to "Pal." My horse was always ready and happy for us to be together.

Ironically, six months later, Lance asked me to marry him. My home life and now work life was a mess, so I thought, why not? I did not think about the conjugal rights part, but I had to do something fast. Father Quinton happened to like my boyfriend, but he reneged on the promise to marry the two of us now. I knew Dad would give us a hard time, but how could I respect his opinion? Mom just wanted to keep me as a chaperone, an alibi, with her and Father Quinton for the public. I had no one to turn to, so I accepted Lance's offer to marry him. Why not? Skip married and was out of the *Poltergeist* house. What was keeping me? My marriage plans upset mother, and she proceeded to slap my face hard with Lance close by. He was in shock! Her imprint was engraved on me for quite a while. Lance said, "Let's get away from here. Your parents are psycho."

I had to ponder this carefully. So given these facts, for weeks, I'd run down to the horse barn at Merryland to be with my buddy, Pal. He looked as if he loved being patted, brushed, and cared for by me. During the camp week, he could be used by the more experienced campers because he was high spirited and swift and galloped more so than the other more docile trail horses. But for those more beautiful moments, my horse and I almost took flight over the hills and valleys. With more heightened senses, I forgot the horrid experiences that were forced upon me by misguided, very dark souls. For that blessed time, I became one with nature and creations as Henry David Thoreau always proclaimed for his life on Walden.

In the same genre, speaking of good literature, *Metamorphosis*, by Franz Kafka, reminded me of my brother so much. The main character, Gregor, if I remember, was so shy when it came to even attempting to assert himself, so much so that he just took his own father attacking him many times! Skip took all of the world's crap too. He never rose up. Skip only escaped, which did keep him going, but he pushed down and refused to accept the part that Dad was bad. Like Gregor, Skip accepted the role of an unnecessary martyr.

Father Quinton, Dad, and Mom all warned me of some rotten secret that *I was never to tell*. Skip was also intimidated not to divulge anything private about any of us. This festered for a time, and then, like Skip, it got smashed down into our subconscious selves. I so badly wanted to let Lance know this stuff so I wouldn't deceive him in anyway. However, each time I tried to muster up the nerve to tell Lance about my boss's advances, someone stopped me. Since I liked his mom and younger sister, I'd refer to their home life experience with Lance and the men. Each and every time, they warned, "Do not tell him any sexual indiscretions." Right there, I should have stopped, but now it was too late. After Lance now witnessed my mother being violent, and the red imprint on my cheek, he was angry.

"Katia, I'm getting you out of this nut house," he snorted.

MY KNIGHT, LANCE

To be completely honest, *looking back*, I wrestled with the idea of marrying Lance because I thought that it would be better to just move out of the house with one of my friends from school. Megan and I talked about getting a small horse farm and being two single women who shared expenses. However, when Lance met at my house to pick me up for our first date, he wanted to meet my parents. I was pretty honest with him about Dad except for the private harassment part. Nevertheless, the night that he arrived at my door, Dad had been drinking and had me pinned down to the living room floor with his knee in my chest, slapping me in the face. Lance heard the scuffle through the door that he was knocking on and admitted that he saw Dad and me a little through the screen door... It was summer and hot. He did not act any different though, because our plan was to run away together and elope. He did not want to give my father any reason to hinder that plan... So he shook hands with Dad, and we drove off for our date. Of course, he asked me about what he saw when he got me in private, and I told him the truth of how Dad beat Skip and me on a regular basis. Lance was angry and wanted to help.

Lance vowed to take me away and take care of me and said he loved me. From what I knew of love, I declared my love for him too. On the day before Thanksgiving, we eloped and were married by the justice of the peace in our hometown. Lance's brother, Beau, and Marlene, his wife, were our witnesses. My whole Italian family and Dad's side found out that Thanksgiving Day. Of course, my cousins told me later that my mother acted like she was going to faint, and Aunt Dory put her smelling salts under her nose. Apparently, she had a reaction to the strong smell, and she started coughing and choking. Cousin Darcy said it was "quite a drama." As an aside, regarding my being (like my mother), this I can say without equivocation. Yes, I was a victim of inappropriate fondling, partial incest, and my boss, unfortunately, had his peep show. I was roughed up and scarred but was a virgin before I married my husband.

I was coming out of the darkness and into the light. The enlightenment? *No authority around me was trustworthy*. Paula Sanford adequately described my emotions then. My positive remembrances were shattered when authority betrayed my trust. "The past now mirrored in the distortion of a million shattered pieces... Authority could no longer be accepted as sanctuary hope or reliable direction... There are no truths to rest in." I became Lance's wife for better or for...

At night, I wanted to disclose everything, but I had become his wife, so too late. Now what? I wanted to tell my spouse all the horrible details, but now, little Donna's words played in my head. *Don't tell.* Again, why was I this container for all the "secret junk" of all of us? I was a child of light, I loved the sun, I hated storms, and I especially hated darkness! God, Father, show me your light!

Another few months went by, and I worked while all the feelings were quickly slipping down into my sick soul. It's almost like someone shot me with a fiery arrow in my heart. My dad, who I adored a long time ago, and then a job I felt so successful in, both plummeted because of evil men—*not* God, but the enemy. I was learning the big difference between wickedness and perversion versus goodness and holiness.

As the savior archetype in *Poltergeist* cried out, "Come into the light, children," I wanted to in the worst way. My raw hurt needed to be dealt with. Pushing it down was next to impossible for me to accomplish. I wanted to tell Lance everything, but... I couldn't.

All of life was pretty normal except for intimacy. Luckily, Lance was going to school, studying, and working so much that he was really too tired most of the time. Even though I did my best to put up a good front, alone in my bedroom, I'd cry just about every night. Oh God, how I anguished. I felt like a part of my spirit and heart had broken off and was hidden somewhere else. I felt ashamed, but I couldn't figure out what I did to cause this. Anything intimate to me was very uncomfortable and painful. A key point I have read in one of my many Christian self-help books was that, for anyone who had been abused continuously or traumatized, physically, verbally, sexually, not only are we emotionally harmed, but also, our spirits are wounded—some can even die. Our spirits are what keep us alive, balanced, happy, and positive. They need encouragement and are very sensitive. Our spirits actually go into hiding, like a little child running to hide from the villain in a story. Like Carrie Ann running away from the evil entity in *Poltergeist*. My spirit was embarrassed, made afraid, tromped on, and traumatized. But I wanted to be fixed, and I wanted to know how to love. I picked up some Christian self-help books. One was by Dr. Charles Stanley on love. *In Touch* became my church. Paula Sanford became my mentor.

I felt bad for my husband, I'm sure at the time, and I made him feel abandoned. I wanted to be intimate, but I felt like too much of me that was private and beautiful was stolen. I could not help it. My exhibitionist father and perverted boss messed up this part of me. I had to find a good father. I heard our Heavenly Father had solutions, and I needed them. I needed relief so desperately. I ached for normalcy, whatever it was. I needed a sage-like Father... I could not receive comfort from Lance.

Paula and John Sanford wrote a book on our wounded spirits, and I got wonderful advice on how to start to heal. First and foremost, I called upon my Heavenly Father. He is so good, never hurts us, and only wants to help and heal. I prayed to Him. I dropped to my knees. I simply said, "Father, I'm so sorry but I can't do life anymore. If you really are a good Father, please, please help me!"

CHAPTER 6

WE'RE MOVING ON

*D*welling with mother and Quinton was strange. Lance and I both wanted our own place. The reason being, compared to my father, Mom was mellow, *but* compared to the average wife and mother, she was a hell cat! Father Quinton, with his food allowances of any and all sweets, was quickly finding out how irritable a diabetic could be. Mom loved sweets and had an "I'll eat what I want" attitude. No longer could I deny what was right smack in front of me, "they let it all hang out." It somewhat sickened me. Unfortunately, California prices were double the area where were coming from. We decided to move south, where his sisters had moved ten years prior. I liked his sister Donna Jr. the best; she was genuine, understated, modest, and darling. The older sister was a bit narcissistic and, like Mom, a drama queen, but we did okay. She told Lance she really liked me. Lance took another government job, and I took another bank job. It didn't take long to make new friends there either, and we all had a ball and still managed to balance our cash drawers every day. Our two male bosses were characters, and the bank atmosphere was relaxed and enjoyable. I loved working there. The other tellers and I were great working together. I had an excellent cash balancing record, so I was promoted to training the drive-up tellers.

Lance's sister and her boyfriend, Curt, who used to be Lance's best friend, were so fun to be around. Little Donna had really good taste in clothes, so she and I went shopping together. She was prudent in the number of items but bought the highest quality. Donna, Curt, Lance, and I went to all the neat and famous restaurants together. We had cookouts on the beach and played with our nieces. The older sister's girls, they were six and seven years old and beautiful. Back then, California was just as the songs and music portrayed, and the scenery was amazing. The lively aroma from all the blossoms and plants hung wonderfully in the air. The ocean scent was wonderful. I loved watching the sea lions. These most enjoyable mammals were watched from the deck in all California restaurants. Lance, Donna, and I observed their adorable antics for hours. We could see perfectly as they swam in the beautiful crystal-clear waters. It really got our attention how they went about trying to come up on the rocks from the water. These adorable creatures would swim full speed and then lift up, glide, and land perfectly each time, so they could perch on top of the flat rocks. Seeing God's nature this way was breathtakingly beautiful. The ocean was a glorious crystal clear with a cobalt blue tint. Porpoises did double flips. It was all amazing to behold and it reminded me of splashing with the kids at the Merryland pool!

CLOSE TO FAMILY

So back to Lance's family we went. This time, even his mom and her boyfriend moved out with us; Lance's father had died. It was nice to have family around again. We bought another house in the upper middle-class area. Lance's brother-in-law was an architect and he became quite famous for his well-acclaimed, mesh-structure architecture that holds up against earthquakes. Even a few Hollywood stars had Robby's designs. He became a young millionaire. He was always in the newspaper for his spectacular homes. The music star Janet Jackson lived part time in the area. She was hardly ever home and had homes in other countries. Tom Selleck was also in the area! I loved *Magnum P.I.,* and Lance did, too.

Now, my brother Skip and his family were somewhat close by, two states over. They too became very wealthy. At least for a few years, they lived with the upper, upper class of people. My sister-in-law was working for a big housing company. Caroline was put in charge of the employees while Skip headed the heliport and boat marina. Their first home looked like something in the Hollywood Hills on the beautiful waterfront.

I decided to go back to school and finish my degree in English literature. I enjoyed going back without money pressures this time; school was great. I had friends my age immediately. We lived in a little ocean city, and we bought a home with a guest house. I still kept in touch with my family back home and I enjoyed being with Lance's family while he went to school also. We were both in love with many things about California and the entire west. The population just seemed "cool." Lance and I were happy in our social life.

Nevertheless, old thoughts were creeping in on me, and I was having nightmares on the sex issues and the vet. I had a neighbor who "happened" to be a psychologist, and we got to be friends. After a few months of visiting back and forth, she let me talk about my past some with her. I even told her about my dad and his sick, cruel attempts to violate me. She hugged and held me when I sobbed, and since she was spiritual, she prayed with me and for me. I told her about my terrible dreams about rats, and she reassured and helped me so much. This was my good friend, Lydia. I wanted to be normal so bad, but I wasn't sure how when it came to intimacy. The only men I was used to being around were perverted, but Lance was not. However, I'm sure he was fed up with my constant headaches, female complaints, or other defense mechanisms. Even though, for the most part, I really relished being with family again and had memorable moments, down deep, I was sad when I was alone. Some days, I did not want to get out of bed due to depression. Lydia and I were to meet up again in the future.

DOUBLE O OKAY

Lance always loved James Bond, and we have a collection of every movie ever filmed on him. So after we left Father Quinton and Mom and moved down to Southern California, Lance took the test to become a government agent. The good news for him was that he passed it with flying colors and was immediately called to go into training to secure the position.

The months he was in classes and away in another state, I stayed with Skip, Caroline, and two adorable nieces. Again, I had a time period reminiscent of Merryland. Skip and Caroline were wealthy by now, and the company they both worked for was in its prime time. Their home was situated on a gorgeous street. Skip had a huge Olympic-sized swimming pool and, of course, having been a lifeguard, this was a heaven-sent dream for me! The two consistent and quick moves had exhausted me—and the refreshing laps and sunbathing the summer weeks did me good.

When Lance's training was over, he was assigned to a Texas office. However, the very next place he had to go was Oklahoma City; the very building where he interviewed and received his work orders was the infamous government building that was bombed just a few years later!

Skip and Caroline invited Lance for the remaining break until he started his government position. The ulterior reason was that Skip was hoping that he could convince Lance to take a government job *close to him and his family*. So was I. I really missed some family, and of course, my big brother was my favorite. Needless to say, I begged Lance to take a job in California (anywhere) so we could be close by to my brother. The answer was a resounding "no!"

So being married and not employed yet, I gave up my dream of living close to Skip and Caroline and did what my husband wanted. But I did not like it!

We flew to meet the new working staff.

Lance's new resident boss in charge was so nice, and his wife and I got along great. Right away, we could all tell, even though the eight agents whom Lance worked around were also from all over the country, we all clicked. Being a Scorpio, I knew that Lance was a born investigator, so right from the start, things went well. I was finding out when you listen to God's word and let the husband make the final decision, things are blessed.

CHAPTER 7

[By] the grace of God, I go.

—John Bradford

MAI TAI THE MAGNIFICENT...
FINDING A FUR BALL OF LOVE

*A*fter really shopping around for the right kitten, I found what I was looking for! A famous cattery with Siamese show cats was just about twenty minutes from where I lived. Lance and I went to get the best little guy we ever had.

The head honcho male cat was named Ching-Chong. The owner called for him, and I thought I was looking at a leopard or something. Chong was gorgeous and huge. He confidently jumped down from the roof, and the way he stomped over, you would have thought it was a goat. On the metal roof, he sounded like he weighed eighty pounds. I just had to see his babies! The three that were left were the most playful, loving, and healthiest little gems I had ever seen.

I was not used to paying for my cats. The one Lance and I picked was the only boy, the other two were girls. We told the owner, Mrs. Flick, we were naming him "Mai Tai," and she assured us that he would get pretty big. After all, Chong was his father, and he probably weighed thirty pounds. We had found the most loving, gentle feline on the planet at the time. Lance loved him more than he did any of our other cats. He slept right between us. Mai Tai was always with us; he followed us around room to room. He was the most loyal pet you could ever ask for! Lance went through three more jobs before things started to happen with our older Mai Tai.

For upward mobility, we packed up and said goodbye to Lance's family. He took a job, again with government; all three of us—Lance, Mai Tai and I—headed for the Yellow Rose state.

What Lance and I could never have imagined was the impact of emotions that Mai Tai evoked in both of us. This is not just companionship; it was more of a deep love. Mai Tai was so affectionate, and like a loyal dog, Lance always talked about the weeks that Mai Tai kept him company all day and all night right after his surgery. The doctors had found a cyst on his lung. At first, we thought it was cancer, but after further testing, it was re-diagnosed as non-cancerous. Oh, I really do love puppies and dogs, but for many reasons of practicality, we always obtained cats. Mai Tai had it all. He was playful, fun, smart, and he always retrieved wadded up paper balls every time we would throw them. All the agent families came over, and Mai Tai entertained them. Several of them had dogs, but after witnessing the Mai Tai show, they added a cat or two to the recreation time. They came over to the cool side with the felines.

The house in the Texas horse community was a lot of fun, but we decided to move to an area closer to two of our favorite friends. The house was occupied by indoor and out-door animals prior to us purchasing it, so needless to say, there were fleas in the carpets. Unfortunately, we had limited time to move in because of Lance's government constraints before the pest control company could come to exterminate. The visit turned out to be a wrong decision; in fact, a very wrong decision in more than one way. Texas was a bittersweet time. Mai Tai and Trust were in trouble

Even after me calling and asking every question I could think of to make sure that these were eco-friendly solutions for treating insects; I feel they lied to me. The horrifying result was that Mai Tai, even after waiting three days before we brought him back to our new home, had gotten a kidney and bladder infection so severe it killed him! When the veterinarian told us he was dying, we took Mai Tai to the mountains with us so that, when he died, I would not have to associate his death with living in our new home in Texas. Sadly, the day he died, he must have known he was going to pass. He dragged himself up on the bed, nestled himself between Lance and myself, and closed his big beautiful eyes and passed away peacefully. This is hard for me, because I believe with all my heart that animals do have spirits. I know that God, our Creator, loves His pets too. I know that when I am home, I will be reunited with Mai Tai and be with him. I will watch him frolic in the light while he chases a wadded paper ball down the golden staircase.

TEXAS HOSPITALITY

The memories of Mai Tai in this house were overwhelming, so we moved back, to the horse community. The home was on a clean and classy street with a two-acre lot. Our neighbor behind us, Bonnie and her family, had horses, and so did the neighbors across the street. Bonnie and I became good friends; within a few months she teared up and disclosed to me that she was date raped. She never told anyone else this, so I tried to comfort her as best as I could. I could tell she was in denial just like I was. I gave her the book of Joyce Meyer's life story. Again, we had a nice pool because Lance allowed us to put one in right from the start.

Not only were the agents and their wives a pretty good group, but they were some of the nicest people I've even known. I laughed and had such a great time with these people. We were always invited to some party, house, park, restaurant, and work baseball games. Most of the guys were excellent athletes. There were nine couples, and we all stuck together. Lance was always an athlete and a star baseball player. Four of the couples become our lifetime friends. C.J. and Lance were, by far, the best athletes. They still "had it" in sports. Lance, like me, was written up and photographed in our hometown's newspaper, but for different reasons.

Lance even grew a mustache and straightened his curly locks for the undercover life. Mirrored sunglasses were really "in" back then; all the agents had them. Our life for the next five years was to be very sensitive. Some days with Lance's assignments, I couldn't know where he was. It was adventuresome but a little frightening, as in *Poltergeist*. Lance was to go through four training schools before he could do the new job.

Nonetheless, a dark cloud was hovering overhead. Meanwhile, my young neighbor was eating food and making herself throw up! The stress and pain of the rape was causing her to feel ashamed. Bonnie bonded with our female Scottie; they loved tossing the ball in the pool for her to bring back to Bonnie. It was a good distraction from her pain.

Do you remember the false accusation I mentioned earlier? The cloud burst on Lance at this time with a shocking rumor; I was kept in the dark.

Placing it on the back burner, Lance went away for one of his training classes, and I stayed in Texas. I prayed that God would give me the knowledge and strength to help Bonnie. We stayed with all of our Texas friends, agents, and their wives for six years. These were the best years of my life, minus one personal incident… I will relay later.

BONNIE

Bonnie was obviously hurting, and she needed a friend to talk to. The eating disorder was a way of punishing herself or making herself unattractive. She couldn't have to associate herself with the past. Bonnie was raped by a guy she thought she could trust right in her own horse barn!

I looked back and over her neat, tidy, freshly painted brown and tan horse barn. The scene was so calm and lovely; it was hard to believe something so violent and nasty could happen right in her backyard. Tears were streaming down her face as she choked on the words. "I hate all men now." Wow, do I understand that statement! After she was finished, I shared my sexual harassment story with her. Moreover, before I was finished, I was crying too. Bonnie, being so dainty and sweet, asked me, "Can I hug you please?"

I replied, "I'd like that." At that moment, she became a sister to me. She felt the same.

Bonnie was talented in a couple of areas. She was artistic, had a wonderful fashion sense, and was terrific at applying "proper" makeup. Bonnie asked if she could practice on me. I said, "Sure," and she taught me some neat secrets from the time she was a model for teen clothes for the best department store in the area.

We prayed together, and her parents were also a comfort to her. Bonnie thanked me with a very expensive, one-hundred-piece makeup set. It was terrific! It lasted over five years for me! Eventually, Bonnie went back into modeling, and she was happier than ever with her Christian fiancé! Sadly, Lance and I said goodbye to all of our Texas friends and again moved back out to California. Lance had a promotion, and we moved into a cute home with a guest house. Mom lived in the cottage some of the year with us, but I had trouble with her, and bad dreams haunted me from years prior involving Dad. Sadly, my involvement with Bonnie escalated my own issues.

BAD FATHERS, DAUGHTERS, THE GOOD FATHER

My efforts paid off with Bonnie; however, my old wounds were gaping with my painful past now. A healed heart takes much time, but for the abused, it takes much more. The trust level of those who have been harassed sexually or have been abused has been so fractured. It is too painful and fearful to receive life from Jesus yet. Again, Paula Sanford had wisdom when she stated, "A daughter molested by her father has related to her in ways that belong to her mother." The daughter's sense "of who she was created to be as a female, daughter, wife, and mother has been shattered, torn, and twisted at the root level." Furthermore, and important for me, Paula continues, "If a little girl feels safe (always) with her father, that builds in her basic capacity to relax in the arms of her future husband." Unfortunately, if the converse is true and the girl has been molested even one time, the girl will feel "betrayed, intruded upon, disrespected, used, unclean, trapped, manipulated, robbed, and trashed." Another thing about the father was that "he failed to understand the sacred trust God gave him to protect his daughter as she blossomed into loveliness." Nonetheless, for far too many years, I was crippled socially when it came to the opposite sex. The only way I could cope was to treat girls and guys equally…and a few times *that* got me into trouble. Men think you're coming on to them simply because you treat males and females the same. But I endured a crippled and damaged self-esteem. Many little girls who have been molested or even raped do become promiscuous or even ladies of the night. The opposite can happen also… and that was where I fell. I became beyond frigid. I was fine with the playful kissing and hugging, but when groping and pawing started, I retreated quickly!! One time, I even called my big brother to come pick me up because I had jumped out of the car to save myself. I walked in a dark parking lot, crying and praying that he would hurry up! That guy was studying at seminary. I found out later, Skip looked for him to kick his butt, but he had quit and moved.

Moreover, Paula Sanford defends victims when she states, "How does a child successfully resist an authority figure who is more than twice her size and strength?" And then, "How does a young girl deal with paralyzing fear?" And third, the young female knows how devastating it would be to the whole family to "discover this nasty secret." I was eight years old and had nowhere to turn.

As the whole family falls apart, she feels the cause, and the guilt intensifies. In my case, it became a living nightmare; the constant watching and waiting and fearfulness of when was mind boggling and made me a constant nervous wreck! When I did tell what was going on, I was shunned and angrily dismissed by family.

Since my situation was a twofold problem (1). An alcoholic father who would beat you with the slightest infraction. (2) He would run you around the house in a drunken rage and try to molest you. I would run and hide anywhere and anyplace I could and escaped for days at Merryland.

The most difficult thing for me, again, was to let my mother know how much she *hurt and angered me*. She didn't seem to care that my father was such an abuser. As Paula Sanford admits, "Perhaps no one is more downtrodden and broken hearted than the sexually abused."

No one in the extended family or my husband could understand, even though Dad did all those things to me, how I could ever care for him, but I did. Down deep in a *child's heart*, I remembered a gentle, loving, and decently affectionate dad who would never harm his Wildflower (Not in his right mind). *Nevertheless...*

CHAPTER 8

If she keeps quiet, the stones will cry out.

—Luke 19:40

"Anyone?" by Katia

There's no peace
My heart sobs
Does anyone care?

Everything is No
No relief
No solace, No god
No comfort

I can't see light
Tarps of darkness
I'm drowning in sorrow
But dehydrated in spirit

For better? Really?
For worse? Maxim?
Eye blackened, heart bleeding
'Til death?

Single-Alone "Skip"
Barhopping, adulterating
One night stands
I can't stand…myself

Oh "friend"—you say?
Behind my back
Two-faced—double minded
A friend?
A man of God? Ha!

Ah yes
Turmoil, chaos…
Heartache—
Such loyal friends of mine

I hear voices
What?
Did you say something?
Quint, "that you?"
Anyone…there?

Love me
Leave me—buy me
Say something
Are you still close?

I can't see, come closer
I can't hear, say something
But I hear someone
God, is that you?

Don't allude me
Don't evade me
Where in this Hell are you?

Anyone there?

A Friend Indeed... And Famous

*W*e moved back to California into to the same neighborhood. Right up the street was a blessing... My marvelous
neighbor. Once again, Lydia was one of the best things that
ever happened to me; of all people, a certified, competent,
terrific psychologist. California is an exciting place. There is
nothing that says you won't run into a movie or TV star in
southern California. The psychologist friend of mine, Dr.
Lydia, did not tell me until later that she was a Catholic nun
who wrote books or that she was a popular clinical psychologist. Moreover, Lydia was in the convent at one time. She left
the convent, but she was perfect to discuss my problems with
at that time. The priests were right next door in the seminary.
With her psychology education, Lydia counseled many nuns
and priests who broke the "vow of celibacy," and she was
understanding about it.

Just being able to unload the heavy burden and dirty
secrets I carried for so long was wonderful! We both were
from the mid-west and knew of Christian values.

She was knowledgeable and assured me, patiently,
not to carry shame about unworthiness or the lies of others anymore. She vehemently stated that Mom, Dad, Father
Quinton, and Dr. C. were the ones who should have known
better than to *abuse their authority* over Skip and me.

Even though Lydia was more or less my neighbor and friend, she wanted to use her expertise in psychology to help me. Once I just let out all the stuff I had buried for so many years, she wanted to help me get on the path to healing. I no longer wanted hide behind anything! The true facts and traumatized inner child came rushing out. Her gentle way and maternal arms were there to hold the tormented, terrified little girl that had been hiding for so many miserable years. God was with me and Lydia. He wanted me free. He put the two of us together, I know.

With my Heavenly Father, Lydia rescued me. After just a few precious cathartic months, I was set free! Now, He was allowing me to start my healing process with a (safe and) compassionate psychologist. She had incredible experience with exactly the intimate issues I was not doing a very good job of coping with… What God did with Lydia and me was a miracle. I owe a lot to two authors that happen to be clinical psychologists, Dr. Henry Cloud and Dr. John Townsend. The reason being their collaborative work entitled *Safe People* made a heavy impact on the keeping, picking out, and choosing those I want around me on a regular basis. Even though Lydia opened my eyes to the "red flags" of destructive types, all throughout my healing journey, I had a fouled-up mindset about boundaries in relationships. For a time, I had what is called a "safety deficit." With my father behaving so horrible when he drank, Skip and I were in jeopardy of being physically harmed and were many times. My father's PTSD, combined with drinking, was like a Molotov cocktail set off in our house! An adult should have removed us right from the start of the violence. Lydia said, "The parental violations were off the map!"

Lydia let me know that Mom and Father Quinton were *not safe* either because they walked away, ignored, or simply refused to acknowledge that Dad was mistreating us, mainly because of Father Quinton's marital infidelity issue with Mom. Since all three paid no attention to what the root of the problems in our house were, the only time Skip and I felt acceptance and love was at Merryland. You can only get heartache from the lonely and self-possessed. I felt normal for running away to camp for what we all desperately needed—a feeling of belonging with love. Skip and I never felt love by either parent after the age of five for me and eight for him. Camp provided love.

My friend Abbie and her family came to Merryland for one month every summer for ten years. They were the best, most loving group of people. They practically adopted me. We all hung out, participating in the all-day and all-night activities. Abbie's family showed me what a real loving family looks like. Since they all loved swimming, my boy cousins that I loved met up with Abbie's three brothers, and they became great friends. Abbie's mom had a sneaking feeling that my mother and Father Quinton had a "thing" going on but only kept it between our families. She was so sweet, and her kids adored her as well as her big old bear-like gentle husband.

I reached out beyond this world for love. I focused on our pastor's words about God's title, "El Shaddai," the gentle role of our Heavenly Father.

Since neither of my parents stayed caring and loving, it thrilled me to know our God, Heavenly Father, and Jesus loved enough and was nurturing more than any mother or father. They promise to take care of us. With Lydia, I had a breakthrough.

With an aching chest, I told Lydia my family background and how much I loved my dad back when I was a baby. I was crying my heart out and told Lydia the true story of just how much I needed and loved my dad at one time. Every family member knew of this one incredible Saturday morning. I too remembered it vividly even though I was only two and a half years old. I relived it in my mind…down to every small detail. Dad had a roof repair to do on the house by the railroad tracks. This particular Saturday, he got his big extension ladder out and climbed up on the roof. He was hammering away, focused on his job up in the sky.

About an hour later into his work, still on the roof, my mother let out a yell. "Where's the baby?! Oh dear God, where's our baby girl?!" she screamed! She flew around hysterically and frantically, looked through every closet, under beds, etc. Finally, she ran outside to Dad, who was still on the roof. She looked up and let out a blood-curdling scream, jumping up and down, pointing. "Jesus, she's up there with you!" After hearing Mom, Dad spots me. I vividly remember how I had left my Handy Andy toolbox at the bottom of the ladder, reached, and stretched each step up the ladder to find my dad, and nothing was going to stop me. Dad was high up, and I needed to climb and walk to find him and to be with him. Lydia's eyes lit up as I continued.

Now on the roof, Dad did not go right to me; he was worried that I'd get too excited and lose my balance! Mom said I was standing straight up and I was walking toward my father. I remember his gentle voice coaxing me not to run but to take a step at a time to him. I remember him saying, "Keep coming, look straight at Daddy, and keep walking, honey. Come on, Wildflower, come to Daddy. Here I am, keep walking very slowly, baby."

I did exactly as he told me, and soon, he swooped me up! We couldn't do much movement with the fear of us both falling thirty-five feet to the blacktop driveway, so there was slow steady movement. But when we went back down, I think my mom was in shock! After all, her two-and-a-half-year-old was on the roof, which caused her to be frozen in fear, and she thought it was a miracle I didn't tumble down the roof! Lydia gently put her hands around my face and whispered, "You loved your daddy didn't you, Wildflower?" When she asked that, I lost it and fell into her arms, wailing.

I believed, as Lydia agreed, *both* fathers were with me. Lydia informed me about many things after this; she had strong faith in God, our Father. Even though, she herself left the convent, she still had an unshakable faith in our Almighty Lord.

After hearing this, all of the extreme attachment to my "daddy," she now saw how devastated I was that my dad turned on me years later. Lydia was the right woman to talk about all my conflicts I had between my two fathers: My dad, who I would have done anything for, and Father Quinton, who would do anything for me, my brother, and Mom. Lydia lived and worked with priests; she was an educated and trained psychologist on top of being a kind, gentle, loving, and compassionate woman. I needed Lydia, and God provided just what I needed. Praise the Lord! Thank God that there was someone I could pour my heart and whole life out to who wouldn't stop me or judge me. What a gift! I was at the other end of the country, and God brought me to be delivered from deep down pain that I had thought would never end.

NIGHTMARES...VARMINTS

Lydia painstakingly made me relive...but she had to. In our first old neighborhood, we were all on the same page. Mom happily agreed and was happy to get away from the noise of the railroad and the threat of the ugly sewer rats that came out of the exposed pipes every night. Several times, when my mom baked angel food cake, she would cool them on coke bottles upside down on the window ledge. Well, sewer rats would be gnawing on the other side of the cake when she came to pick them up. I remember her screaming, "Oh no, not again!" We had four adult female cats that hung around, so we fed them.

My dad said, "Don't feed those cats anything and you'll see the rats disappear!"

From the age of five, I used to have terrible nightmares. I told Lydia how realistic and frightening they were. Lydia informed me that because the dirty varmints I was dreaming about were rats, I was probably having those nightmares about the people in my life that had harmed me. I'd put my arms out, and all of a sudden, I'd be lifted off the ground and, with my arms straight out to my side, start to fly over the rats. Lydia thought that this could be a foreshadowing of my future freedom from the abusers in my life (unless they changed).

RESCUED

Lydia was wonderful. She was such a great listener. When she could see that I was stuck or hesitating to come forward with something embarrassing or shameful, she'd help out. Sometimes, she would turn the light off at her house and take part of my father or boss and say some frightening words, which would force the truth out of me. At times, it was hard. But with her gentle trustworthy way, we got to the root of many of my fears and defense mechanisms that were blocking my joy in life. When I got to the molestation with

Dad and the indecent exposure at my first vet job, my voice cracked and my bottom lip quivered. I told Lydia I wanted to just scream! Surprisingly, she said, "Go ahead, I do it all the time."

I was dumbfounded. "Scream, really? I could yell right here, right now?" Wow! This took me off guard! I asked again to be clear on what Lydia said. "I can scream!?"

She cutely shrugged and reiterated, "I'm waiting on you, or would you rather me go into the other room so you can really let loose?"

When she left the room, I used a pillow and really let it all out of my system. I stopped when my throat was sore and my voice was hoarse. Jesus truly delivered me from anger that I stuffed down for so many years! Just swallowing all the hurt wasn't an option any longer!

After hearing the story about Dad, me, and the roof, she let me know that just as people themselves can suffer and hide in shock for many years, denial is the result. I was denying my hurt deep down and the excruciating suffering that my childhood endured. The cold, hard, 180-degree turn with my dad was incomprehensible to me, so I sunk under the perverted weight of it. I was not near over Mom and Dad's undeserved mistreatment—the residue came out through depression. *Dad's lost love devastated me.* The result was I became a target instead of his precious Wildflower. What's more, the PTSD from World War II and the extreme jealousy over Father Quinton caused my dad to become a violent alcoholic.

I could not see it at the time with my young mind, because Father Quinton wanted to be Mom's husband and wanted Skip and I to be his own kids; he was mostly good to the three of us. However, I see now where Dad was the odd man out. I told Lydia about Skip. She needed to know how he "handled" all the stuff with our dad. My answer was Skip was an escape artist. He learned quickly that if he was never home, he'd never be in trouble or be a target of Dad's deep-seated anger. Every club in school, every party by classmates, all year round at camp, whatever—he'd go. One year, I remember, if he was home two weekends, it was a rarity. Being almost three years older, he could go. I was forced to remain in the snake pit. My home was my prison.

Skip would try to divert Dad's attention to his favorite subject, baseball! Skip wasn't an athlete except for horseback riding. Skip was entered by Father Quinton in horse shows. He did barrel races, western pickup stuff, and could even break in colts and fillies. He later got to continue his life with horses with his two adolescent daughters. Skip had the most terrific personality. People were magnets to him.

Accordingly, Skip had a way with Dad, that which could take his attention away from anything. In every fight between our parents, if Skip was forced to choose a side, he'd always sided with Dad. At the time, I did not understand this.

I told Lydia that Dad would sometimes be distracted by Skip. But I told her the one of the many times he had to endure Dad's wrath. It happened when Skip was sick with a 104-degree fever and symptoms of the flu. I don't know what he did to upset Dad, but he made Skip go down to the basement to get something for him. Mind you, my brother was dizzy from his illness. My father seemed to be totally clueless when it came to "mercy."

First of all, Skip should have been in bed resting until he got over his sickness. That stuff never mattered to Dad. Since he hardly ever got sick himself, I guess he thought nobody else did either. Skip was being outwardly obedient and did what Father said. He headed down fifteen steep basement stairs. Skip said he felt woozy at the top landing, and all of a sudden, he couldn't help it, but he threw up all over the steps! Like always, here came my dad, half inebriated, and he tried to grab my brother because he was angry at the mess he made. He reached and knocked my brother down the vomit-covered stairs! Down Skip went, and Dad slipped on a few too. He threatened Skip to spotlessly clean the steps or else. Dad seemed to add "or else" to everything to instill more fear. Unlike me, Skip never fought back or tried to defend himself. Almost like an emotionless martyr, Skip took Dad's abuse. I was uncontrollably sobbing.

By this time, Lydia also had tears in her eyes of compassion. I told her Dad also treated his whole family as though we were in the army. On weekdays, to wake us up, he wouldn't say, "Wake up or get up." He'd say, "Roll out," and sometimes even act like he was blowing the Reveille trumpet as he tooted the tune to the wake-up melody. He was very regimental with his behavior. He would say things like, "Kids should be seen, not heard." The only opinion that counted was his. However, he refused to ever talk about his days in the war. Skip could converse with him better than anybody else, and he always tried to appease or humor Dad. Sober, Dad was nicer and somewhat normal.

When I finished telling this true story about my brother and the steps, Lydia sat stunned and then asked if Skip ever managed to clean up the mess? No, but I remembered Mom and I came home from shopping just minutes after it all happened. I felt sorry about what Dad did; both Mom and I helped Skip mop up his vomit, and we helped him to bed. Mom was fine when it came to illnesses. When Skip or I ever had a cold, she'd iron our sheets and we'd quickly climb under them as it was very warm and toasty. Mom was so mad at Dad; she was on him all night about how mean he was to my sick brother. Skip never forgot it but stuffed it all down deep in his spirit…to his regret. Keeping all the hurt in caused my brother terrible stomach problems all his life.

Homework was another nightmare in our family. I especially hated needing help with my math. I asked Mom at first, but she'd tell me she was never good with math. Skip was the next choice, but he was always gone. I was left with my father. He happened to be a wiz in math. But it was also very scary and nerve-racking. If I didn't get the answer right, I'd get whacked right across the face! After about three or four times of this, I got smart and just did the best I could by myself. With Lydia, I could easily remember more and more junk. It was all rising to the surface with a safe, caring woman. I could never talk to Mom because she didn't seem to be interested in helping; she was too busy.

My homework was not always correct by any means, but at least I didn't have to suffer insults, slaps, criticism, and/ or name-calling from my father. It was hurtful enough that I chose to get Cs rather than go through the ridicule and pain. Ironically, I became a bank teller and even trained people to become bank tellers. Maybe it wasn't the math I hated.

THE REFRIGERATOR INCIDENT

Next, it was my turn to let out the fear and hurt from Dad. This was a day Mom was away. Skip was away, and I was left at home with my father. I always made attempts to be out of the house too, but this day, I couldn't find anyone available to drive me or hang out. Many times, I just wandered around the woods and climbed trees. For the first five years, our neighborhood consisted of eleven boys and two girls. I was one of the two. I was very much liked by the boys;

we all played sports together. But if the other girl, May Jo, was around, I would skate with her or ride on our bikes. At night, the whole gang would play "ghosts in the graveyard" or "spud." I loved being with other kids! Camp life taught me how to get along great with other kids. As an adult, I had one problem with a neighbor, and she was a known psychotic!

In the same realm, this dark day, a terrible storm threatened. I really ticked my dad off. I think I compared Dad to Father Quinton in an innocent way. But that was not a good thing to do, especially when Mom isn't around to help. I hated to be alone with Dad! The storm clouds looked threatening. I was seeking out places to take cover. The dark sky was ominous over our house.

Dad, around this time, was drinking hard stuff. We had a built-in window box where he kept all his whiskey and other liquor. It was right next to the refrigerator. Mom and Skip were not coming back for a while longer. "Drat!" I stayed out of Dad's way the best I could. But he would not hear of it; he wanted me to be like we were when I was little. He kept on it and on me. He even reminded me of the roof story! I cried then, but not for him to see.

I even tried to go to my room, but he wanted to talk. I had really a bad feeling about this day. So I went back down to the living room in order to keep him calm. I always wanted to be close to an exit, just in case. He wanted to talk in the kitchen, so I obeyed and sat, but I didn't like it. He asked if a priest was more important than a father. I kept quiet. He then rose up and yelled, "You better not mention that priest's name in this house!" He pointed his finger as close to my eyes as he could get, visibly shaking from too much alcohol traversing though his veins! He'd turned into an alcoholic rage-aholic, so I had to be very careful not to anger him.

As I continued talking, Lydia was very focused on not only my words but my body language. When I kept coming to the parts where I expressed fearful happenings, she commented to me something I'll never forget. Lydia said, "Look down at how you are recoiling and pulling up your legs and wrapping your arms around yourself." Then she elaborated on body language being so important for "key signs to our fear and distress over being bullied." Then she said, "Katia, your father was a bully and stalker in your own home!" I'm sure my jaw dropped, and my eyes got as big as saucers and teared up at truth.

The sad part is I knew she was right. Lydia, was making me recall everything. I suddenly became freezing and visibly shaken. Mind you, we were in sunny California where the temperature was 82 degrees and our A/C was not needed, but I asked her if I could pull the afghan over me that she had on the back of the couch that I was halfway sitting on. It was summer, and I had frigid chills.

Lydia gently consoled me with a hug. I told her all the things that happened in the house I grew up in and that emotionally drained my strength just by recalling the vivid details. I continued while holding tightly onto a bolstered pillow Lydia had on her soft corduroy sofa... I clung to the pillow while telling Lydia how I lived in terror of Dad and what he might do.

There were countless case-in-point topics you could not talk about with my father, or he would fly off the handle. I picked the safest topic—baseball. Somehow, something was said to upset him still, and he was about to blow up like a volcano. At this point, because I accepted Father Quinton at all and worked for him like the rest of my family, he couldn't handle it. He said, "I understand your mother and brother being turncoats, but not you." His movements were intimidating, and when he angrily spoke, his nostrils flared. Then he reached over my head to the window box and grabbed a bottle of whiskey. Well, something rose up in me, and I knocked it out of his hand! It went crashing to the steps in the kitchen, and Dad simultaneously grabbed me like a ragdoll and started to bash my head against the refrigerator a couple of times! I was fading in and out of consciousness. I don't remember much, but it didn't take long to feel like blacking out. I recall my crazed father muttering something like, "*Why did you desert me, Wildflower? Why?*"

I remember that my head felt buzzed and my ears rang. I had a weird *cold* feeling come over me. I recall I cried out as he pulled me up one more time, "No, Daddy! No, Daddy!" and I must have passed out. I think Dad left and must have grabbed the whiskey I knocked out of his hand. The next thing I recall was Mom and Skip came back home, and they saw me passed out, lying in front of the refrigerator. I think Mom took me to the hospital. I couldn't really remember, I told Lydia. A bit stunned, I remember she remarked on how much I'd been through, and I remember Lydia and I both looked up to the sky, thinking it's a miracle that I'm still here. We were both crying now. She said that in her practice, she heard many sad childhood stories, but she scared me when she said my childhood was comparable to the movie *Agnes of God*! Meg Tilly and Jane Fonda portrayed the women in the film. It was riveting. Lydia, with a flash of anger in her eyes, said my father was a terrorist and should have been locked up!

Summing up, I told Lydia that after that, I think Father Quinton stayed completely away from the house. Nobody said a word about him for a few years. Mom still traveled with Father Quinton, she just never mentioned it, especially around Dad. I had bruises, and to this day, I can't have anyone comb my hair because my head became very sensitive after that incident. I trusted Lydia and told her all about Dad, and the time he came into my room drunk and tried to seduce me. She said, "The *constant* drunken violent attempts had to make you a nervous wreck." She was right. Lydia held me whimpering for a long time after I disclosed each harmful encounter.

I'D RATHER BE ANYWHERE ELSE!

Skip and I left home and stayed at friend's houses as much as we could. After age twelve, I had many overnights at camp or anywhere else with my girlfriends. Once, I told Lydia that *fear* was my constant companion. For most of our elementary days, Mom would get home from work about the same time we got off the school bus. But this all stopped when she had "meetings" with the boss of our camp, Father Quinton. Sometimes, she would barely make it home to make us supper. Our dad got off by six but didn't come home until six thirty or six forty-five. Mom wouldn't worry about what Skip and I did in the meantime; we were seven and ten years old at the time. Several times after school, the house had been broken into, with jagged glass everywhere! They only robbed us of little things, but to come home to an empty house turned upside down with ransacked toys and stuff was scary.

I tried to stay calm as I told Lydia about my past as an adolescent with my dad. I begged and cried, but I had to eat a horrible meal, most called it "shit on a shingle." It was a spam-type meal served with sickening white chalk-like gravy. It was horrible! Dad staggered over after drinking, saying I had better eat his favorite meal or else. I asked for anything else. He wouldn't hear of it. I said I wasn't hungry. I just wanted to do my homework. As soon as the request was heard, *ooh hot!* He pushed my head down into the meal! I had to go to the bathroom to wash off, but the gravy burnt my face. I noticed that this was the first time my dad never came after me. Where did he go, and what was he up to?

I was so hungry, so I ran into my cubbyhole closet with a Zero candy bar, Fritos, Reese's Cups, soda, and other sweets I stashed away. I always had a backup plan. When I went down in the morning, Mom was nowhere around to fix breakfast, but to my surprise, I saw my dad there already dressed for work. I did a double take on the kitchen table to find the gross meal of last night's supper. I said, "I'd rather die than eat that crap!" I was thirteen and belligerent, and I'd had it with this insanity. My father proceeded to force feed me with a spoon and butter knife. I didn't have to push away because I immediately threw up all at once. I always ran upstairs to my room with my cats for comfort. They were always willing to be my friend and love me when no one else would. They loved my Cheetos!

CHAPTER 9

LIFE GOES ON, AND GETS BETTER

I filled Lydia in on my marriage life. My husband graduated from college and was offered a job with the federal government. He took the job, and almost immediately, our financial picture changed for the better. As both families declared, "With government, he'd have a job in the future." Lance always achieved success in whatever he took on, whether it was at home or at work, he was a mover and a shaker!

Within the next few years, my husband had one promotion after another. Then, having the bug to travel to see what might be out there, we decided to take a job up north, three-hundred miles from our hometown. For me, not being in the same hometown where I was traumatized would be beneficial. Perhaps it would give me a new perspective of the world. I was willing to try. So we packed up, visited everyone, hugged, and shook hands and left for our first adventure away from away from a town of horrors.

I also knew how to be a bookkeeper and camp hostess, two of my side jobs during the camp season. So I applied to get a job at a small-town bank. I always made friends pretty quickly; we had several couples that we befriended and went around together. We so much enjoyed the excellent restaurants, and we were right on top a major city, Pittsburgh. The small town and the government offices were full of friendly folks. Lance wanted dogs, not cats as much, so we went to look for a few. Scottish Terriers were always my favorite, so Lance saw them and agreed. We bought a pair and named them Bonnie and Bailey. They were so cute. I loved them too. Nonetheless, Lance got the travel bug again,

My husband did not like to attend church. For a few years, I did not attend church either. With Father Quinton, the church, and Mom and Dad, I wasn't really ready yet. I wish I had gone back then. I felt unworthy to go. Even though I was confused, scared, and lost, I could not make the trek back yet. All the guys I ever dated were Catholic. Before I met Lance, I never took any of my relationships seriously. Mostly, the popular guys I dated were used to their dates "putting out." That was something that was not going to happen. A few boys remarked that I was a "cold fish" or an "ice princess" after the kissing part. I dated a lot but mostly to get out of the house. I did go to a few proms, and although I did have fun, I just went through the motions. Remaining my tomboy self, Mom forced me in many dresses and fancy gowns, but they were not my comfort wear.

Two older boys I dated said that I was pretty but a cold freak of nature when I would not cooperate with their racing hormones. I put on a pretty good front and let guys flirt some, but I treated the guys like girlfriends. And they'd get the wrong impression and think I was leading them on. I just wanted to get out of my house away from my parents when they were constantly at each other's throats. Mom told me about ten years later, she confronted my dad about what he did to me at night when she was gone. A little too late, Mom! My father told her he was just checking me because he used to be pretty rough and aggressive. *Ha!* I'm just happy that he never discovered my cubby hole in my closet. Thank you, God! That could have turned out for me like poor Joyce Meyer. Wow! What she had to overcome, what a champion for women everywhere! I have several of her books in my library on self-help sources. She is one of my favorites!

After Skip and I both married, Mom wasn't home with Dad much. And I was married about five to seven years when we eventually moved out to California. My mother and Father Quinton had then bought a gorgeous place out west. At this time, Mom was living part year in our hometown and part year with Father Quinton out of town. We drove out to stay with them. Hotels were expensive, and Mom begged us all to come. But why do I still, after all he did to me, say, "What about Dad?"

I expressed to Lydia that the house Father Quinton bought was absolutely beautiful. We were told an actor owned it and rented it out to upcoming actors. He used to give acting lessons there. It had a huge living room with a balcony overlooking the dining room, family room, and den. Its kitchen was long with white cabinets and pot hangers twelve feet up in the ceiling. The floor was black and white checked. It was something off a picture postcard.

There was a large, kidney-shaped, black-bottomed, stone-trimmed pool. The view from it was as high up as we were—it was spectacular! But as many years as Father Quinton was around us, I could not cope with *them,* in my mind, being this Richard Burton and Elizabeth Taylor-type couple! But they were gracious enough to us, and the house was a knockout! On the other hand, their night-time departure was shocking to me as they retreated hand in hand in the extravagantly decorated, Queen Victoria-embellished master bedroom. For the first time, it hit in the pit of my stomach... My mother was the adulteress in *The Scarlet Letter*!

THE KING'S WIFE, THAT JEZABEL

THE THORN BIRDS... BACK AGAIN

Father Quinton and Mom wanted to rendezvous with Lance and me, so they visited us at our apartment. They surprised us with wanting to watch the miniseries, *The Thorn Birds*. The MC for the movie explained about the thorn birds, which are a type of songbird. They know when they sing the loudest and best is when they have impaled themselves on a thorn bush and know they are dying, so they cry, singing out until the end. Perhaps Mom's marriage did die. My father was the worst to her—to all of us. But I couldn't visualize this relationship between Father Quinton and Mom staying alive either. It had a death toll ring to it.

My psychologist friend, Lydia, laid it out for me. Like me, she read God's scripture and, as a nun, continued it throughout her life. I trusted her, and she enlightened me on how wrong my thought process was. In some ways, I felt the blame for what happened to me because I was told so by many authority figures that I was the problem. So the truth really did set me free. The difference of now realizing the truth and *not* being "the problem" was astronomical in my growth as a happy Christian. Again, the weight of my dad, Mom, and Father Quinton was on me because I was used as the target, scapegoat, or alibi. They selfishly did not want me to know the truth. Had I known, it could jeopardize their "secret dastardly deeds." Shrikes are that way. They always find same unsuspecting one to pounce on and dismember, even if it is one's own family.

A NEW "ISM" WORD

A word that not many people hear of is shrike. Shrikes are very nasty, destructive birds that impale their prey on a thorn and then proceed to methodically peck it to death. People in my family have acted similarly to this bird when it comes to gossiping about their so-called loved ones. They tear them up verbally one side and then down the other. The victims are lucky if they have any respectable reputation at all. I like what the pastor and author, John Sanford, says about verbal shrikes. "They lacerate with their tongues." These wicked folks demolish the other's character and divide friendships. They chip away and use force to get their victims right where they want them and then go in for a slow, agonizing kill. This boils down to an extreme pride issue; the person's behavior is called "shrikism." The best way to describe this is "a person who establishes their own personal righteousness at the expense of others." In other words, the shrike can only look good if others look bad (Sanford). A shrike will constantly push himself or herself to outperform everyone around him or her. They must get all the glory, applause, and credit. Unless God does a radical interruption in the shrike's life, like He did in Saint Paul's life on the road to Damascus, they will not make it into heaven.

As victims of shrikes, we do forgive, but you do not forget. Remembering prevents one from falling into the same situation or traps. We chose to forgive our enemies, but when we do, our Heavenly Father is not finished with *them* yet. If they do not repent, and repentance is not just saying you're sorry but also to avoid repeating the same offence again, God will seek vengeance (Psalms 7:12–14). In other words, they must change and *have a change in heart.* That is true acceptable repentance in God's eyes. We must forgive all, and then God will take on those who do not admit their sin who have harmed His own. In God's words, "Vengeance is mine, I will repay" (Romans 12:19).

In regard to habitual sinners, 2 Thessalonians 6 states you must, "put the person away" for a while. Tell them what they did, and if there is still no repentance, have nothing to do with them until they have stopped their destruction. It's Biblical.

MY MOTHER "QUEENIE"

That is not disrespectful. She loved that name, Queenie. We found out that Mom's boss and significant other bought my parents their lovely house on the lake. But even though Father Quinton and Mom had so much in common and really cared for one another, she could never make the giant move to divorce my dad. I know Father Quinton would have given up his priest vows if Mom would do this. Our Catholic family would have freaked, especially Mom's Italian father and Quinton's nephew, Tyler. They all had a problem with Jezebella and Quinton. My mother had an issue with starting rumors about others… It threw people off.

Too many townspeople were talking, and the rumor all over three counties was that Father Quinton and Mom were having an affair. Dad remained in denial…but knew he did not want Quinton around all of us. This really bothered Skip so much so that he stopped coming home from Arizona. I do understand, however, now that we were living back home, I was upset with this! I always wanted to see Skip and Caroline. Mom and Quinton's relationship, to all watching, was a copy of Liz Taylor and Richard Burton crossed with the couple in the miniseries, *The Thorn Birds*. Not only did they look like the *Cleopatra* Hollywood couple, but they acted and dressed like them. After I was married and realized Mom and Quinton were an "item," I asked her if she was trying to imitate Liz Taylor, and she just smiled in response. The actors in *The Thorn Birds* portrayed a priest and a married woman who had a very long relationship. The son died, and the daughter lived and had a good man as her boyfriend. This movie had many parallels to all of us. The female main character had a husband and two children, one older boy and a younger girl. The boy was the priest's hidden son.

I asked if Mom wanted me to get something out of *The Thorn Birds*? Father Quinton retorted, not mom, "Just how the world reacts to a priest having a girlfriend or wife." He then shockingly told me that Mom and *he* went through their own private ceremony and that *they* were married!

I gasped. "Say what?! Isn't there a civil law against having two spouses at the exact same time? Besides that, what about the Ten Commandments? Does my mom know you all did this?" Now I was really confused! With them breaking all the Biblical commands, being with my mother and Quinton no longer worked; it was seedy, sneaky, and wrong! I was just discerning. But…down deep, this crushed me!

Still shocked, I asked, "What about your *husband*, my father?" I was ignored and dismissed with a roll of Mom's eyes. Over the years, Father Quinton bought several houses in garden spots in the country. He had five hideaways that he rented out when he and Mom weren't staying in them. He bought Mom anything she wanted. She had so much genuine silver and gold jewelry that she had to store in a chest of drawers rather than a jewelry box. She wanted to wear several pieces at once that coordinated and looked good on her. Her Indian jewelry was her best. It was real. Father Quinton also bought her diamonds. Mom, unlike me, did not care for fine, delicate jewelry. Lydia agreed.

Mom loved to wear shiny, sparkling clothes. And lots of red and purple. She probably, at one time, had fifty pairs of heels and forty studded purses. Mom loved things. Father Quinton had a nickname for her—Queenie. She loved the movie *Cleopatra*, so I believe Mom wanted to imitate the fashion in her own wardrobe.

A DIABETIC WHO EATS SWEETS!

Life out West in this gorgeous ocean city was fantastic! Lance was constantly looking for a job. He really wanted to get out on our own. My mom and Father Quinton turned into Liz Taylor and Richard Burton right before our eyes. Mom always, in the face, looked like Elizabeth Taylor. I believe a few people told her that, and it went to her head! The town's people were nice. Now that the two of them were footloose and fancy free, they didn't have to hide their feelings for one another. We constantly saw them holding hands and kissing everywhere. Father Quinton being like a servant to my mother, he actually held a fan and fanned her at the beach in the sun! They were thousands of miles away from anyone who threatened their bliss, but Lance didn't like it. I remained confused and worried. Where was there a good father—a selfless one? I was sick of it all! What will happen to my dad? Am I going crazy? Where do I belong? I had lots of questions—and lots of wounds. And now my own mother, "Jezebel," was in bed with Father Quinton.

Father Quinton would dote on Mom, giving her anything she wanted. This included cakes, ice creams, sweet
breads, pancakes with syrup, etc. She was off her sugar-free,
diabetic diet, and my mother had a bad temper. Lance and I
wanted away from it all, whatever it was. I loved the beauty of
the ocean city, but I did not want to be with Father Quinton
and Mom anymore. Like Skip, he became just "Quinton" in
my mind now. I still cared for both my mom and Quinton,
though it was time for us to find our own place. I was being
called to "come into the light" and out of the darkness,
Poltergeist-style.

CHAPTER 10

You will know the truth, it will set you free.
                                        —John 8:31

SKIP, DAD, AND ME

Going back, I told Lydia that, as kids, when trouble with Dad was looming, I would usually signal Skip covertly to sneak out of the house. Dad always had some reason to go after me. I'd run around the dining room table a couple of times, which made Dad dizzy in his drunken state, to escape. I would not allow my dad to tear up my brother verbally nor abuse him or leave him with no dignity. I felt sorry for Skip and I hated bullies! I was to be involved in the future, with my own kids, again with bullies. I've had many experiences. I hated when my dad called Skip "sissy" or "panty waist."

My dad knew I never listened to him when he was drunk. Dad wasn't a sloppy drink; he was a demonic one. Skip knew all about that but refused to ever complain or tell anyone. Dad was his dad, and Quinton was "not his dad." Skip let Mom know that, but she tried hard to win over his affection all his life. Skip kept away from our parents except for Christmas after he married Caroline.

CAROLINE HITS THE JACKPOT

Lydia wanted to know about Skip and his family. Throughout the time of Skip's marriage, something fortunate was happening. Skip's wife was doing well in her job. Movie stars, music legends, and famous people lived in their area, but my brother always wanted something more simplistic and genuine. Privately, he told me he always wanted to have a hardware and feed store. He always loved horses and fixing and improving cars. Caroline's boss invited Skip to join his worldwide home building company, so they moved their kids and seven cars west. They lived life in the fast lane and traveled to just about every country in twelve years. Skip was good to Dad as he always sent him expensive shirts, sweaters, and jackets back home. He never missed a birthday or Christmas.

The business put Caroline on the board of directors of the entire million-dollar company. It had a brand-new jet and a staff of four pilots by this time; they also hob-knobbed with the rich and famous people, socializing with governors, attorneys, and even senators.

Skip's two girls had nannies in their beautiful waterfront-style mansion. Skip and Caroline worked from Las Vegas, LA, San Francisco to Colorado. They went to the Virgin Islands for cruises, they went on mountain expeditions, safaris, ski slopes, and much more. They lived extravagant lives for twelve years. I was very happy and proud of him; Skip was also very generous to extended family. He never forgot his humble roots though. Every Christmas, he sent really generous checks. Skip was always thinking of others.

Sadly, only I knew that, deep down, Skip *wanted* a simpler life because of his Camp Merryland background. Unfortunately, Skip's hardware and feed store weren't in his future as Caroline ran the show. But he did enjoy his collection of vintage cars and new Jaguars. That was one dream he did get to realize. He bought a farm where he could ride a tractor and even grow corn!

As I mentioned, my brother and I both had stomach problems by the time we were teenagers. Skip actually had bleeding ulcers the first few years he was married. I can't imagine what Skip went through! I was told to drink milk before eating chili or any kind of Mexican food—my favorite food ethnicity. Skip loved Mexican too, so he'd have to drink his ulcer medication before he ate. He also loved putting hot sauce all over his food. I thought he was crazy for challenging his stomach like that.

Like me, Skip's inner child was confused and shy when it came to him asserting himself. We both swallowed our pride many times with the domineering, aggressive people in our lives. The problem was our hate, anger, and resentment of our parents had to go somewhere. Our stomachs suffered the damage along with our self-esteem. Even our loved ones and spouses took advantage of our so called "easygoing" personalities on occasion. For example, I never wanted to move, and Skip didn't want to work for that big company. He did it, but he did not like it. I wish he would have stood up for himself and gotten his hardware store.

CURSE TO CROSS

Our Heavenly Father knows us so well. Amazingly, he knew us before we were even born. In His own words, in the first chapter of Jeramiah, God lets him know, "I knew you before you were formed in your mother's womb." That also goes for us. I wish I had known so much more about God's words and promises. Each and every line is valuable information that could have saved much heartache and brought comfort. For instance, also in Jeramiah 17, The Lord warns us, don't depend on man. I should have never gone to Father Quinton for advice. He was in no position to help me while he was sinning with my mother. Exodus 20:14. In fact, God said in Jeramiah 17:5, "Those who trust in man and depend on human strength are under a curse." Gasp! So that's what happened to all of us! I have found that we also need to repent for the evil circumstances we end up in, even if we didn't cause or start it. It's still sin.

Through our Savior, the necessary arrangements are made for reconciliation with our Lord. The wait is worth it. Jesus is our bridge to our Heavenly Father. I love the female pastor and author of some of my favorite self-help books. She says, "We are not humans with spirits. We are, rather, spirits having a human experience" (Paula White). I believe this. That's how we can be Holy-Spirit-controlled. It's God's spirit meeting our own, which opens doors for his promises, blessings, and supernatural intervention. "No one comes to the Father except through the Son" (Matthew 11:27).

Reprogramming

As a result of coming clean with my friend Lydia, I started breaking out of my shell. I started to allow myself to enjoy every moment in the moment. I did not feel like I was a bad girl anymore (like Mother said). I didn't let men, or anyone for that matter, walk all over me anymore. Lydia helped me realize that I was the victim of the situation in my home life as a child, *not the cause of it*. She described it as "pseudo guilt," and I shouldn't burden myself with it.

Letting out all of my gut-wrenching pain that I had carried for so long gave me relief. Lydia helped me find solace in my Heavenly Father, who lifted my burdens and helped me let go of my self-pity and self-destruction. I felt as if my new job now was to not allow my emotions to drag me down. With the help of God, I could now pick myself back up, dust off the dirt, and allow him to wash me clean. My goal was simple: Deprogram the old negativity, rebuking the horror films replaying in my mind over and over. I had to give my heart to Him. I began to claim all of the positive affirmations my Real Father says about His children. I am not pathetic or unfixable. I am loved. This didn't happen all overnight, but once I made my decision, I began to feel a weight had been lifted… I was, in fact, happier.

Furthermore, I was on a new mission to find Christian-based self-help books. I frequented many used bookstores, thrift shops, and many garage sales in my feverous search. First, I collected the books where other authors used Scripture to entail the solution to my problems. I began to see that my Heavenly Father had launched me out there and created my blueprint for emotional and spiritual healing and set forth my unquenchable thirst to become whole. I wanted to keep unloading the unwanted baggage…and reach for the light. In *Poltergeist*, the characters are encouraged to come into the light.

My search was continuous. Though my family would not listen, my newfound freedom in Christ had pushed me to go on and discover who I really was inside. It has been completely astonishing, the many wonderful and compassionate personalities that I was privileged to meet along my path. So many times, I seemed to be in the right location for the *perfect book* that would combat the private issues that I had been dealing with at that moment. I'm not ashamed to disclose that all of the authors helped me by writing about their own research of the Bible and the promises that I so desperately needed to hear. One of Leslie Vernick's books she wrote on destructive relationships says that *"the maturing person allows others to act as mirrors that reflect the truth of his or her own life."* I agree, I learned many private ways that these writers used to move forward that worked for them. Their methods were already used and successful. Most of the writers of my collection were either a pastor or a psychologist or both. One thing we all had in common was that we were all Christian. My friend Lydia was truly a special "gift" to me! She was a Christian, a psychologist for domestic violence victims, and experienced with the clergy. Lydia did it all in Christ and for a hurting daughter, this was pivotal and a miracle.

A MAN OR A MAN OF GOD

Now, Lydia wanted to learn about Quinton. Since the age of five, I've had a real dichotomy with Father Quinton and Mom, who apparently were "involved" ever since I was in kindergarten or before, I think. I admitted this to Lydia and that Mom felt all eyes watched her, even though she and Quinton took every precaution to keep their affair a secret. After many years of knowing Father Quinton and the whole situation, he told me to call him Quinton; after all, he was just a man, but as much as Quinton and Mom were really in love, Quinton had a deep love for God. I know. In search of my Heavenly Father, Quinton and I discussed this. He had an approach conflict, and God was one of his conflicts. He is the one who gave me my first Bible. I read it some myself at night. I could not put this Holy book down! It fascinated me so. I hated the blood and gore, but I seemed to want to change within the first months of reading it. I had to find this wonderful yet elusive being that everyone called God. I was twenty-five at the time.

I think forgiveness for some people is gradual, especially if things done to the person forgiving were traumatic and ongoing. The Bible always refers to our belief in Jesus and gives us peace of mind. What is so incredible is that when Jesus looked down from the cross, writhing in pain and suffocating from the blood that filled his lungs, He asked God to forgive His murderers. *How in the world do we imitate that?* Jesus is how.

What is so neat is just making the *choice* to want to forgive an offense, an insult or abuse is that just choosing opens doors. I personally had trouble with Father Quinton even though he did everything humanly possible to win Skip and me over. We both knew it was all because he wanted to make Mom happy first. She included us in on the deal.

Dad *had a reason* to act out and drink and do all the evil, horrible, destructive things. He did, however (and I'm not excusing it). He was what the Bible called "the afflicted." His PTSD would kick in, combined with the threat of a competing force of Father Quinton taking his kids away from him. Furthermore, with the worry of a public scandal, he drank to obliterate his thoughts and not face reality. When he was sober, he was an easygoing and very nice man. Even back when Dad was acting his worst, I felt sorry for him. When Mom went for help for the two of them, she got more than good counsel.

In the old days, the women used to say of their drunken husbands, "Don't listen to him. He's got the spirits." I guess Dad was in such a terrible predicament because his competition was a "man of God," he got inebriated to numb the pain.

My dad believed we were put on earth to suffer, but I don't believe that. There is a lot of suffering in the world, but I don't think we were *put* here to suffer. In fact, anytime I hear the word *suffer*, other than what Jesus did for us, the pain, trouble, and suffering are all things God uses for good. Greater is He in us than he who causes most of the suffering. This, of course, is the enemy of God, the devil. In the "Our Father," God forgives us our trespasses *as* we forgive those who trespass against us. Most Christians *do* know when they have sinned, so it is for those of us and, this is a 50\50 benefit… This is freedom.

I HAD A DREAM…

I disclosed to Lydia that something very weird happened to me. After a few years visiting with my mother and Quinton at various locations throughout the United States, something strange happened. Each and every time that Lance and I were with them, my conscience started bothering me to the extreme. Even though my dad was an alcoholic and abusive as a parent, I was veering away from Mom and Quinton's secondhand lifestyle.

In fact, to be more explicit, I was becoming revolted inside with the pseudo-marriage carried out between the two. The straw that broke the camel's back was one night after a weekend visit of staying with them in one of their hideaways. I had a very disturbing and defining dream. Actually, even though I was deep sleeping at the time, the vision became crystal clear as to what my next steps were.

I dream in color, so the scenery was spectacular and beautiful. My mother was in the dream with me (just the two of us). We were standing on a small cliff, peering over a lovely ocean, and motioning in almost slow motion with our hands. With Mother being Italian, the hand gestures were quite common. The difference was I took a hold of her hand and led her off the cliff and into the air. Fortunately, instead of both of us plummeting downward, we took flight as we held hands and were gliding over the ocean. In this dream, no wings were attached to us, but we both had long silky night gowns on. As we flew, our garments gently flapped in the tranquil wind.

Suddenly, appearing out of nowhere, was this huge forested mountain. Mom and I, still flying, looked over at one another. No words were ever spoken, but I took control and broke away from my panic-stricken mother's outstretched hand and, veering right, missed the mountain ahead. As I looked left, she had disappeared out of sight, as if the mountain was a huge split between us. I kept going on the right side of the mountain, flying solo now. Mom was nowhere around or in my sight. When I awoke, I was crying but somehow knew that this indicated I had to be true to the Word of God and now to myself as a new creation in Christ. This definitive dream set the course for the rest of my family and extended relatives in my mind. I knew in my heart that our Father is also a Gardener and was pruning me for anything that wasn't to His liking in my Christian walk. Ever since that dream, I have begged for spiritual discernment as one of the gifts so that I could get and keep on course following God's commands. Lydia verified, "You're on your way, Katia."

I had to separate from my family to get back to my moral and spiritual balance in my life unless they chose to change. Because of the threesome in my childhood, Dad was not the only one who acted out in anger. Mom was always bitey, looking over her shoulder like a nervous wreck most of her life. She used to take Librium, a tranquilizer, like candy.

I remember her having two of three bottles of them in her purse. The Word of God commands you, in the name of the Lord Jesus Christ, that you withdraw from every person who walks disorderly or habitually mean or sin-filled. I obeyed my Heavenly Father (2 Thessalonians 3:6). Both of my parents were abusive, so I kept away from them for a good while. God was dispelling the evil.

CHAPTER 11

Come out from them… Be separate.
—2 Corinthians 6:17

FATHER QUINTON, QUESTIONS FOR ME?

*O*ur short time in California presented me with a sudden but weird visit with Father Quinton.

I relayed this to Lydia. As a priest, Father Quinton shocked me with something regarding his faith and beliefs! He asked me, "Do you believe in the devil?"

Well, I quickly blurted back, "Of course I do! Don't you know my dad?"

Quinton threw his head back and laughed his deep resounding laugh, so I laughed too. However, his extreme persistence with me made me nervous. No one else was around, and ever since my trauma with my previous boss, I didn't feel comfortable with any man alone, even kind, somewhat caring Father Quinton.

Suddenly, the conversation turned very serious. And he asked again, "No really, I need to know. Do you believe in Satan?"

I said, now being very careful with my words, "I think he exists, but I don't 'believe' in him. I believe in Jesus Christ." I continued with reminding him "the devil walking to and fro upon the earth" (Job 6 and 7).

He persisted with, "Come on, you know what I mean." He asked again, very serious and focused. Then he said something to me which is bringing water in my eyes right now. These three people, my mom, Dad, and Father Quinton, could still get to me. He asked me if my dad ever abused Skip and me because of him.

Tears welled up in my eyes, and I answered, "Dad was very angry at everything, so I can't really say."

Father Quinton then got up, grabbed me, and hugged me very tightly. He told me I was a very good person.

He sat back down, and he questioned me at this time, and some of his questions and answers really surprised me. He once again asked me, "Do you believe there is a 'being' that is the devil?"

I remember rapid thoughts were rushing through like, *Father Quinton didn't you watch The Omen? How about Amityville Horror? Remember the temptation of Christ in the desert? Wake up and smell the coffee. You loved Jesus Christ Superstar!*

Lydia said, "What about it, Quinton?"

After pausing in disbelief at his real question, I politely said, "Yes, the enemy is very real." He came back by saying he didn't believe he even existed. Thinking to myself, I thought, Father Quinton, *therein lies your problem*. I referred to the eight hundred and ten places in the New and Old Testament where the devil, Satan, the dragon, Lucifer, the leviathan, father of lies, the snake, the serpent, the enemy of God, the "the fake morning star," and more were located. It took a while. Then I asked, "Do you still believe in God?"

Sadly, he said, "Hon, I don't really know anymore."

So that day at my house, Father Quinton sat with me and wanted to know all I thought about God, the Holy Spirit, Jesus, heaven, hell, and eternity. He knew I was in an all-out search to *connect*, whatever I had to do, to the Heavenly God. He asked me if I believe that people can really go to a place called hell.

"Yes, yes, they can, and I, for one, am doing everything to sidestep that place!" Then he wanted to know if there was a rapture coming, with a second coming of Jesus? He wanted to know if God really forgives sin. Is there an antichrist coming? Further, he wanted to know if we can *really* forgive our enemies. After that one, he finally took my hand, and I knew what he was going to ask next. I interrupted and gently assured him, "Yes, I can, and I do." Then he cried.

THE LAST STRAW

I continued with Lydia and told her after that incident with my father coming into my room at night, Mom *finally agreed* to let me live with Aunt Bev and Uncle Gino. It was the best decision she ever made for me.

I spent many months reliving some very sad, painful, and heartbreaking things. She said, "Katia, maybe a movie will be made out of your life." I laughed and thought *anything* is possible. She also said that she could see my spirit coming alive. Lydia relayed, like Sanford, that she thought my inner self was hiding before this. Lydia smiled and commented that I had a great personality and quick wit. I thanked her and said, "Despite the head pummeling I got from Dad." She giggled.

I had one more story to relay to her. The last event I spoke to Lydia was about my boss and the way he revealed himself to me. I told Father Quinton the truth that day but omitted rough-sorted details I could not bring myself to tell a man. After trusting my mentor and dear friend, I told Lydia *everything*. I felt like my whole life had changed. For the first time, I felt good relived and really happy.

I was starting to feel better about myself. I let my hair grow very long and put highlights in it and wore more fashionable clothes. I'm not ugly, but what mattered to me was *intellect*. I knew I got my parents minds; they were both very bright. Lydia assured me that I had this too. Lance said I was extremely quick. *This* meant everything to me.

Lydia filled me in on her opinions all along. Since Dad would do such a number on me if I made mistakes, it made me hate school. I didn't exceed like I could have until later. My mother was incredibly smart too. After graduating from high school, she'd never miss reading the newspaper; she was well traveled, creative, and had a memory like none other. She was considered the smartest in her family. My husband even said I had the same "save, seal, and steel trap" memory. I'd remember things as though I was a computer. If my husband wasn't irritable, he'd remark that I was very deep and very intelligent too. Thank God Dad's abuse to my head didn't harm my brain!

NEW FREEDOM

Lydia ended our last visit saying to talk, cry out, and not let hurt build up. Just go to God honestly. It felt good that I was cared about. I can't really explain it, but there was a warm and loving sensation every time I picked up my Bible and read the beautiful, nurturing words. Now, many years later, if I don't start my day ingesting this love letter from my Father, I realize that there is a void in my heart. On the other hand, each and every time I do read it verse by verse, I get strength, energy, and feel empowered to take on what the new day has in store for me and those I come in contact with. His word transforms me... His cross freed me! God was transforming my life and Lydia was a huge help in that regard. There is *no* going back. Victims are delivered to triumph!!

I let Lydia in on things I was worried about. Ever since I was fifteen, I had a sensitive conscience. I always wanted to do what was fair and just by others, especially those I loved. But the people you love do wicked things. I'm also a self-examiner; if I had done something off color, I was quick to apologize for it. Truthfully, with my boss, I sort of detected his liking for me more so than what a boss should. His compliments didn't make any difference to me as I have heard them many times before. Stupidly, I ignored the red flags until it was too late! I learned a valuable lesson there with my boss. There's a time to see the truth and run i.e. the veterinarian.

Again, our time in California was too short. My husband was interested in moving again. He did not want to stay working for the government but wanted to get his PhD in education. He landed a teaching job in Virginia, so the plan for him was to go back to teaching and secure his PhD. I hated this! Our moves were getting on my nerves; I wanted to stay with Lydia and Lance's family. I felt safe with the women.

Nevertheless, trying to be a cooperative mate, a few weeks later, I said goodbye to Lydia. She left me with the decision to fill my husband in on the boss. Lydia didn't know Lance and our marriage well enough to tell how he'd react. I decided to tell him myself, thinking it would be a huge load off my shoulders, but I was wrong! When I told him, he had a few choice words and said he needed to go on his own for a while. I think he was fed up. Still, he also said he always suspected there was "something between" my former boss and me. So much for his understanding. There was *nothing* between us *except* what was between him and *his baggage*! We moved fifty miles further up the coast where Lance's mom and her boyfriend were. But now he wanted to "think about stuff." Oh gosh! I really wanted to stay close by Lydia. However, she assured me very maternally that I'd be okay. "The Holy Spirit will be with you." We prayed the days before we left... No more guilt! I was *free*! Lydia told me a puzzling thing. "I believe, in the future, your dad will call you *Wildflower* again."

I was better but I needed kindness, a gentle touch, while beginning to heal.

Lance's family was still there with me, so we with visited each other. Lance's sisters weren't surprised that he just left after hearing the facts about the vet. They reminded me of how jealous all the men were in their family. I let him go, not because of what they said, but because we did need to break off from one another for a while. Surprisingly, I had a great summer! I took a theater course. A professor who played in Hollywood war movies taught the class. I so much enjoyed the whole experience. I knew I wanted to continue my higher education; I was bitten by the university bug.

At the end of the summer, Lance said he missed me and I missed him. Although I did not like his attitude toward my emotional issues, we agreed that I would come to the university where he had his job and finish my master's degree in literature. We were testing our marriage. The university was one state from our hometown. Slowly, I was communicating with my parents again. We made a few trips back to see family and friends. When we returned, we leased a home from a professor right by the school where I did my own thing and Lance did his. Our relationship was still very strained. The general attitude he had with me was "what else was I hiding from him?" I guess I couldn't blame him, but it still hurt. It was easy to remember everything with Lydia; I was opened up to her. I was opened up, but now I needed comfort while gaining confidence. (Lance was not there for me yet.)

All that unburdening to Lydia made freedom happen for me—I was becoming alive! I could already sense I was becoming more liberated and I was loving it! After being held "hostage" my whole childhood, I was free to be whatever I wanted to be. Lance was doing his own thing. College for me and teaching for him was quite rewarding. The other professors and the wives were becoming our friends.

Moreover, I was having a ball in my classes! The English professors were fantastic. I had four different teachers teaching seven classes, all literature! Two of my professors had great senses of humor, and I fell in love with Literature all over again! Since my husband was also a teacher, it was a kick to be invited to all the university and staff parties as a couple. The faculty was such a good group except for the few troublemakers. Lance was an especially big hit with the women faculty. They had a good time teasing him. My husband was having the time of his life. His female students were taken with his youth and good looks. Like any man, he enjoyed every minute of it.

Around this time, I started reading the Bible. Three of the four professors I had were Catholic or Christians, and they chose either Christian authors or stories with good morals to them. Because of this, I studied the Bible. The campus had a chapel, and I also began attending church again. I enjoyed going with my friend Niva; she was from Madrid.

She lived with her uncle, who was a professor in social studies. She was wealthy, and her family owned a fifteen-bedroom mansion with seven servants that were hired and worked for her family in Spain. Niva was exiled from her region because she refused to marry an up-and-coming diplomat. Her family was well-to-do, and so was the fiancée, but Niva grinned at me and added, "Katia, he was a dolt." I laughed so hard! Her Spanish accent was fantastic and intact—coming out of her like that struck me so funny. She quickly retorted, "No keeding, Katia, my parents wanted to keel me for refusing to agree with the marriage ceremony! No keedin', Katia," she added, "I'd rather marry Reeki Van Shelton." By now, I was roaring with laughter! What a character! I loved Niva! Something that is a must for me—my friends have to have a sense of humor! I also love women from any race or culture. I'm glad America is a melting pot of people. When the semester ended, I took Niva to stay with Mom and Dad at their house at the lake. Mom loved her. Our university was six hours from our hometown. I ended up graduating magna cum laude during the time Lance and I were separated... But I felt the Comforter with me.

Now, back home, Niva and I were having a good time, just two young women running around in my old hometown. I took her to my favorite aunt's house, Aunt Bev's. They all thought she was very pretty and kind, even Father Quinton met her and offered her a job at the camp. That was funny too; Niva was loaded with financial security!

After a few weeks with my parents, Lance called and said he had a present for me. It was a wedding band set—a 2k marquis-cut diamond! I don't know what happened, but Lance was different. He wanted to get right back together and made all kinds of promises. He even said that once were we together, we'd remarry in a church. We bought another lovely home on a street where all the rich kids from our high school lived. Lance knew the area from his band days. The Big Swimming Club, where all the doctors and lawyers were was right down the street. Real estate and finding good deals was his hobby. He found a lovely one across from a private golf course on a lake.

I loved our home; it was wonderful. Our neighbor was a preacher, and he always gave me scripture brochures. He also gave me my first Bible concordance. He and his wife prayed with me, for me, and for Lance. Lance had a bad thing happen to him; he was overdosed by his doctor with thyroid medicine, and within a few months, he developed breathing problems. It made him very uncomfortable around people. But we still had our extended family over all the time. It was like the old days at Camp Merryland! Every race, color, and religion were welcomed at Merryland as well as at our home... *New freedom!* Niva and I were going to stay overnight at Quinton's farm, but that was suddenly deep-sixed! A large black snake was crawling across the steps. Niva was devastated! Other cultures say this is something evil. She refused to stay, and so did I... This was a bad sign.

HOMOGENIZED

I kept in touch with Niva and was honored she considered me a best friend. Another good thing both Father Quinton and Mom did for me was with their world travels I was very open to all nations and peoples. In the Webster's dictionary, the word *homogenized* means, "of the same or similar kind or nature; of uniform structure or composition throughout."

I think homogenized described the relationships that God wanted us to have with all our brothers and sisters, no matter what color their skin. I am very proud of my mom, Dad, Father Quinton, and Skip because we all treated *everyone* the way we would want to be treated. The Bible is very clear on this! The problem with so-called Christians who claim to obey all the commandments and think they are "holier than thou" (is when they turn around and treat God's children from other cultures and color with disdain and disrespect). Jesus called these people "hypocrites."

Talking about other countries... I was so lucky for the many years prior to working out in the world. At Merryland, I was privileged to help seven Spanish missionaries from Honduras and Barcelona. I worked side by side with them for several summers. These women all sang together as they worked, and together, we had some wonderful times. As I sat at their feet, they told me stories of their homeland and their childhood. These saintly women taught me what I did learn about kindness, character, and love. I wish I could see them now, but they all went back to Spain with their own families. They were only hired by the Catholic Church for the seven years.

I needed a comforting shoulder to cry on, the Spanish ladies were very much a comfort and were very nurturing with their devotion to the Holy Trinity. They lived and breathed godliness. I believe they and Lydia are why I love my Father in heaven so much. They, all eight women and God, opened the door for me.

In writing this, I don't feel "poor me, poor baby." I feel blessed and loved beyond this world! I have been homogenized nicely; this was a very positive thing that came out of my own hometown experience. I *know* "all men are created equal."

MOM SHINED QUINTON ON

After some huge disagreement, Mom kept away from Father Quinton. When the holiday season came, we received some bad news. Father Quinton got into an argument with his nephew, Tyler. Tyler always acted so nice and subservient to Father Quinton, but behind his back, he disliked him immensely—the dagger was hidden. Since Mom and Tyler worked together, she had to be very careful about what Tyler saw with her and Quinton. The rumor was that Tyler was out to expose Father Quinton, and Quinton knew it. He wanted Quinton out of the picture. I'm sure Mom was torn... She loved Tyler for many years, working side by side with him as her assistant and Father Quinton's favorite nephew.

There was even talk that Tyler was planning on going to the church to tell on them. Not to help or do an intervention, but to ruin him. You see, Tyler took over Father Quinton's job as head of the camp and part-time boss of the retreat center. I always wondered why they picked a "lay person" for the retreat part. They were now regretting this move. Upper mobility and promotion was on Tyler's agenda for the year. Skip was pushed aside for the job ten years ago. The job should have gone to a chaplain/priest. Mom did her usual and got her way hiring Tyler. Mom needed a deliverer... She was in a *moral mess*.

Furthermore, the family would always say that I'd get into the biggest messes, I'd royally screw up, but somehow, I'd land on my feet. For many years now, my feet have been planted on the one immovable force, "the Rock of Ages" (Isaiah 26:4). I honestly got so worried if I got off track with God in some way, I'd cry out, "Father get me back, I'm falling. Lift me up now, please!" I desperately wanted away from all the darkness and to be healed. Nevertheless, very soon, something shady was approaching again, but for Father Quinton, Mom, and Skip.

I THOUGHT I WAS THE BOSS!

Quinton and Mom stopped seeing each other for a while over Tyler again. Quinton started hearing rumors that Tyler was going to take over his job as head honcho. I think Father Quinton liked being the one in charge. Pomp and circumstance was more my mother's thing, but Father Quinton would do his male "peacock" dance for her. Being the outdoors type, I don't think he himself really cared for the glamour, but he was always out to impress her, even after thirty-two years of being with her. How could my mom and dad be so mismatched? But since Quinton was preoccupied and out of the picture, Dad started to relax and be nicer and not fight with Mom. Lance and I were still at the university and loving it!

Simultaneously, back at the camp, Tyler, Quinton's nephew, wasn't going to let up on the high-power-boss job that he apparently out maneuvered Father Quinton from. In fact, rumor had it that a couple of Mom's extended family had a meeting with the church. It did not look good for Father Quinton.

First, he lost my mom, and now, he was losing his career. I never felt so bad for anyone in all my life. All this stuff happened during that same year. The doctors had Quinton sent down to mental clinic because of "severe depression." They said they tried counseling him and psychiatric therapy, but they couldn't get him to respond; he'd just stare and kept saying he was so sorry. Mom was not communicating in any way to her old flame.

Father Quinton's nephew, Tyler, with his smooth talking and manipulating ways, was now occupying all of Mom's time. Mom and Dad were in their seventies at the time, so they needed help with their grocery shopping, yard work, house cleaning, etc. Tyler's family volunteered. Somehow, that didn't surprise me. His wife, Nelly, did do cleaning and sewing for some households…but this was becoming annoying to other family who worked for Father Quinton twenty years! Tyler knew exactly how to "work" Mother also.

HAMAN/TYLER

About this time, my Bible group happened to be doing a study on the book of Esther. In case you don't know, or don't remember, she was a young Hebrew girl who married the king of Persia, a pagan nation. It was a fascinating story with intrigue, undercover situations, plots of murder, and Machiavellian characters. One in particular, the antagonist in the story, was a proud and greedy man named Haman. Haman wanted to be moved up to a high position in the king's court. He would do anything to secure that position. Several thousand people's lives were in jeopardy because of one man, Haman. He convinced the king that the Jewish people were going to take over his kingdom. Haman said it would be a defensive move to get rid of them first.

This seemed to be what Tyler was doing to Father Quinton, Uncle Gino, and all the extended relatives. After the doctor had Father Quinton analyzed and diagnosed, none of us were allowed to call him, but he could make calls. He made one call to our house, and I picked up the phone. He sounded very strange and said he was on several antidepressants. He wasn't making much sense; my husband came to the phone, and I passed it on to him. Lance did a better job communicating. I even heard Lance invite Father Quinton out to stay with us, and I agreed. Father Quinton said he'd probably do that. He even said he'd build onto our garage and make himself a nice apartment, and he'd pay for it all. Lance said it was okay and fine. That night, Quinton said, "Goodbye, and thank you for caring. I'll call you soon."

OH DEAR GOD... NO!

That last phone call was strange, but when Lance told him to move in with us, he thought Quinton would. A few days later, Uncle Gino called, all upset about Tyler. Uncle Gino said he knew what he did, and now, Tyler was the new and permanent CEO of the Merryland Camp and Retreat Compound. Tyler was taking away all of Gino's yearly bonuses, his camp car, all his supplies for his maintenance crew, etc. Uncle Gino said that "Tyler is really hurting our family financially" to make himself look good to the church community. Tyler was saving money for them by cutting down on his own friend's perks was the guess.

The sad rumor was they ordered shock treatment for Father Quinton.

Thunder and massive lightening was in the forecast. We did not hear from Father Quinton the whole week regarding moving in with us. I was taking a big chance letting him do so as I could lose my dad again. It's important to note that I did not know that mental hospitals still did things like "shock" treatment. At one time long ago, Quinton helped me, and I was ready to help him, and Lance was too. I was very proud of Lance for offering Quinton to live with us. Sadly, three days later, we got a call from Uncle Gino right before Christmas. He told us Father Quinton had been shot! I dropped the phone, speechless. I remember Lance saying something, but I wasn't listening as I was traumatized! We all wanted to know if he was in the hospital, but Uncle Gino said, "He did not make it."

Everyone said Father Quinton had died by his own hand. He had my brother's and my picture as well as news clippings of "poor" kids on his dresser. Right now, over fifteen years later, I still can't get over that. If there ever was an active, life-loving, daredevil of a man, it was Quinton. I know he loved God, but he was angry at the church for not allowing priests to marry. He believed there would be far less molestations and sexual assaults by priests if they were allowed to live as normal men and marry as the apostles did (Matthew 8:14).

CHAPTER 12

[The enemy] sin is crouching at your door
—Genesis 4:7

DID FATHER QUINTON REALLY MURDER HIMSELF?

*T*his question regarding the "suicide" of Father Quinton still remains a mystery. The reason I say this is…the police found no fingerprints anywhere in the vicinity of his home or on his bloody body. Not even the gun revealed prints of any kind. Records show "suicide." We wonder. Lance and I cared a lot for Father Quinton. We do recall that, during the two times before his death when we spoke to him, loud music was playing…but it was "off in a distance" kind of sound. The music was very old fashioned but intense. Father Quinton said, "I've never been more afraid." What did he mean? In the past, my husband and I also talked about him visiting from out of town and allowing us to stay in his guest cottage. I had horrible memories of that house because it was overrun by mice…everywhere. Father Quinton never bothered to exterminate the varmints. There were rumors about the "soldier cemetery." It was said that the cottage builders removed only headstones and left the graves. Then the *big black snakes* that Niva saw were there. Father Quinton was strange in many ways, and my mother disclosed to me a few years ago a sad thing. Apparently, Father Quinton himself was molested, while he was young, by an elderly priest. A tear rolled down my cheek with these words.

Tyler's mom was Italian. She and our family were close friend's years ago. Tyler married Nelly after she saw him play drums in Uncle Gino's band. After Quinton's death, my mom fell apart for a while. However, she quickly leaned heavily on Tyler and his family. He and his wife practically moved in with Mom and Dad. Years before, Tyler had a problem with my husband, so we never saw him anymore. Tyler was a drummer, like my husband, in my Uncle Gino's band. Well, one night, Uncle Gino asked Lance to play along with them… Lance was an excellent drummer! Everyone stood and clapped for him. Unfortunately, Tyler's wife said aloud, "Now, that's a REAL drummer." Tyler did not take kindly to this and never forgot.

MOM, QUINTON'S NEPHEW IS HAMAN

It was the moment of truth; several months later, I had to tell my mom about Quinton's nephew, Tyler. Uncle Gino agreed, but since Father Quinton who, for thirty years, controlled all the financial strings, was gone, Mom was left with it all.

Just like the Haman in the story of Esther, Tyler seemed out only for himself and did not care how many lives were hurt in the plan. Sometimes, even your own family becomes your worst enemy. I dove into reading how Esther handled it all, and with God's help, she outsmarted Haman. The trap

Haman set for Esther's gentle Jewish Uncle Mordecai came down on Haman's *own* head instead. Literally, Haman lost his head at the gallows, and the king ordered it (Esther 7:9–10). A Scripture I'd be reading would be very similar to what was happening in my life! The problem was my mother took the "I'm always right" stance, so I had to let the chips fall.

I intently prayed about my mother and Tyler. She just lost the love of her life, and I asked God what I should do, if anything. It did not take but a few days for things to hit the fan. We received horrible news that Nelly, Tyler's wife, had passed out while they were at a dance together. The ambulance came and got her. She had been cleaning and sewing for Mom while Tyler was running the camp and retreat house. Mom gave a lot of stuff to Nelly and her daughter for helping her. She always helped Tyler more than Uncle Gino, her own little brother. Suddenly, bad things happened for Tyler and his wife Nelly.

They said Nelly fainted and cracked her head on the wooden floor. Tyler was trouble, but I didn't want her to be hurt in anyway; I remember having a good time with her. Nelly was a beautiful country girl. She never had a farm but referred to herself as the "hillbilly who married an Italian." She resembled a very tall Deborah Kerr. Really, Aunt Bev resembled and acted like a petite Mary Tyler Moore. By the way, she was one of my favorites, and so is Aunt Bev even to this day.

It had been three months since Nelly was taken to the hospital. They kept her for three more months and then sent her home with a frightening diagnosis. She had an inoperable brain tumor. At first, the whole family was devastated. The prognosis was grim; the excellent doctors did not expect Nelly to survive. She hung on for two years in the same comatose position. It took a big toll with her kids and Tyler.

Sadly, two years and three months later, Nelly died. They had her cremated. Mom needed us now.

Living so near to my parents after all those years away was unique. Of course, my mother was great with her grand-babies. She had two gorgeous twin baby girls from my brother Skip and his pretty wife Caroline. They came to visit at least once a year. It was always so much fun and nostalgic to be with them. Skip, Caroline, Lance, and I always got along so well. We had many terrific nights sitting around, talking about every subject under the sun. I loved Caroline like a big sister. I listened and watched her to buy quality clothing and apparel. She did not look at price tags like I did.

For twenty years, no matter where we were, every holi-day, I'd go home to see my parents and my Uncle Gino's fam-ily. I still felt very close to Aunt Bev and called her about once a month. She never had any extra money to buy nice clothes, so I'd give her mine. Although she was shorter than me, she could still fit in some of my clothes. She always said she loved the way I dressed. So throughout the years, usually spring and Christmas, I'd send her two or three boxes of clothes, shoes, purses, and jewelry I rarely used, and she loved it.

Do You Remember, Bro?

Reminiscing with my brother over the phone became one of the most special times of my life. Skip and I had some of the most honest and straightforward conversations. I loved my brother, and he told me, "I'm really a genuine fake. If I'm happy, I'm acting."

I told him I thought he was the much quicker one; he was always ready to plan an escape route in regard to Dad. I said I was not as sneaky and inevitably would get caught.

We'd discuss specific times when we thwarted Dad's traps. Many times, I'd let Skip know when Dad was closing in on us, preaching, "Danger, Danger!" like the robot on *Lost in Space* would alert young Will Robinson. We outsmarted him many times with the warning.

We were both laughing at some of the closer calls. For instance, when Skip came home so drunk he parked the car in the middle of the lawn! He was sixteen and I was thirteen, but I drove the car back up on the driveway, so all was normal. Skip was a pacifist, I was realist. He remembered how I rescued Otto and Ollie from the blizzard one winter. I didn't know he even knew that! Skip even mentioned Dad's being flipped to the ground with the clothesline incident. We laughed and cried together so many times.

CHAPTER 13

BECOMING THE REAL ME

*O*n the serious side, I went digging for scriptural help for Skip. I researched and read the Bible, studied, and have been on a constant path to be transformed in the spirit, soul, and body of Christ. I feel I've been like Joyce Meyer, Stormie Omartian, Paula White, Sheila Walsh, and many other fantastically enlightened women who went through the wilderness and desert. We also have been spread out on the Potter's wheel, peeled off, and finally molded from the shattered pieces of hearts and lives. I personally have been in recent affliction and am working my way out of my own personal fiery furnace. But just like these other brave and persevering women, we will get the victory!

I owe a lot to two authors that happen to be clinical psychologists, Dr. Henry Cloud and Dr. John Townsend. The reason being, their collaborative work entitled *Safe People* made a heavy impact on choosing and keeping those I want around me on a regular basis. These two compassionate Christian writers bring it all together for those of us who have had trouble deciding who to be chummy with and those to avoid. Mom and Father Quinton were not safe either. Because they walked away, ignored, or simply refused to acknowledge that Dad was mistreating us and sexually harassing me mainly because of Mom and Quinton's marital infidelity issues. The charade was finally over… I was finding our right from wrong—good from evil.

When I read in *Safe People* that God wanted us to "hunger and thirst for righteousness" and reach out to others for what you can't get from the selfish and self-possessed, I felt normal for running away to camp for what we all desperately needed, which was a feeling of belonging and love. Skip and I never felt love by either parent. We felt as if we were a burden. This is not the way it should have been, and he admitted this.

I discovered that I had a fearful and warped attitude whereby I developed a complex and dislike for any private touching. In her wonderful book, *Healing Victims of Sexual Abuse*, Paula Sanford again is brilliant, deep, and concise on her experiences trying to draw out the extreme emotional truth regarding incest or even inappropriate touching by a male authority figure. She states that "frigidity can be the result of wounding, unhealthy attitudes and even physical impairment." Many times, she and her husband John, also a pastor, conclude, "We routinely consider the possibility of suppressed memories of abuse. Many times, something inappropriate occurred but was repressed." Until I discussed it with Lydia, I did hold it all in. With my sessions, I learned much, but I had to make the choice to take my mask off that hid my misery.

In a sense, my father's mind stayed imprisoned as he could not get all that ugliness and World War II carnage out of his head, so he drank. As I mentioned, the Native Americans say that consuming liquor is drinking in the "spirits." Most know that people, when they drink, do not behave as they normally would. They get reckless. They may drive recklessly, hit people they normally wouldn't, they may have one-night stands and not remember it the next day, etc. In other words, they become a different, usually "negative" spirit. Even a "happy" drunk doesn't stay that way.

The vet, my former boss, was also a drinker, I came to find out. It's funny; once you make up your mind to forgive and drag all the mistrust, anger, abuse, hate, and disrespect to the cross, it just doesn't matter anymore. Therein lies the victory. It does not always happen instantly. I'm sure I wore deep ruts to the cross with my cart of turmoil.

MY BIG BROTHER, SKIP

What can I say about someone so rare? Skip was the cutest, kindest, and sweetest person; and compassionate too. He had it all. He was fun loving and amusing; I don't think he had an enemy. He was my protector, my partner in kid crimes, like our "sting me, sting you" towel fights on the beach and while doing dishes. It was Skip and me against the world of darkness. Oh God, yes Quinton, there is a devil!

Unlike me, Skip never challenged Dad. I never really knew why not, but I jumped in and did it for him. I could not stand how he'd make Skip stand in front of him with bloodshot eyes, drunk, and berate and insult Skip for twenty to thirty minutes. I had to break that up. Meanwhile, Skip would just stare at the floor in embarrassment. I'd try to distract Dad like a decoy duck; I'd warn Dad to "leave my brother alone." This would turn Dad's attention to me, and Skip would have a way out to escape. Now, he was not only having marital problems, but he was also being sued by several people for something the mother company did. Skip, I know, did nothing wrong. He had nothing to do with the "charges" the mother company was accused of! Nothing!

Skip was sent to a psychiatrist because of his depression and threats of suicide. In response to issues with prescription drugs and alcohol, he was sent to a rehabilitation center and attended AA meetings. Of course, like me, it stemmed from childhood issues. So who better to talk to than me, the one who lived under the same roof as him? He used several prescription drugs for depression and nerves. When we visited three months earlier, we noticed his cabinets had several bottles of pills. I was very worried about my brother. Caroline said she had a fight with him, so she locked him out. Well, Skip broke the big bay window and broke in! This was not the Skip I knew… He was never violent.

For several weeks on and off, Skip called me. Things were not getting better for him. The worst part is that Skip had a girlfriend outside of his marriage, he told me, and his wife was wanting a divorce or to dissolve the marriage. Caroline accused him of being "just like his mother." She called me also. I took no sides but wanted to help them both, especially my big brother Skip. However, he would not listen to me! Skip begged me to fly out to him… I could not. Lance was going through horrible health issues because of his thyroid problem. I felt *so* helpless…and torn. The violent storm from *Poltergeist* was quickly rolling in.

Skip and I knew many secrets about our family…and the years of pain and abuse had to surface in order for him to cope. When he was later questioned about our parents by the psychiatrist, he was leery to tell the truth. I don't know if it was extreme loyalty or fear, but at first, Skip avoided all of the questions. Finally, I convinced him that he had to come out of denial or it would ruin his life. So with my continual prodding, he disclosed Dad's mistreatment of him and me.

Feeling insecure, I asked him whether or not he thought I was smart. He responded that I had the looks, brains, and personality. I thought, *Oh! Wow!* That was very kind, and I thanked him. He said he liked that I was like "Pollyanna;" however, we were both too "passive," but to us, just surviving was a plus. I thanked God.

NO THANKS

Meanwhile, more bad things on the western front. Mom called me on Thanksgiving morning. We were all supposed to get together for a big family Thanksgiving dinner. Poor Mom, she found out that, years ago on Thanksgiving, I eloped. The family said she got so weak in the knees they had to put a chair under her so she wouldn't collapse on the floor. Now a horrible call came from Skip on Thanksgiving too.

My brother called her and told her that he quit work and his wife left him with their two girls. Again, my mom was hysterical and fainted. Everyone still met at my other aunt's house, so Thanksgiving was not ruined for everyone. However, Mom, Dad, Lance, and I stayed glued to our phones. This was the worst. Skip was 2,000 miles away threatening suicide. Skip called again. We all took turns talking him out of this; we heard him spinning a gun barrel in the background. This was my brother whom I adored! I screamed through the phone Lance was holding, "Put the gun away, Skip, please! Why are you doing this? Come home and stay with us until you're well. I need you in my life, Skip, please stop it!" I yelled so I could wake him up; he was slipping away. I had to help. He sounded so strange and made no sense. Evanescence's song that I love, "Bring Me to Life," kept playing in my head.

I felt so helpless, and Skip was so hopeless, that the miles seemed so much further. He seemed to be slipping into a dark hole to another dimension. Just a few months before, he said he and his new girlfriend may "get married and have a new family." What had happened to cause this 360-degree turn? We all knew Caroline was planning on taking the two girls and already had moved out.

Mom was being hysterical again, and Dad had not been any help at all as we talked to Skip over Thanksgiving. I turned to Lance to see if he could help my brother. I needed my brother alive and well! He was the one in the hospital. The doctor was kind and gentle with Skip. So maybe he could help my big brother; I was very desperate, and Lance could see that. No matter what it took, somebody had to help Skip! My brother was always a light in my life. I could not bear him being so sick.

COMING OUT OF THE PAST

The doctors kept telling us there was not much they can do when Skip won't open up with the truth. Due to my father's extremely authoritative style with me and Skip during childhood, we lost out on a very important aspect of growing up called "individuation." We both had no real guts. Notice I said "had" no guts. I have them now, but it took years to assert myself. Skip only now showed despondency or anger. He wasn't capable at this point to do any more. He was withdrawing…from alcohol, tranquilizers—life.

The Gestaltists say, "Kids raised in rigidly controlled environments lose spontaneity." Children of alcoholics, PTSD, etc., stay victims within themselves. They do not know how to embrace life because their psychological body armor prevents the vibrant self from coming out. On the other hand, as children, Skip and I got our released side out when we took off for *summer camp*. We were gone and stayed gone until the last second. We did our jobs at the camp, but we were free to be ourselves, and we did so with gusto. I honestly believe camp life kept us both sane. "Merryland" fit the atmosphere. Skip and I were very happy there. Our hearts were "merry" (Proverbs 15:15).

In a phone conversation, Skip told me, "Watch this movie!" I had a ray of hope he was seeing others' pain. In the movie, *Prince of Tides*, Nick Nolte did a fantastic job of playing the main character who had brothers and sisters that all came from a very violent family environment. I don't want to ruin it for you, as it should be a film that you don't miss. My brother called me to tell me to rent the video and watch it because of all the similarities in our childhood. Finally, Skip felt that it was a sign to disclose his past to the psychiatrist who ministered at the rehab center where Skip was inducted. In the movie, the younger sister was the one who was suicidal, and the brother had sexual dysfunction. The psychiatrist was portrayed by Barbara Streisand who counseled Nick Nolte, and a transference took place between the two of them. The movie worked on many restless and traumatic feelings within both Skip and me. Our lives were a combination of this movie, *Prince of Tides*, *The Thorn Birds*, and *Poltergeist*. Skip finally agreed. The movie greatly upset him and evoked old painful thoughts. I was happy… I thought he had a breakthrough. Oh, how I tried to encourage, even push him to disclose things that could free him. Remaining in denial would make things impossible for resolution.

CHAPTER 14

"COME INTO THE LIGHT CHILDREN"—POLTERGEIST

SHADE TO LIGHT

*J*ust recently, my good friend Dinah came to me when I was three-fourths of the way finished with this book. She knew I was a bit concerned about some of the things that I had disclosed about others. However, just at the time I began questioning again, she brought me a book that she pulled off her shelf that put a fire under me again. The book was *Rising Strong* by Brené Brown, PhD.

I gleaned several good points from what she wrote regarding our loved ones. Her writing that "the heartbreak associated with addiction, mental illness, behavioral disorders, and physical health struggles can be termed protracted heartbreak. This is when we feel helpless; when we watch those we love suffer even if that suffering pulls us down." She goes on, "Staying hidden in darkness and not bringing the hellish things out in the light is very damaging. Silence and pretending don't work anymore." This is where I came to myself and cried, "No use." I absolutely couldn't pretend or be with pretenders anymore. I wanted Skip to do the same. He wanted a simple, beautiful dream life, and only I knew what that was.

Brené Brown has a good term called "stealth expectations." This is where so many important things we missed out on because of someone else's neurosis, pride, or jealousy, disappointments, and cancelations of reunions, celebration, holidays, blocking or stopping normal social activities. It also includes continual, significant, endless setbacks. Skip and I, because of the demands of others overriding our desires, were full of these.

I could not do much more for my brother. He was taken to a rehabilitation hospital, and I told Caroline all I knew about our past to try to help her understand. She did her darndest to get the best help she could for Skip. My mission after divulging everything painful to Lydia was set... I was going to continue and get rid of even the residue from my broken and shattered past. Just having it brought up and out into the light put me on my spiritual path to healing and wholeness. From this season of excavation and reconstruction, I included my *real Father* in with all of me. I wished so much I could get through to my big brother. Sadly, he had too many pills in him... He did not want to live anymore. This freaked me out and scared me to death!

Both Skip and I were English majors in college. He loved to read, and my voracious appetite for reading turned into a passion. Skip read mostly history. Our family history was haunting Skip; nothing was getting through! Skip! Listen to me!!

OH GOD, NO, SKIP!

A humungous black sky blanketed overhead. About the same time my brother started having marital issues, Caroline's company started to go under due to the owners being charged with felonies. Court appearances, fines, and lawsuits became my brother's fate. I felt horrible for the whole family. Skip and Caroline were personally sued several times! This was more than Skip could handle! He barely got to see his girls, and Caroline wasn't being merciful with him anymore. Skip screwed up and had a fling with a girl in his office. Caroline was finished, and since one fling happened, rumor was she threw the book at him said he was unfit to be around their almost teenage girls. This ended it for Skip… I begged him to come home!… No response.

This was the final nail in the coffin. My God, I could not believe all of this. Was our family cursed? I wondered and cried my heart out for my brother and his family. On Independence Day, my wonderful big brother *shot* himself! *It devastated me!* My legs went out from under me. "Oh, Skip! No, no, no, no!" My wonderful big brother killed himself! I just kept crying, I wept and wept until I had no more tears to shed. He was my childhood soulmate. Oh, God, take care of my brother. Even now, I can hardly stop the tears flowing from my eyes. He made a statement that we will carry on in our family forever. How can Skip be gone…really not to come back? The news of Father Quinton was so terrible, but now my big *brother* is gone! For weeks, "this can't be happening!" was my only mantra. My heart broke for the two girls he loved so much. My heart sobbed and was shattered. For months, I was useless, like a dishrag. Numbness befriended me.

TRANSFORMING TRUST

For months, I couldn't do anything but stare outside and cry, weep, sob. After a long period of grieving to get back into life without my big brother, my constant confidant, I had to get my priorities straight. Without Jesus, we don't know how to love correctly. Like me, we love at the wrong time, we love with lackluster, we love too much, or we put other people in front of the Trinity. Jesus was balanced, Jesus was sinless, and was perfect. I've learned why God said we should imitate Him; luckily, He already knows He has to guide and lead us because, otherwise, we wouldn't know the entrance from the exit of His plan for all of us. Sadly, Skip may have chosen other things in front of God. I wasn't judging… I just wanted him to call me…talk to me. Oh, how I miss your voice big bro. Who do I trust now? You hated storms too... Skip...it's storming.

The dictionary definition of "transformed" is change in structure or appearance or character.

Our Heavenly Father states that when we are changed, we are taken from glory to glory. Transformation, to J. L. Marcum, MD, takes place when "the light of God's love enters into a darkened life. We begin to experience how we were designed to feel." We begin to be aware of the destructive health habits we need to set aside. "We are able to offer forgiveness (because we have taken our sins to the cross already). To others, anger can begin to be changed into acceptance. When God's love illuminates a life, a transformation can begin." I had to forgive Skip for leaving me, then I had to forgive myself for not doing more for him. *That* hadn't happened yet. I had terrible guilt that I had not hopped on a plane to be with my big brother. I hated Lance for stopping me. I know it was not his fault that the thyroid medicine almost poisoned him, but Skip was in dire straits. The murky pool from *Poltergeist* was engulfing Skip... He needed me. I wasn't there.

Honestly, every day is valuable, and when we deprogram all the negative that has held us back, we must reprogram and renew our minds, which is another way to say open our hearts to God's words and do what His love letter says. We must trust. I trusted Skip... He trusted me. Now, I had to make myself trust God. I know Skip is with God the Father—the Good Father.

Skip would let the other person always have the last word. He did good deeds, like the time he stopped in a snowstorm on a freeway and helped stranded motorists get the help they needed with stalled cars. My brother was very generous. Both Skip and I love to give things: presents, pets to good homes, money to those who need it. In fact, several times, Skip left soft drinks and beer for the garbage men when they took things for him they didn't usually take. He always tried to please everybody, and so did I. Could God use people pleasers?

Years ago, Skip volunteered as big brother for the boys in scouts who did not have a dad to be with them on their projects or excursions. He also helped pay for the school clothing they needed to go to class presentably. He even bought and fixed up a truck that had a personalized license plate that said, "BIG MAX" on it. Dad kept that truck and loved using it for yard supplies for twenty years! Skip tried to please everybody. He even tried to be good to Mom and bought her fancy ceramic soup tureens, expensive platters, and hors d'oeuvres trays made out of sterling silver—all the best dining room luxuries.

Remembering back when Lance went to the various government training facilities, Skip invited me out to his house to live with them the entire summer. I never had to pay for one thing… I had my own suite with my own bathroom. My two nieces were so cute, and they were with me wherever I went. Skip and Caroline had to work every day, so I got to swim with the little girls, take them shopping with the nanny (who I really liked), and then run around with Caroline after work and eat at the best restaurants. She would not let me pay for anything! Caroline and Skip were sharers with others also. Actually, Mom and Dad were both pretty generous. So I guess that's where Skip and I got it. Caroline was kind to even our extended family. Checks were sent to our cousins as well as the whole family, especially when they needed help. What a horrible tragedy! However, Skip… I'm letting go… It's time.

Ann Lander's Poem

After A While
by Veronica A. Shoffstall

After a while you learn
the subtle difference between
holding a hand
and chaining a soul
and you learn that love
doesn't mean leaning
and company doesn't always
mean security.

And you begin to learn
that kisses aren't contracts
and

presents aren't promises
and you begin to accept your
defeats
with your head up and your eye ahead
with the grace of a woman
not the grief of a child
and you learn
to build your road on today
because tomorrow's ground is
too uncertain for plans
and futures have a way of falling
down in mid flight

After a while you learn
that even sunshine burns
if you get too much
so you plant your own garden
and decorate your own soul
instead of waiting
for someone to bring you
flowers

And you learn
that you really can endure
that you really are strong
and you really do have worth
and you learn
and you learn
with every goodbye you learn

CHAPTER 15

TRIALS MAKE OR BREAK US

I do not believe that, in World War II, my dad could help himself. He witnessed something so traumatic for three years in the service. His comrades and others were blown to pieces; he had to pick up the parts. His family did nothing to get him professional help. Dad should have gotten help from the VA. Mom made the choice *not* to help him, so he was never calm in the home where Skip and I grew up. My spouse always blames Quinton and Mom, not Dad, for most of the dysfunction.

Some people reading my little story can see that, in most ways, because of my youth, I was more of a victim than a participant. However, I still needed to change my thinking process that was *so out of balance*. I also had to keep unloading the duffel bag of hurt and dig up deep-rooted resentments. One by one, they died.

As much as we all try, we cannot just say that, one day, I'm going to change myself. Jesus Christ has to be there to nail the old us and let us be reborn as new creations. The old self slowly dies away so the new spirit man or woman can take over. Then we go from victim to victor! When I chose to dig out all the hurt deep down that I had stuffed, I started the regimen of *Live the Let Go Life*, as Joseph Prince reiterates in his wonderful book. I started to live my life for the first time by faith rather than by my flesh. Joel Osteen and his gorgeous wife, Victoria, are excellent examples that preach after disasters and dysfunctional backgrounds, and how to handle it all.

The Bible calls a half-dead spirit or a hiding sleeping spirit a slumbering spirit. With Skip's death, I got to the end of myself. As in *Poltergeist*, I literally fell to my knees and cried, "God help me!" Within a few months of surrendering all I was and had, He got room to move into small pieces of my shattered heart. I had to open the door a crack first. God is not pushy, and He suffered along with me. My spirit was crushed, and He was ready and eager to save me and those who are crushed in spirit (Psalm 34:18). Mom and Dad's neglect and abuse were bad, but my heart was never the same after Skip killed himself.

Skip's unnecessary and early departure…was almost too much! My spirit was useless for a long time. As much as I loved Skip, I didn't want to fall apart. I somehow had to go on, let go, and leave everything in the Lord's care. Now I staked my entire life on the Living Word of God. How power filled it really is! *This* was another pinnacle reached in my life. In all heartache, you *learn* why the Bible says "the circumcision" is of the heart.

"Let us therefore be diligent to enter that rest, lest anyone fall according to the same example of disobedience" (Hebrews 4–11). I let go of any sin I ever knew; and I slowly let go of my lost brother. It took a long while. But what I have learned is all along the path, God transforms us as the Holy Spirit enlightens our minds to become more pleasing to our real Father. The time of tyranny and chaos was settling down.

FORGIVENESS INITIATIVE

Confused, I prayed a lot, and true to herself, Mom dove back into life with her Italian family. Dad had not gotten over his son's suicide. My resentment was vanishing, but my deep-down, gut-wrenching hurt was still raw. One night, weeping and on my knees, my prayer was constant and deliberate. "Oh, Father Most High, set my bitter heart free." It was my everyday prayer for months. How could I have to go through so much so young? My own parents were the ones I had put away. Nevertheless, down the road, I still had to forgive—this was a hard thing. No, impossible is more like it. I had heard so much of the gift of forgiveness, but how to obtain it was a puzzle to me. For a time, I did untie myself from all those who had deeply hurt me; but now do you *ask* for a gift? Moreover, how do you let go of the revenge you feel inside for all the years of lost happiness? Every time I thought of Skip and how stoic he was, I broke down into sobs and crumpled to the carpet.

Again, returning to my Bible, I found it. Another king discovered what to do when enemies (even in the form of family or friends) come to attack you. The Psalms literally fell at my feet while looking at books in a used bookstore. If it had been a whole Bible, it probably would have broken my toes… I had on flip-flops! However, it happened to be a single thin leather book of Psalms alone. What a find! Over the years I prayed the same prayers about forgiveness and revenge God's way probably at least one hundred times. My subconscious blamed Mom and Dad for Skip. They had beaten him down for years. I had hurt and hate in my heart.

"Hear the sound of my cry, my King and my God… Hold them guilty, O God, let them fall by their own designs and counsel, cast them out because of the multitude of their transgressions" (Psalm 5).

Now I better felt that I could *legitimately* pray for my abusers to the One who could intervene, and it was called love, but tough love.

"Oh Lord, My God, save me from all those who pursue and persecute me and deliver me" (Psalm 7). Too late for Skip...but I guess he's with you.

"O Lord, You have heard the desire and the longing of the humble and oppressed...to do justice so that man of earth may not terrify anymore" (Psalm 10). Those unfair lawsuits really brought my brother low.

It was such a release to be able to bring the Mighty One in to avenge me against the adults who abused Skip. These next Psalms really worked.

"O Lord, my Rock. Hear the voice of my supplication... the wicked with malice and mischief in their hearts... (*Aha!*) Repay them...according to the wickedness of their doings... Render to them what they deserve" (Psalm 28). I let God work on my heart attitude. My work was to focus on spiritual dynamics, my Supreme Father's plan, and my "lack" in both while lifting my burden.

Do you see how our Creator took care of the "release valve" for our deep pain and anger and made an outlet for retaliation? *He* is to take care of business, and we are to surrender it all to Him. With Skip gone, I wanted peace. Mom and Dad never spoke of Skip again. I was to do things God's way. Man's carnal way only keeps us with no peace.

We forgive the abusers, betrayers, liars, abandoners, and God comes in when we cry out. He knows far better what to do and how to correct—wickedness.

I can't remember where, but somewhere in the Word (it might be Isaiah), the Bible declares and warns. You do not want to fall into the hands of our angry God! Father knows Mom and Dad's hearts. Maybe they talk to You, Lord. You are the only fair judge. I need harmony so badly. *Is* there any way to restore what should have been?

MY PARENTS... WE'LL SEE

This devastating loss of my loved one had sidetracked and frightened me for a long time. It was surreal to me that my brother was gone. I did my best to be a comfort to Mom and Dad. I still felt complete emptiness in the pit of my stomach. Somehow, I had to forgive both of my parents, but I was still struggling about Skip. For some reason, I could do this for what they did to me. For Skip, it was harder to mute the rewind tape. I sobbed and grabbed my stomach, rocking back and forth.

My mother reported to all of us that Dad completely quit drinking shortly after Skip's passing. Dad was messed up, but Mom...who really knew what the reason was for her uncaring attitude? Dad loved Skip, but so did Mom down deep in her womb. I needed to quit going back and forth. I think this is where we know we wrestle with hosts of wickedness.

An extremely helpful book in this confused season was *Battlefield of the Mind* by Joyce Meyer. In my spiritual yearnings, the signs all pointed to make up, and I knew I had to be the one who started the reconciliation. Letting go of the hurt was definitely the hardest for me. How can my mother have the nerve to ask us children what we have done to cause our father to be so angry to the point of abuse? She then would slap or pinch us when we disagreed. Old hurts and incidences came into my mind. One by one, I took it to

Jesus. Forgiving those who have passed on is a must also. We need Jesus to set us free.

Choking on my tears, I kept saying Skip is gone now. I need to be there for them. They needed unconditional love, love that they may have never known before. I again dropped to my knees and cried out to the Lord that I forgive them and all of their sins against me and my brother and to forgive me. Jesus, help me let it all go. I didn't want to resent them anymore. I remember the relief and the feeling I got instantly with my simple declaration to my real Father. I took more than thirty-five years of serious hurt and deep bitterness, and I placed it at the foot of the cross. The release and exhilaration were overwhelming! A few weeks went by before I called my mom. She was the one who always answered the phone. I told her I wanted to get together with her and my dad as soon as possible. And so it was done, the first step in reuniting with my parents and making peace at last. I had to rise higher than my human instincts and love my parents. Jesus's love pierced my heart and allowed His mercy to flow through my spirit to both Mom and Dad. Jesus was becoming my Healer and my Divine Brother. I wanted to try to help bring our family together again.

In that respect, we moved back to our hometown, and Lance found us a lovely big home by Mom and Dad. With Father Quinton gone, something developed with my parents. I noticed after we moved in that my father started saying, "I might come over for a visit." That was music to my ears. I was very eager to be on friendly terms with Mom and Dad, so I invited them over for dinner. Lance said I was always a good cook, and sometimes, I'd spend half the day whipping up a gourmet recipe. For my parents to come over, this was really a thrill for me for them to eat my food at my table. But they had to be nice. I remember I was half really excited and half really scared to death! They dressed up and were compatible with each other. I made prime rib, baked potatoes, hot slaw, asparagus, and German Chocolate cake.

It was a date, and the first visit went so well. After dinner, I pushed away from the table, and I motioned to go to the family room. Dad never made a negative comment the whole night. He never asked for beer, wine, booze—nothing. He just nicely and calmly talked with Lance and me; it was wonderful! You could tell he was happy that we lived close by again. Dad and Mom were affectionate and enjoyable at my home. It was wonderful but too surreal. The cathedral where both my mom and dad attended and belonged to for forty years gave a fiftieth "wedding renewal" offer to the new old couple. Shockingly, Mother agreed to remarry my father, and so did he. I really thought this was a diversion tactic. The announcement was made, and over three hundred people came to Mom and Dad's wedding. It was a gala event, and I was finally happy that they were going to make a go of it again.

MEMORY HEALING

Much of Skip's and my bitterness and resentment stemmed from my parents, but now, I loved them both. When we receive God's unconditional love, finally, we can pass on the same love to those who have hurt us deeply. It's been many years since all the insanity of Mom, Dad, and me. It's like it all never happened.

I'm all about healing through forgiveness with Christ's love. The Holy Spirit directs us. Our Lord "walks into the darkest of hells of our existence." Leanne Payne, as author, wrote, "As past trauma unfolds in our memory, we look with the eyes of our hearts, and we're actually able to see Jesus. The fantastic result is we receive his healing word, glance or embrace we've needed so long." I guess when you have forgiven so many, you become experienced in calling on Jesus and crying out to our real Father (Psalm 89:26). Even though we may feel justified in our feelings, if we are to truly imitate Jesus, we *must* forgive everyone.

As soon as I called for Jesus, I felt like I was let out of an iron jail cell. I know this is what is meant in the scripture, "I want you to say to the prisoners, 'Come out' Tell them who are in dark cells they are free" (Isaiah 49:9, NIV). Unforgiveness, hatred, and bitterness keep us from the light of freedom.

OH NO, ALL MY BABIES!

One problem, for years now, because of the physical and psychological abuse, I had much trouble trying to have a baby. I finally got up the nerve to ask Lance if we could adopt. When we were talking about adopting, Lance would not agree to it unless I got new homes for all of our pets. This shocked me! I don't think I ever forgave Lance. We had a pair of Rottweilers, a Ragdoll Himalayan cat, a beautiful dwarf Siamese, and a gorgeous sleek black cat we named Mrs. Preston. Lance found her just ready to cross a busy street and lured her over to him with hamburger meat. He saved her life, and I loved her. She would only follow me around. Mrs. Preston was demure, gentle, and gorgeous. I named her because of the movie I saw years ago with Doris Day and Rex Harrison. Toy was our Himalayan, a beautiful, sweet boy. He would have no problem finding a home for he was purebred. A little old lady saw him and fell in love with him. It was a perfect match. Shogie, short for *Shogun*, another movie, was my special guy. He had slight asthma and was a very tiny Siamese. The couple that came to adopt him loved him right from the start. Shogie, within a few minutes, was climbing on the man's shoulders. I still cried for months; he was such a cute companion.

Baron was our long-haired Rottweiler. Talk about gentle! He was so big but very sweet. One time, Mally, the aggressive female, went after an opossum in our side-fenced area. Mally's parents were police-trained drug dogs. I think this is where Mally got her aggressiveness. So Mally cornered the opossum, which got near her food bowl, as I watched out a window. Being an animal lover, I went out to stop Mally from potentially killing it by removing the opossum from the yard. About twenty feet away, I saw Baron in the corner with his back to us. It was obvious he wanted no part of Mally when she's "on one." But we found her a wonderful home with a single mom and two athletic teens. Mally loved playing catch and romping in the park. They promised to take very good care of her.

Mally only loved Lance. She could have been a problem, but Baron, the male Rottie, was very friendly. Baron was the last to find a home. That one got to me. The young guy I chose had three acres in the country and lived alone. The cute thing I remember was when I called to check on him at his new home, the man that adopted him said, "Oh my buddy and I just got our baths together in my big tub." I felt much better after hearing that. His "buddy" was Baron.

This still was a killer. I didn't speak to Lance for days. He tried to tell me two reasons he said were valid—you will be so busy with the babies, the animals won't get the attention they're used to, and they could (especially the dogs) hurt the kids, but I was still beyond devastated!

CHAPTER 16

There shall be showers of blessings.

—Ezekiel 34:26

OUR BABY BOY IS HERE... SUNNY DAYS ARE HERE AGAIN

I loved our new home. It was wonderful. Our neighbor was a preacher, and he and his wife gave me scripture all the time. He gave me my first Bible concordance, he prayed for me, and he prayed for Lance because he was overdosed on thyroid medication again. He developed problems breathing but still helped tremendously with the adoption procedure. I never missed a meeting and went to all the reunions with the other potential families of the children. Lance came to some of them when he had a good health day. His labored breathing caused a delay.

I went next door to my friend's house and prayed about it. I poured my heart out about starting a family, and while Lance and I were walking, he agreed to keep his word. I vowed to God and Lance that I would be a terrific mom. I had already envisioned my son, so I went to a moving sale and got about $1,500 of baby boy furniture!

I admired Lance at this moment. He was not breathing right again, but he jumped on the phone and called a lawyer. Meanwhile, I had already filled out forms for the caseworker weeks before. We had our application finalized, and again, we met with other adoptive families. Before the year was up, we got our baby! He was a boy, just like I wanted first. We named him Jonathan, and he was gorgeous! I had such a good time buying clothes for him. I loved to put him in little baseball uniforms, and I took him everywhere with me—to shop, to church, etc. Even men wanted to turn around and look at him. He was a prince. Women thought he was adorable and should be in TV commercials. The baby furniture, clothes, toys, crib, and changing table were so sturdy and perfect. It was very high quality and new that I bought from a neighborhood moving sale.

Mom saw Jonathan for the first time when she was on her porch. Holding his arms, I sat him down right in the middle of the big table across from her. She immediately kissed his chubby little arms and legs. I had him in a pale blue baseball shorts outfit with tiny green high-top tennis shoes. She never forgot that day; my heart melted. I think it was one of the best days with Mom, ever!

Lance was doing much better with his breathing by now. He still had difficulty, but it was much improved. He wanted his friends to see Jonathan. Everybody who met him loved him just like everybody loved Skip. I chose having Jonathan first because I wanted the brother to be older, just like Skip. All the family marveled at how much he was like Skip…even though Jonathan came from the farthest part of the world.

Once Jonathan was brought home, my life became sweet. I had no trouble with him, even though he was several weeks premature. He was tiny but perfect in every way. With me being part Italian, the first plan of action was to "fatten him up!" He could not tolerate milk, so we gave him formula. The doctor told us to sweeten it with Karo syrup. Well, that did it. He loved it! By the next doctor's appointment, he was almost normal height and weight. I was thrilled!

Jonathan was no trouble at night either. Almost every night, he slept from 8:00 p.m. to 7:00 a.m. without a noise. He was a happy baby, and I was in love! We have many DVDs of the baby years, and I'm going to make copies for him and his family in the future. He'll get a kick out of the DVD where he runs back twenty-seven times from the living room to check to see if his bathtub water is ready. He has twenty-eight toys scrunched in his fat little hands and pressed against his chest, all ready to toss, giggling as he throws them into the water in the tub. He was two and a half years old, and this is a showpiece DVD! After the twenty-sixth time, he says, "Momma, weddy yet?" He could have done TV! Every time I look at Jonathan, I see a miracle. Skip and Jonathan would have been chums!

My Prayer for a Wonderful Son

My son, you may not see it yet, but you and I are going to hit it off fantastically. My big brother and I were very competitive at times because I was a tomboy. So bring on the baseball bats and gloves! I'll teach you all about one of the most fun water sports. I know we will have a pool; your dad knows how much that means to me. The most important passion I have is God. I'll teach you all about Him and His kingdom. Of course, you'll go to church with me and grow to love Jesus… He's wonderful!

We'll go somewhere, maybe festivals, where you can ride ponies too. My brother and I loved riding the big horses together. When you get a little older, I'll try to talk your daddy into getting you your own dog. I already love having you with me everywhere I go; women especially think you're quite a handsome and well-behaved little guy. That makes me proud. Speaking of proud, I think you are going to be so smart. I see it even now in how quick you are to pick up on what I'm saying to you.

Oh, Jonathan, I'm so glad you're here-I'll be there to kiss your cuts and bruises. I'll be good to you and take care of all your needs. Your dad has a whole list of guy toys to buy you. Nevertheless, he can't have you only to himself just because you are both males. You are my guy.

You have helped the pain of losing Skip, and when I see how much you are like him, it makes me smile. I don't know if you see my pictures of you on our refrigerator, but it says, "Son, you are my sunshine." I love you madly.

ANOTHER BLESSING

Our Italian side of the family had two very apparent health conditions. Eight of them suffered from diabetes, a few more had lower back disc degeneration. My brother Skip suffered from this immensely and could no longer ride horses as he would have liked to. Now, I had a Jonathan who needed to be cared for and carried with me wherever I went and no family that was well enough that could lend a helping hand. I knew I needed some help. Aunt Dory, through her network of people, helped find someone who could help me.

Lance hired this woman to clean and help me around the house. Her name was Etta. Not only was she fantastic at tidying up, but she was also terrific with the children. Jonathan was an infant at the time, so I appreciated all the help. Even Lance liked Etta and depended on her just as much as I did. The biggest thing that she ever did for me was introduce me to the whole Biblical salvation plan. In our religion, we never talked too much about salvation. Of course, we knew Jesus was our Savior and had died on the cross for our sins. However, Etta was the first one that sat me down and explained how important it was to be "saved." That little seed of knowledge opened up a whole new world for me! Over the years, I was always very grateful that Etta had come into my life. She was a woman of strong faith and was a *true blessing* to me and my family. I could not have made it without her. She was a true friend and a godly woman who married a godly man. They are probably the only truly religious couple I had ever known. I was honored to be able to call Etta my best friend, and her daughter, Joseline was a wonderful babysitter.

She sparked my first real interest in the Bible over twenty-two years ago. I've never quit learning from the marvelous Word of God. As I have mentioned earlier, Father Quinton had given me one of his paperback Bibles. I had it for many years, and even though it was not a King James, as I was used to, it became the one that I read and studied every day. Many family members and friends could not understand how I could forgive Father Quinton since most of my beatings were because of Dad's misdirected anger from Father Quinton's and my mother's relationship. I can't really explain it; I just really pitied him for some reason. Under all the daredevilish demeanor, I believe there lived a very misguided soul. I did not want to add to the heavy burden he was already carrying, so when he asked me if he was the reason that my dad turned and took his anger out on me, I only told him part of the truth. I just couldn't be the reason he would feel worse than he already did. I had to take it several times to the foot of the cross. I forgave him before he had passed away. Although it was very difficult, I forgave all of them, totally.

As time went on, Jonathan got to know his grandparents. He ended up calling Dad "Pawpaw" and my Mother was "Grammy Jezz." Mom and Dad both loved having the chance to be grandparents again. Seeing the kids happy with them, it just felt right to forgive...so I did.

A breakthrough burst forth when Mom assured us that Dad "had all but stopped drinking completely." Wonderful! He came around almost humble now. After this, we had many dinners at one another's homes. Of course, my parents loved our baby Jonathan. He was the life of every get-together. He was so cute; Mom, like me, could not keep her hands off him. The only thing he did a little later on was walk. He was very smart, and I think he figured out that if he didn't walk, we'd carry him everywhere. Dad loved that we were a family and Quinton was not in the picture. He even played with Jonathan! Jonathan loved to play with trucks, cars, and airplanes like all little guys do... Jonathan's favorites were Jaguars.

Now, I was getting ready for Jonathan's sister, little Gloria! I wanted to shout and tell the world, but instead, this Bible verse jumped out at me. "Sing, O barren, you who have not bore a child, break into song and cry aloud, you who have not labored with child" (Isaiah 54:1). Alleluia!

Now, my second dream could come into play. I was going to adopt my baby girl. I had already gone to a snazzy kid's consignment shop. You can get the best new, adorable, and stylish baby clothes there. My purchases consisted of dresses, doll baby tops, ballet shoes, baby booties, lamb blankets, and tights. On the flip side, I bought an army tomboy look. They have the cutest clothes for babies and toddlers. I got her baseball caps too. I even got camo stuff and the cutest stuffed animals you'd ever seen. My Gloria was going to make a fashion statement right from the start. She was a few months away from arrival. I could not wait! I counted the days. Nevertheless, I smothered Jonathan with all the love I could. Every time I had him in my arms, the love just flowed to him.

OUR BABY GIRL IS HERE!... SOMEWHERE OVER THE RAINBOW

Nine months later, a liaison brought Gloria. We met at the airport... My second *miracle* baby was with us! I remember how I put her name in the back of my Bible years before along with my son's name. My beautiful Gloria was beyond my wildest dreams! I even wrote a poem two years prior to her arrival titled, "My Gloria." She was such a sweet, loving little doll baby right from the start. She was also Jonathan's half-sister. She loved to play peek-a-boo with her dad. Jonathan was careful not to share too many of his toys, yet... especially his sporty ones.

Oh, how I wish Uncle Skip had stayed alive to see his nephew and niece. I know he would have fallen in love with them like I have and come to his hometown more often to see us all. Jonathan loved cars, all cars, as did my big bro Skip, but both preferred Jaguars—all colors, all years.

I vowed to God and Lance that I'd be the best mother I could be. I vowed to not make the same mistakes my mother made with me and Skip. I'm sure she didn't mean to be neglectful, absent, selfish, and disloyal. Life just happened, but the Lord knows I have forgiven her and my father. Father Quinton also knew just before he died that all was forgiven. I think of all the horrible things we go through in life, but then

God gives us something *so spectacular*, like my two children, that seems to dry up all the tears of the painful past!

MY PRAYER FOR MY PRECIOUS DAUGHTER

My promise to you, sweet Gloria, will take our lifetime to discover. I will do my very best to protect you from anything dangerous, painful, or unloving. Sadly, there is a cruel strain of wicked folks out in the world. However, as long as I have breath, I will be there to defend and rescue you. I'll cheer you and your victories and love you like no other mama could. You can come to me. I'll love on your skinned knees and Benadryl your bee stings. Oh, I love you so much, that you and I are the same gender. I will do all I can to guide and encourage you where you need it. My shoulders will be there for your tear-filled moments; there may be some of those. Nurturing, feminine, strong arms will wrap around like your favorite baby blanket, and they'll be mine, your mom.

Thank you, my angel, for floating down from heaven. We are going to stick together, and we'll have so much fun! Dressing you in the clothes is just a start. We'll bake cookies, and at Christmas, gingerbread men and women will be on the menu. Heart and star shaped pancakes will taste yummy.

Perhaps, like me, your mommy, you will love cats. I know when you see your first kitten; you will want it more than your favorite toy. On the other hand, all of us will play baseball and swim together. Ponies will be part of our outside family along with kittens.

My little Gloria, I promise to be a very good mother and know you will love my mother, Grammy Jezz and "Pawpaw". She has calmed way down and is ready to be a terrific grandmother to you and Jonathan. If you don't mind, I am going to teach you all about God and Jesus. I hope you honor Them in your life far before I had the chance to. I'll be nudging you to be a capable and strong girl and I believe already, you were brought into our lives for a very special purpose.

Live out your dreams and don't let anything stop you and come to me in the future if you need anything at all. I'll try to be there for you when you're heartbroken. You are my heart. I'll love you into eternity!

Momma

CHAPTER 17

LOVE THY NEIGHBOR... REALLY?

The couple that lived next door had three children under the age of ten. The mother had an obvious alcohol problem that we detected within a month of moving beside them. The father was quiet but trouble because he liked to pull out all his truck parts and the greasy chunks of metal and motors landed on our driveway rather than on his. The dad loved old-fashioned fifties music and wanted all the neighbors to enjoy it also. He cranked it up as loud as the boom box would go on Sunday.

The eight-year-old boy also loved to play soccer with several friends after school and weekends. The whole team ended up in our yard more than their own. The activity and these antics went on for three straight years. One other nighttime activity that the couple participated in looked to be very strange. Just about every night, when the weather was decent, other couples and singles would come and sit out on their back covered deck. Borrowing Lance's job binoculars, I peered over and focused in on the scene as much as was possible to see at night. Lance, on the other hand, used his infrared camera and snapped pictures. It appeared that there were three or four tables whereby the group held lighted candles and would very quietly pray or chant. I sensed something evil about the gatherings. The wife and one child always wore black.

The bigger problem came when there was a dispute over how far their driveway was over our way. Surveys showed that there was a thirty-five feet encroachment of them onto our side. The front lots were not that wide—about seventy-five feet. So not only did we try to nicely address the situation proving there was a "glitch" on the boundaries, we said, "I'm sure we can work something out." Their Lassie-looking collie tried to chew our family up…and she was trespassing in our yard!

Shockingly, the woman went crazy over the boundary dispute! For the next months, there were nightly assaults to our property and the array of evil stunts. The kids next door bullied Johnathan and Gloria… That was it! Police came constantly.

I tried so hard to get along with our neighbors, but sometimes, it was not possible. By now, the couple had become more than obnoxious with all kinds of pranks. We had no choice but to take them to court, I felt. Lance did not want to do this.

Lance actually insisted, "Let's just move away from these crazy people." The only problem was Mom and Dad. What would I tell them? The German, stubborn side of me suddenly appeared.

"NO!" I vehemently declared. I had enough with people pushing me around and trying to scare me off! I put my foot down. I wanted the kids to stay near their grandparents.

Approach, Conflict

Lance was still saying we should just move in order to "get away from these psycho neighbors." Nonetheless, my parents were pressuring me to stay in my house and to not get pushed out. But Lance was right; this was no life for two little kids. These messed up neighbors would carry on forever, and our kids deserved better. Since our reconciliation, both Mom and Dad, and I'll add Aunt Dory, were relentless to entice us to stay.

Aunt Dory, Mom's next oldest sister, both Lance and I loved. She was loved by her community for her service.

She was a mayor's secretary and involved herself with the people and did more than the mayor did. She was more country than her Italian sister (my mom) who imitated the "Liz Taylor" lifestyle. Aunt Dory was more of a "Ma Kettle" personality. She hung around farm people. Quoting Nelly, "Her folk are hillbillies." She sided with my mom in order to keep me right where I was, and they'd offered to be witnesses for us if it ever came down to court. Aunt Dory loved Jonathan and Gloria. She and Mom babysat them both for several years. They both declared that watching and playing with the toddlers was the best times of their lives!

My husband Lance was so fantastic during the case. Their hotshot lawyer was very intimidated after questioning Lance's previous government work. Every evil tactic she used had been shut down by him. She only got to ask two questions and the judge overruled her! But a double-playing prosecutor messed up and the case was "dismissed."

Since the case was dropped within a few days, we decided to lease out our house and quickly go. I told Lance I wished I would have listened earlier and never stayed long enough to take her to court. But leaving my mom and dad was so difficult. Dad was just starting to get used to me being around. It upset all of us to think we had to leave and we had to go from the whole county. The last night at my parents' house was very sad and painful. I hugged my dad before our departure, and he quietly turned his head and cried; it broke my heart. However, it seemed that evil surrounded me in my hometown—just like the family in *Poltergeist*. The signs were unmistakable; it was time to go. My dad was the one I was so worried about. He and I were buddies again, and I had never been so heartbroken. When we put the "for sale" sign in our yard, the wife pointed and laughed, "I always get my way. Bye-bye!" What a witch!

Mom was sad too, but she had her brothers and sisters. None of them were further than twenty-five miles away. Lance was fed-up; he wanted us to go as far away as we could. I, on the other hand, had left part of me back there. Lance never seemed to care that this all broke my heart. The six years we were there were some of the best of my life! I missed them all, but my kids were my first priority, so we leased out the house. We said our goodbyes to everyone and met our new leasers. However, we did warn the people who leased the house of the neighbor prior to completing paperwork. But the people who leased the house said they could handle them. I hope so!

CHAPTER 18

BE GOOD TO THE CHILDREN

I firmly believe that children are gifts from God. We, who have chosen to adopt our children, know this well. Our Heavenly Father had only one begotten Son through the Virgin Mary. We, as His children, are adopted also. He created and loves each and every one of us (Galatians 4:3–7).

Parents are to love their children and take care of them as we need our Father's help and guidance. His Word is the best on the how's and what's of bringing them up in the Lord. When we leave God out of the picture, in any area, we become overwhelmed by the world. God cannot be left on the back burner. As Joel and Victoria Osteen always say, "Keep God first" (Revelation 2:4). The churches that were lacking in the end time prophecy left their first love—Almighty God.

Even up to the time we adopted our two miracles, Jonathan and Gloria, I enjoyed all the games, DVDs, and kid shows. I love the innocent fantasy-like magic that surrounds a child… I really can't excuse any reason to do harm to any child for any reason. My pastor is so wonderful and Biblical and is of the notion that children should never be punished while the parent is angry. Rather, think about reasonable consequences but have the sense to explain to the child where they messed up. Take time; they are all very smart and they'll get it. This worked for me because I had to figure out a way to be a good Christian mom and still get the kids to do what they were supposed to do. Reading the children's Bible stories to them and then graduating to the teen's Bible and so on helped a bunch. I also thought the *Veggie Tales* were terrific. I thought they were pretty cute too… I plan on following this same routine with my grandchildren, at least when I get to babysit them.

JONATHAN AND GLORIA STEAL THE SHOW

Right before the holidays and prior to our departure, the fiftieth wedding anniversary took place! Part of me was sad that Mom was married to Dad again. Wasn't the first part miserable enough? Nevertheless, the wedding reception was awesome!

All the extended family saw Jonathan and Gloria for the first time. It was close to Christmas, so I had them both all decked out. I remember exactly what I put on Gloria. She had a past the knee, dark green, velvet dress with lace around the collar and sleeves. I put on her white tights with black, patent leather shoes. I had her long black shining hair partially up in a band of thin white lace; she looked like a baby China doll out of the box. She was old enough to walk, and when we strolled in, hand in hand, all the people, family and friends, gasped and looked straight down at Gloria. She looked so beautiful. I was never so proud of her!

I had Jonathan in navy blue slacks with a white shirt under a navy blue and burgundy sweater vest. He was about three. All night, everyone came up to Lance and me to compliment the kids until we all left. My heart sung! Our children are such a blessing; every time we'd go anywhere with them, it was always a joyful occasion. Our Heavenly Father really took good care of us by blessing us with Jonathan and Gloria. But again, staying around my family was short-lived. A pattern was appearing. There always seemed to be dark cloud over our hometown area.

KICKING BACK FOR R & R

Lance, myself, and our kids decided to travel for the whole summer. We checked every amusement park that we could find, from east to west and north to south. The kids were only five and four years old, so we decided to include any petting zoo and race car tracks we could find. We visited Lance and our government friends; this took us from the mountains to beaches and deserts. We visited with my family and Skip's girls and then ended up staying with Lance's family on the west coast. It really turned out to be a wonderful summer. We stayed in our favorite hotels and motels, and the kids loved every minute of it. They got to swim indoors and at the special hotels. The outdoor pools were quite empty, which was nice because we had the pool all to ourselves many times at night. It was relaxing, but we had a busy schedule. While driving all over and visiting everybody, we played all of Amy Grant's music, and the kids watched *Veggie Tales*.

After the very adventurous and exciting summer, we temporarily rented in an adorable little town in the foothills and forests of Virginia. We attended the local church, which looked like it came off of a postcard with its cute little steeple. The pastor was crippled, and his cane was more like a staff. No kidding.

A REAL HOME

We had come to the same county we visited five years prior. We leased optioned our house and trusted the contract that the house was in the condition it had stated. But it turned out to be false. On the real estate contract, it clearly stated that the house "never flooded and had no known problems." Four to six months after we moved in, my husband started having breathing problems, and it happened in certain rooms of the house. The house did have a fireplace, but they claimed it was never used. As days went on, Lance got sicker and sicker. The basement was *full* of mold.

Lance had a law background, but he is not a lawyer. We "rescinded" the contract and gave the house back to the owners. Thank God we were able to get out of that mess. The sad part—the sellers were church elders.

A real good house was just a stone's throw away. Just up the street at the very top of the hill, there was a ranch-style home with a swimming pool and fully finished basement. I fell in love with it, so we bought it outright. We had good neighbors, and the kids went to the best schools in the area. The kids had several friends that came to our home to play and have snacks after school. Jonathan and Gloria, like me, loved to swim. Of course, friends came to swim and play in our pool all summer long. It was Merryland all over again!

SOMEONE TO WATCH OVER THEM

Trusting takes time and must be earned. For a few years, I verified that our two children were safe at school. I wasn't the only doting mother on the school grounds. There were several of us who constantly volunteered for any and every school activity. I always was a room mom, alternating every other year for Jonathan and Gloria's classrooms. Then, with both, I was on the construction and decorating committee for their yearly or bi-yearly school plays, skits and projects.

I was cafeteria monitor for several years. Following the pattern of Merryland festivals, I worked every year in the school carnival booths. Some years it was the ring toss, some years it was the food booth (with, yes of course, pizza!). Finally, in honor of the famous Beverly Goldberg, I too became "spy mom" on the playground. I did my best for the kids to know my support, love, and affirmation regarding them. Jonathan and Gloria had excellent grades all through school; both were on the honor roll just about every year. The rewards seemed to always be video games; however, I do *not* like the violent ones. School kids picked on Johnathan and Gloria some, so neither child rode the school bus for very long at all. We all drove to school and back, the speakers blaring our favorite CDs. Some of our favorites were the best Christian artists such as the incredible David Phelps with the Gaither Vocal Band. We also loved Avalon. Janna Long is one of my favorite female singers.

We loved the Booth Brothers, and Darlene Zschech is marvelous too! The best was to watch over the two gorgeous and intelligent wonders that He lovingly placed in my life!

A Defining Moment

Rita already knew of my extreme interest and intense study of the Bible. I was a member of the church choir, and I sang my heart out to my Heavenly Father enthusiastically. Rita, I noticed in our many religious discussions, had a wonderful, peaceful demeanor, even when she was in the middle of struggle. I witnessed this several times regarding her problems dealing with some not-so-Christian personnel and rowdy school children in the cafeteria. So in other words, she appeared to have it all together. She was another school mom in Jonathan's class, and I had sat with her at many school functions. She also was very compassionate with Jonathan and Gloria as she was a cafeteria mom. She was as vigilant about child bullying as I was. Several times, she intervened to stop pushy boys from messing with Jonathan by gently pulling them out of line or scolding them for harming him.

Her son, Kent, and my son ran around and played at recess with each other, so I felt a double comfort with Rita. She also was good to Gloria and gave her extra portions of the "foods she liked" as she was very picky about some of the others that were offered.

One day, when we were in the car together, she invited me to her all-women Bible study at her church. She had talked to me a couple of times about how much it helped her and that she loved all the other ladies; they were so sweet and nurturing. Hmm, my ears perked up. "Nurturing?" Wow, I'm not sure I would know how that really felt. Being the woman of intrigue, I accepted her invitation.

So the date was set; it was this afternoon! The same day she asked me! I followed her to the cute little Baptist church. I was greeted by several other women very warmly with handshakes that led to hugs. The ages were anywhere from twenty-five to eighty-five, and I was already feeling welcome there, but it started to rain.

We were in the church itself, and there was not one man around. We sat on a big shag carpet right up next to the altar. The women all appeared to be mothers, and a few were grandmothers to be sure. Every one of them had an almost glowing aura around them while they had smiles that beamed as the raindrops hit the windows. In my spirit, a tiny voice was telling me, *Don't be ashamed, you're in safe territory. Speak out.* I think this was "direction," and I obeyed it.

Rita asked me if it was all right to tell the woman about my children being Asian and bullied and how I had to leave the kids grandparents and why. I agreed, and by now, I was crying again as she told my true story to the other women. I broke out sobbing, almost uncontrollably when she disclosed the pain I felt about Skip's horrible suicide. That small, intimate circle of women came to me, and we all had a giant group hug. I longed for that closeness with nurturing women, and I had it now. I relished every second. It was as if I had known them before. It was incredible; the sun came out and a rainbow as well. I scarcely could take in the harmony and love!

So at that moment, with several sobbing and crying with me, I gave my heart, all my troubles, worries, hatred, and love to our Savior, Jesus. They did not have to ask me. I blurted out, "Oh, Jesus, I need you!"

You see, up until that time, I talked and prayed "about" Jesus; *now,* I gave myself as He gave Himself for me. He was the Lord of my life. It was a wonderfully ecstatic time, and I had several Bible studies with them after that, and my insatiable appetite for more and more truth from God's Word has continued, and that truth is in His letter reaching out to all His children. I take Him at his Word. Not only was there relief with a release of the junk I still held in, but I knew that this was the most vital decision that had haunted me (Romans 8:8–11).

As the wife of a famous pastor said, "God speaks loud and clear through His written Word." Bobbie Houston states, like me, "God was on my case and speaking to me from all directions." In my car, with a sister in Christ, even that rainy day, light burst through the clouds adorned with brilliant colors! I was saved, and I danced in the rain.

KIDS AND PETS

As a child, I never pretended that I had an imaginary friend, but I had my cats, kittens, horses, and other animals to keep me company. At camp, Skip and I had tons of friends around us all the time. On the other hand, when I was hidden in my cubbyhole by myself in darkness, I would whisper to my Real Father who could "fix things." In my total desperation to secure protection, I cried out to the Powerful One, God. As a child, I couldn't fathom the Holy Spirit quite yet, and the "*crucified*" Christ was very scary to me as fear dominated my spirit.

A very good friend of mine told me that she wanted to read more about my kids. If I started on them, it would probably take another whole book! Jonathan and Gloria were the best angelic souls I could have ever imagined coming into my life. From the very moment we went to the airport to bring them into their new home with us, I have never stopped smiling. They were, and still are, my sunshine and rainbow all in one beautiful loving scene.

Not birthing your children is not a flaw; adopting children is the greatest blessing there ever was! Since my church and I believe there was a heaven and earth age before this, I think God handpicked Jonathan and Gloria for Lance and me. Every stage of development with both children was more exciting than the one before! Having a two-year-old and a one-year-old at home at the same time was fantastic! Every new word and every new step in life, I was right there with them. They were companions and playmates for each other every day. Even in preschool, they were in the same classes and had many adorable friends.

As their mother, knowing how important it was for them to have a sense of belonging and fitting in, I never missed an event. There were birthday parties, swim parties, field trips, festivals, Fourth of July celebrations, Christmases, or driving to their friends' homes and to school. There were a few incidents where Jonathan and Gloria were both bullied by children in their school. As I declared before, I would drive my kids and be a spy, help to grab the future delinquents, and put them in the principal's office. I did not let my kids ride the school bus where they were so easily picked on. However, both kids had many sweet friends that swam in our pool and spent nights at our house.

Our kids' favorite foods were Italian. Jonathan's favorite food was pizza, and Gloria's favorite was spaghetti. Of course, having an Italian family, they all loved that these were their favorite choices. The irony of this is that their grandmother, who is Italian, favors the Chinese cuisine most of all. Again, how boring would our lives be if America was not a fantastic mixture of all the different races and cultures...and *foods*!

When I think back to my kid's childhoods, I am reminded of the pets we have shared. Gloria is much like her mother (me). She absolutely goes nuts over kittens and cats! For her tenth birthday, you would not believe the magical events that took place just to get her present—her very own purebred Siamese cat. The kitten was from a cattery in Pennsylvania, and the twists and turns that started to deter the whole birthday surprise had somehow miraculously turned out as destiny should have it. Originally, the kitten was to be placed in the airplane kennel from Pennsylvania and flown to us. As a series of unfortunate events unfolded, it started with an 800-mile journey to secure a pet. Our home had been struck by the flu bug, bad weather, scheduling conflicts, and so much more. Our new Siamese addition was just about ready to be *scratched* from Gloria's birthday present list. As destiny should have it, our Father must have intervened here. "Simon" (as Jonathan got to choose the name) was hand delivered to our house. *Out of the clear blue sky*, the owners themselves drove Simon to Gloria. The owners had some friends of theirs that were having a Christmas holiday wedding. As it should turn out, this was only seventy-five miles from our home, the cat's destination—us. Gloria had the best birthday ever!

Years ago, we had lost a very dear cat, Mai Tai. Since Gloria had bonded with Simon so well, he stayed in her bedroom. I wanted my very own cat again. My husband had agreed with me. It was decided that we could get a Siamese girl cat.

As you saw, before we adopted Jonathan and Gloria, Lance had made me agree to find new homes for our pets. I had one cat, Shoggie, that was handicapped. Naturally, I focused more on him. He was a tiny, blue and grey Siamese who had asthma. Getting rid of him crushed me. I loved him so much and worried about his future with someone who may not be as patient, caring, and loving with him. I did, however, find Shoggie a forever home. But I always missed him most of all, so the search was on. The kids were entering the sixth and seventh grade when Jonathan came home with a request of his own.

As for the kids, in middle school, Jonathan signed up for the cooking club. His buddies asked him to join for "girls." I became a mom sponsor, and Jonathan and I had a really good time together. We still have the delicious recipes from forty-five families, grandmas, aunts—the best of the best! Jonathan loved the variety of dishes and had a ball with ten guys and thirty-five girls in the class!

SAVED BY THE BAND

Gloria did pretty well with kids too. She actually buddied up with more boys than girls. She was like me until she was about thirteen; she was a tomboy. I could not get a dress or skirt on her—even for church. She was so cute though, in her camo pants, T-shirts, and high tops.

Also, in school, both kids joined the school band, which changed their lives completely. Jonathan and Gloria were only a year apart, so they were in the same band, and they enjoyed school. I don't think I missed one concert when they were in middle school. They had about four concerts each year. Their father was an excellent drummer, and they were both taught to play well by him. They had more friends than ever during this time, and Lance and I were most proud of them.

SONGS IN THE HEART

After ten years of living at our lovely ranch home with a swimming pool, the outside paint needed refreshing, so my husband turned the task of finding an "excellent but fair priced" painter over to me. Normally, those things are next to impossible to occur together. My never-give-up attitude got the assignment accomplished after calling and interviewing eleven painters! I prayed that my choice would be a good one, and as usual, our Heavenly Father blessed us during the process.

Robin and her two friends were my choice; she was an excellent painter. A blessing was that she introduced me to the best Christian music. Darlene Zschech was one. The last

DVD (*Here I Am, Send Me*) that I watched of her was absolutely an encounter with the *Holy Spirit.*

My mom and I are crazy over David Phelps's singing. He is the most talented tenor I've ever listened to in my entire life! Lance loves him; my daughter, Mom, and I really enjoy his marvelous singing. David Phelps writes beautiful and sensitive lyrics, and God has truly blessed this man's voice! My friend Shella just listened to his new CD, *Freedom,* and said one word, "Terrific!"

One of the other Gaither singers wrote the most gorgeous song about Jesus. "Mary Did You Know" describes the Christ that is "God" in such a fantastic way. Power-filled. Robin also introduced me to a really wonderful band who was right from our area. The Booth Brothers write most of their songs. I wake up and go to bed listening to them, and their rendition of "Christ Alone" is the best I have ever heard. For me personally, their song "Wildflower" impacted my soul more than any other song ever! It came out on CD close to my visit with my dad at Christmas. I love *that* song!

Avalon with Janna Long can really belt it out. I listened to it when I drove the kids to school and back. What a powerhouse band! Their CD, *Faith, A Hymn Collection,* is excellent and inspirational.

"Hillsong," with Brian Houston Ministries, is excellent too. His wife, Bobbie, is great to listen to her preach. Her book, *Sisterhood,* makes you feel so good that we were created women. I wish we girls in the United States were as loving and caring as she and her church in Australia/New Zealand are. What an affectionate group of Christian followers they are! The pastors that are highlighted on their program dig deep in Scripture, and I love that. Christine Cain and others are very down to earth and are enlightening evangelists.

I also love a Christian singing group who were in the audience of the Gaithers when they were young guys. The name is "Signature Sound." What harmony! The songs all stayed in my heart. I have enjoyed listening to them and will continue to.

Until I met Robin with her CD gifts, I didn't appreciate Christian music the way I do now. I think our Heavenly Father may smile and snap His fingers when He looks down at His children praising, worshiping, and adoring Him through this beautifully uplifting music. Doesn't it blow your mind that a supernatural Father desires our love as much as we desire His? This love is revealed in this next story.

I MISS SKIP SO MUCH

Skip's been on my mind. My birthday is tomorrow. He and I always called one another on our birthdays. As I write about Skip, I can't help but to burst out crying. I miss my big brother; I have wonderful baby and adult pictures of us in gorgeous sparkling frames. He was so neat, funny, loving, and sensitive. He loved his two girls with all of his heart—at least, with the big part that was not shattered from our past. Skip was a latchkey child like me; he was beaten, verbally assaulted, cruelly criticized, and was told he wasn't valuable. But just like me, he did his best. Oh, Skip, what did they do to you? I wish I could have been with you; maybe we could have outsmarted them all! I wish we could talk. Tomorrow's my—never mind, Skip.

Nevertheless, something spectacular happened to me about eleven years ago. My darling daughter was with me in the kitchen as I was fixing supper. As I was opening a can of food with our electric can opener, I stopped, dropped everything, darted into my room, and burst out sobbing. I was crying so much I was heaving. My precious daughter ran in with me. She was so concerned that she hugged me and I squeezed her back. Gloria was about ten years old and asked me what was wrong. I told her it was about my brother, Skip, but I was sobbing so much, all I could say was, "My brother, my brother Skip."

Then the most amazing thing happened. She said, "Mom, Skip said he forgives you."

I gasped. "What!"

You see, when my big brother and I were in the kitchen as teens, washing dishes, something very sad happened. Skip always used the electric can opener to open the dog's food. This he did at the time I was doing dishes. He did his usual teasing and clowning around with the towel sting tactic, so I tried to keep away and jumped by quickly turning, but as I did, the knives and forks I was holding accidentally stabbed him. He was hurt pretty bad, and I exclaimed, "I'm sorry, I'm so sorry! Are you okay, Skip?" and I insisted he needed to go to the doctor and get stitches. He bled and bled while I cried, but he didn't cry. He would not hear of stitches and convinced me to keep the whole ordeal from Mom and Dad. I reluctantly agreed. So I took care of cleaning, medicating, and gently bandaging his poor arm wound. He wore long-sleeved shirts for a few weeks while it healed. *Nobody* but us knew about that.

He teased me for years saying, just to me, "Yeah, my little sister loves me, but she stabbed me with a knife." Skip was always sick and, even though a big guy, fragile to me. He had a heart murmur and constant colds and nose bleeds too. Later in life, he developed a bleeding ulcer, but he remained very stoic about it. He did not get to live out half of his life. He never complained, ever.

I know that, because we both came from the same chaos, Skip was a nervous wreck inside. He never showed it, but we were both emotionally and spiritually hiding. Like Sanford had witnessed, when abused and constantly traumatized, our spirits "go into hibernation." We can be stuck in denial or block out so much we can't remember what happened because we don't want to. Why did alcohol even have to be invented? So much pain comes from it. I believe it is a tool that the enemy uses as his elixir.

Skip had killed himself on Independence Day, ironically. I know, just like me, Skip threw all he had into raising his two girls. We had to do it right as a way to right all the wrong done to us. Somehow, we both loved. We doted day and night on our kids. Our spouses were the disciplinarians; we couldn't be.

That marvelous evening, I believe a miracle occurred when my sweet Gloria surprised herself speaking out about what she heard, the time with the electric can opener. I do believe God allows for His children to be wonderfully comforted when tragedies happen such as a lost loved one. Not only is our Heavenly Father the Creator of everything, but He is compassionate about His creations. I honestly believe Father Quinton and Skip are in heaven. I know that Skip has forgiven me now. Thank you, Father; I had to know that he did! Thank you, Skip. You made *my birthday one I'll never forget!*

I also believe, from what I've read in all kinds of places in the scripture, that whatever talents we had on earth, we are given them back in heaven too. The best part is, we never get sick or age; let's hope they have chocolate. I know there will be Milky Ways!

CHAPTER 19

TRANSLUCENT—TRANSFORMED

$\mathcal{W}$e, as Christians, are to be the Holy Spirit's translucent vessel that, when unbelievers see or meet us, they can see "a spark of the heavens" shining through us in the world. The Holy Spirit was glorified that incredible evening of visitation. I felt a spark of sweet love with Gloria and Skip like I had never felt so strongly before! Our three spirits met for a reunion!

The more light around me, the better, and I love the sun, swimming pools, and peacefully floating and staring up at the marvelous sky. I remember one partly cloudy day I decided to make a go at catching a few rays until it was time to drive up to school and get the kids. This is the day the concept of translucence made more sense to me. It was also the day I started seeing light and dark in a new way.

One of Jesus's titles is the "Sun of Righteousness" (Malachi 4:2). It is not S-O-N, it is S-U-N. When I looked up at the sky with the sun brightly shining, I thought of Jesus and God's brilliant way of letting Christians know, even at playtime, that Jesus shines on us.

Suddenly, a very dark cloud blocked the sun and transformed the scene. It hit me that that's what sin must do in our souls. On the other hand, within a few minutes, the sun, bright and shining, broke through the darkness. Isn't that what happens when we repent? When Jesus comes to live in us, our souls become translucent; it's just as if He harnesses the darkness and casts it away. Now the enemy never gives up, and I was about to discover how ruthless he can get.

STRANGE SYMPTOMS—A TESTIMONY

I have read, in many of my books, that right after a Christian is saved, Satan gets to work sawing out the floor under them. Recently, there was another great enemy in the journey of this life that I was to face. This enemy was the worst and most challenging trial I ever had tried to handle. In fact, I did not handle it very well, because physically, my body gave out on me. The trauma and stress had weakened my immune system, and I collapsed in bed.

At the start of 2009, it was Lance who had the health issues. He had heart issues and broke out with rashes and welts as if beaten with a riding crop. He also had breathing issues when he stayed on the computer or stood in front of the microwave for too long. Out of the blue, Lance could not tolerate any soy products, sugars, dairy, and fifty other foods. He was told by a doctor that he had very low blood sugar. However, just like a diabetic, he had to cut out sugar from his diet. He even developed allergens to processed foods from fast food restaurants. This happened after we lived in a certain part of the country and came upon him suddenly. He could not figure out what was going on.

Then in September of 2010, I started having strange symptoms too. It started with fatigue, but then I started getting hot flashes, but I waved it off as early menopause. I also began having heart problems, and it was frightening. I still tried my best to continue my daily routine of driving the kids to and from school. I did as many activities with the kids as I could. Each and every day, it became harder to do so. I was having a terrible time digesting my food; it got to the point where I could only eat a few foods also. I knew something bad was happening to my whole system. Kind of like Lance, many foods were going by the wayside. What was happening to us?

The *Poltergeist* theme song was playing in my head. Oh no. *It's baack!* My face, arms, and torso were constantly feeling like they were on fire. I had a constant fever but no rise in temperature. I had flushes and dangerous heart arrhythmias that never seemed to leave. I'd have to use the commode three of four times a day because of excessive diarrhea. The worst symptom was I was constantly breathless. This lasted for six months straight!

By Christmas of 2011, I had the worst health crisis that one could ever have. The constant diarrhea caused me to drop ten pounds every couple of months. I dehydrated horribly. After two more years of going through these symptoms, I had become so frail and weak that I couldn't get out of bed. Lance did some traveling as he was better but still could not be around microwaves or cell phones. It appeared to make our symptoms much worse.

Lance moved out of the master bedroom because I kept waking him at night with my symptoms, and somebody had to take care of the kids. They were teenagers but still had to be driven everywhere.

My Near Fatal Illness Predicted...My Testimony

Our bizarre and frightening symptoms had become quite debilitating. The first few months I had my scary symptoms, I still had continued with business as usual. This included going to church with my two teenagers where they attended youth group sessions. Well, one Sunday I decided to talk to the pastor right after church and ask him to bless me. I waited until the last song was over and went right up to him before he made it out the door. Now understand, at this time no friend or doctor nor any person knew how sick I was feeling. But the most unique thing happened when he blessed me. He looked at me and said, "Katia, I don't think doctors are going to cure this one." Then he continued with, "In fact, I'm not sure they will know WHY you are having these symptoms. *This malady is going to be up to God alone.*" When I left him, I'm sure I was in a daze. How could he think that? I never even talked to him or anyone else at church about how debilitated I was becoming. I was afraid the whole church would think I was crazy, so I kept quiet until I saw the pastor this Sunday. I left baffled and anxious. I tested positive reactions from 52 foods that I used to eat routinely! I was in shock by the pastor's prediction!

What was worse was that my thyroid was stuck. Nevertheless, he was right. Mayo Clinic and other highly educated doctors were totally stumped at what was causing my strange and horrible symptoms. I was suffering from malnutrition. Only the one Holistic D.O. who prayed with me could have a clue of what was ravaging my traumatized body...and even his knowledge was very limited. He guessed that the last government facility had extremely high powered utility towers, which harmed us both. Since the damage that had already taken place was depleting every cell, neutron and atom in my system, it was a miracle that I survived this far. Right after that last church visit I stopped driving. That was the start of the things I had to give up. Within a few short weeks, Dr. B. discovered that individuals such as myself and my husband, were *overexposed* with high amps of radioactive power. These surges, plus dangerous electrical grids, cause the same damage as a person who has been struck by eighty thousand volts of lightening! No wonder both of us got so ill. The thing was, I was exposed for many more hours than Lance because during the time he took this job stent, I was a stay at home housewife and Mom. Furthermore, we were living next to a street of such *high-powered* energy facilities that were right next to a swimming pool. The combination of all these radiation and electro-magnetic fields to empower the specialized equipment were lethal to a human body (Take the time to research those electrocuted or struck by lightning and radio frequency illness.). It is very real!

During this crisis period, my spouse and I researched all we could find about being highly sensitized to radar, electronics, and Wi-Fi technology. For example, cows in a pasture are known to give poisoned milk when they are fenced next to high-voltage power grids (the ones that power up our homes on a daily basis). Just like radon harms and even kills people over time, electromagnetic and radio frequency fields harm and can kill in an instant! The medical phenomenon of amalgams poisoning our blood through tooth fillings was also a big contributor, on my part, for the destroying of the remaining decent health picture. I tested having extremely high metal in my blood. The prognosis without being admitted to a hospital for immediate blood transfusions, adrenal aids, and nutritional remedies was grim. The irony of this: The hospital that would normally save someone's life was a death sentence for me. The hospital equipment, x-rays, and heart monitors would have stopped my heart. A heart doctor told me. Don't be so surprised. Our hearts are electric thus "electronic pacemakers." Lance had heart issues before I did. He had palpitations and skipped beats first. Since he left the facility to go into the city to work, he avoided 70 percent of the killer emissions. This unwelcome debilitating intrusion hit my system mixed with the poisonous mercury fillings that had ruined my blood. The metal poisoning throughout my skin and bone was making me a "walking antenna." This is exactly what Dr. B. said. Do you remember the movie, *Powder*? Well, sadly, I felt like that poor old soul. I believe the enemy took one last shot at me, and he "hit me with his best shot" (Pat Benatar). Even lamps and lights had to be put off around me as I would become feverish and perspire tremendously. The darkness again was engulfing me. This time, the enemy was warring to kill my flesh. My vision was dim, almost invisible. The light I craved so had to be kept out of my reach!

THE WORLD FADED TO DARKNESS

When this started, I began to identify with the brave people who are blind. Patience is what God freely gives you when bad things go on. I have found that, while in the fiery furnace (literally) of affliction, "it forges an eternal hope, and it is God's patience for the tormented soul," according to T. D. Jakes. It is the highly underrated and over taxing word, "long suffering." In my case, when all the stores, school activities, church activities, concerts, and family celebrations abruptly ceased, the whole earth as I had known it broke off and drifted away out of my reach. Anything and everything worldly was gone. It had vanished into a dark place. My poor little family. I was on the broken away island that was opaque, gloomy, and lonely.

It happened like in the hallway in *Poltergeist* for Jo Beth Williams. In the movie, while the rest of the neighborhood carried on merrily, Carol Ann's family was attacked by satanic forces, and the physical and psychological issues they were forced to endure took a huge negative toll on all the family members. They also had to endure their world turned to darkness. Lance and I both had severe physical symptoms when any 220 appliance or furnace was used! We were both lepers (outcasts) from the bustling world of techno power.

We had to limit the number of lights beaming brightly in three-quarters of our house. Mine and my husband's illness was hard for the four of us. The kids didn't complain much, only when they had to give up their Wi-Fi technology for a while. However, Lance and I looked sickly, skinny, jaundiced, and felt like we had walked through hell, just like the family in the movie. We looked like zombies.

The whole scenario shifted for Carol Ann's mom (in *Poltergeist*) as soon as she cried out, "God, help me!" And after weeks of enduring just like the movie family, I did exactly the same thing. God heard my cry. "Enough, please." Our lifetime had all four of the Hollywood movies *Poltergeist*, *Prince of Tides*, *The Thorn Birds*, and now, *Agnes of God*, converging on our crisis situation. I had to have the Son of God come into my fiery furnace as He did with the Hebrew children and wait on the Lord. I no longer could make light of my symptoms. They were excruciatingly real and awful. I did not deny it, and it was frightening! My horrid childhood home life was bad enough, but now this??

I was forced to give up all the things I enjoyed doing in the past. I loved net surfing, but it caused nausea and hot flashes. I could not watch TV unless I was at least twelve feet away. I could not cook, which was one of my passions. I could not sit out in the sun and read. I even became allergic to the sun's radiation. Lights and lamps had to be far away from me. I became very depressed. The kids, and all that came with raising them, had taken most of my time, and that was gone. Perhaps I was remiss when it came to my spiritual side. I made up my mind to still have computers and phones for the kids, but we had to go back to Ethernet lines in replacement of Wi-Fi.

I FEEL LIKE A FEMALE JOB

I could not help comparing myself to Job. I tried to keep my cool, but there were times when I felt sorry for myself... Like Job, I identified completely with the enemy coming at me from all sides. In the Old Testament, I remembered that the Bible prophets felt like giving up. Job cried, "I hoped for good things to happen, but something evil came" (Job 30:26). Mine was Satanic too. "I looked for light but all I saw was darkness." Oh, yes, I even read by moonlight. "My insides are always churning. Nothing but days of suffering" (Job 30:16) are ahead of me. The nausea was worse than morning sickness. "The days of affliction take hold of me...and my gnawing pains take not rest" (Job 30:27). "My heart is in turmoil and I cannot rest." I could not get a regular heartbeat for three years. "My skin has become dark... but the sun didn't do it" (Job 30:30). Radiation burnt me inside to out. "My skin grows black and peels." It did so for four years. "My body burns with fever..." Every time I was around Wi-Fi and appliances. "My bones burn with fever." Mine too and my flesh. So yeah, Job, I know what you mean.

My medical issue was in full throttle, and as much as I was thankful for Dr. B., I had a long way to recover, if at all. For instance, cortisol is an adrenal hormone that we cannot even survive without. My level was hard to find and hardly registered at all. There was, however, a stumbling block regarding my visits with the doctor; my insurance didn't cover him. But as far as physicians go, I'd gladly take him. He was the only doctor that could help find a way for me to recover, and he was only ten minutes away. Although his help was true, I still had trouble driving to him because I had gotten so weak. Nevertheless, God led me to Dr. B so whatever it took; I was going to stay with him. The wonderful news was our health insurance finally agreed to pay 65 percent! Thank you, God! Due to my illness, I had become a shut-in, but I still continued my Bible studies. I was too weak to go out in public. I had become like the "lepers" in the Old Testament. Sadly, no family member, friend, or even kids would even try to understand my illness. It was too bizarre to comprehend. Other than Lance, who had one-fourth of my symptoms, I was on my own. We had to have all of our computers wired in. No more Wi-Fi. No one could use a cell phone around Lance or me. It was as if we were thrust back thirty years in technology time. The only privilege I had left was I could read by flashlight. The only foods I could tolerate were pinto beans, brown rice, and cooked apples. All other foods, I reacted to.

Casting all other cares away, I focused on God's words on healing. I had just about every good Christian self-help book. I have probably read over 1,400 books in my twenty years of reading on self-help. Many authors have walked a desperate path like I did: Paula Sanford, Paula White, Beth Moore, Joyce Meyer, R.T. Kendall, Cloud and Townsend, Marianne Williamson, Charles Spurgeon, Charles Stanley,

Tommy Tenney, John Sanford, Andrew Womack, Warren Wiersbe, Charles L Allen, E. M. Bounds, and Dodie Osteen, Joel Osteen, Douglas Pessoni, Stormie Omartian, Joseph Prince, Sheila Walsh, Derek Prince Christine Caine, Bobbie Houston. In fact, Steven Furtick and Lisa Bevere's sermons were very encouraging regarding telling my story. I needed to fast forward from my comfortable religious stance and dig deep to uncover the mysterious ways God rescues and delivers.

I owe so much to these authors because their books and CDs have worked. Pulling out all of the exact healing and helping quotes from the Bible can be daunting, but they all did so beautifully. My Christian self-help books have been my counseling mentors. Many writers even prayed for us. Any time I went through distress, God's grace had gotten me through and kept me going. I kept praying back God's promises to Him and trying so hard to meet the conditions. If we all adhere to the "ifs" before the promises, I believe more prayers would be answered. I was about to search for the Great Physician Himself...desperation drove me.

THE THIRD PERSON

The Holy Spirit is the Paraclete. Andrew Murray, an author, describes the spirit and the inner man better than any. The heart thirsts for God and will sacrifice the world for all that God reveals. The Holy Spirit does God's will in us. The Third Person comforts us, and we transcend trouble. The word *transcend* was never in my vocabulary until recently. This fellow brother gave his testimony and said some things that resonated loudly with me. He said, "Any crisis or tragedy emotionally affects each one of us terribly. Nevertheless, as soon as we turn it over to God and stay in faith that He sees and knows exactly what to do, we 'transcend secular solutions.'" Paul L. Walker and his wife tragically lost their son in a horrible car accident on a Thanksgiving Day. The son was a young pastor and was killed.

Dr. Paul Walker reports regarding hanging on, "We turn to the deepest resources within us and draw on the rudiment of our own faith to sustain us." Like all of us who feel like we can't go on another day, Dr. Walker continues with, "To become a transcender, we go beyond the limits, to step over boundaries, to surpass the limiting factors." We push "to rise above the hindrances, to cope with the uncontrollable, and to know that regardless of the circumstances, we are more than conquerors through Him who loved us" (Romans 8:37). I had *two* fronts going on—Lance and my crisis with our health, and Mom and Dad's future. My parents were distraught, and no one was willing to assist them. Their finances were jeopardized.

Ever clinging to God, with the fiasco regarding Dad and Mom's estate, I had to remember that our relatives were a bit ruthless about my parents' assets. I had to *know* that God was for us in helping to retain and secure for them what wasn't already taken. I prayed that the extended family I loved were not part of the crimes against senior citizens. *But* I did not know. Lance and honest bankers came to their rescue.

More importantly, God surely did give us all the victory. Dad and Mother lived quite comfortably in a nice assisted living facility for seven years. Mom and Dad went back to church together and, as always, tithed their 10 percent. Now my quest was to pray for the Great Physician. I was slipping away…

Moreover, after I dusted off my books on the Holy Spirit, I got started studying about His position in the Trinity.

Another male author whom I have grown to admire and use his work is R. T. Kendall. I've read several of his books, but one of my favorites was *The Sensitivity of the Spirit*. Okay, in the title alone, "sensitivity" connotes God needs to be welcomed in calm territory. Hmm... How in the world can I be tranquil when my world as I've known it is being disconnected and all but "powered off?" Nonetheless, I dug my feet in and researched all I could on healing of the flesh and the prerequisites to save it. My feverish search kept my mind off my raging symptoms. I would not tell my parents. They are elderly and frail.

Children who loved Hayley Mills's movies know that she never gave up; she found a clue or something that achieved her goal of being successful and on top of the situation. I started my search to find out the energy connection to the source of real power—the Holy Spirit of God. I needed to be careful not to run off the Spirit in any way. I did not even know it was possible that, once we were Christians, we could make the Holy Dove "flutter away" (R. T. Kendall). Maintaining a calm attitude during this torturous time was very challenging.

I found someone trustworthy to talk to; I prayed to God. Now I was dealing with new emotions and feelings, and not too many around me understood what I was going through. "Oh yeah right. Turn off my cell phone. I don't think so," was what Lance and I heard over and over when we would ask those around us. My heart went out to the leper in Bible times. They were rejected and shunned. I know some of how they felt.

Coming into the light is disclosing sin and evil. Now I had to literally fight my way back into the light—back into life.

SINS OF THE PARENTS...PLEASE DON'T FALL UPON ME

Scripture has backed up many of my questions regarding my illness. Even though I was in good standing with Mom and Dad, I used to wonder if my parents' sins would somehow lead to me being punished. I would catch myself in these thoughts and quickly draw them in and read from the Word. The verse that stands out to me the most is in the book of John.

In the book of John, Jesus clears it up for us when he walks through the story of the blind man. Jesus, with his disciples, came upon the young man who was born blind. The disciples asked, "Rabbi, who here has sinned? Was it his parents? Or him?"

Jesus answers them, "It is not because of the sins of the parents this has happened, it's so God's work could be witnessed by many in his life" (John 9:1–4).

I often referred back to this when I would begin to question, "Why me?" Then a small whisper came to me, *Why not you?* This is a chance to witness God at work. "Be still" and trust, hope, believe. That's easier said than accomplished. Sometimes I felt so bad I wanted to scream out! The Holy Spirit would fire back to me with 1 Corinthians 10:13. But how long, Lord? I think I'm at my wit's end!

Another great author who has been used to heal others through his books on scripture and healing is Derek Prince. In his books, he says things that hit very close to home for me. When we read the Word of God, believe it and claim it in simple faith; our Heavenly Father will intervene. He writes, "The Lord will use every difficulty, need, or illness as a means to show Himself greater to us than He ever has before." He shows up with his saving love. I couldn't help but think back to my dad when I was climbing up a ladder at around two and a half years old, climbing each step up to get to his arms. Along with Derek's words on how *faith climbs* up on difficult obstacles, it is overcoming the difficulty of it that gives us increased faith and spiritual character. Amen. May I have the strength to continue to climb and never forget my Heavenly Father's love is forever unmatched. He forgives us for everything we have done and does not hold us accountable for what our parents have forsaken Him for. God's word clearly states, in Philippians 2:12, that we shall stand alone to be judged, not with our parents. Maybe Dad and Mom both repented... Who knows?

I sobbed my heart out over Skip's death. It seemed so pointless for him to just one day to be here on Earth, laughing, swimming, horseback riding, and so on, but now, in a twinkling of an eye, he's gone—out of my life. How could it be a curse? Mom and Dad had been were so nice and good to my little family for several years now. I had long since buried their blame for anything.

An untrue statement I have read and heard all my life is that generational curses can come to believers. For several years, I wrestled with that one. Look at my Italian family and Mother and Father Quinton. If I believed that, I'd be up the creek (lake) of fire without a paddle! Conversely, God cursed those who hated Him and all those after them who do their best to take God *out* of the four hidden dynasties. Those are education, finance, politics and religion. Yes, if He is left out, blessings, grace, and mercy will be also. Can you blame Him? (Per my pastor) The closer you get to God, the enemy tries to lure you to him. My parents were back in church and tithing. They were model grandparents. A curse was unimaginable.

The reason I say that our Creator will not hold any of us accountable for our parents' sins is proven in the Bible also. Believe me, this promise I anguished and searched desperately to find. Thank God, there it was. Our Father loves to use analogies. In the book of Jeremiah, the prophet says, "The Lord announces the days are coming when I will plant the nation of Israel and Judah again. I will plant it with children and animals. I watched over Israel and Judah to pull them up by the roots, I tore them down (enemy nations captured them) I crushed them... I destroyed them (and their false god) I brought horrible trouble on them... *But now* (since they have repented and turned back to God alone), I, the Lord, will watch over them to build them up and plant them announces the Lord. In those days people will no longer say, '*The fathers* (and mothers) have *eaten sour grapes but the children* (me/you) have a bitter taste in their mouths.' (No longer) Their sin is *not* our sin. Instead everyone will (only) die (spiritually) for their own sin. Conversely, those who (follows in the same sin) will die for their *own* sin (not their parents), the one who *does* do the same sins and who eats the sour grapes (does the sin) will taste how bitter they are!" (Sin is the curser. No sin, no curse.) Fortunately, Galatians 3:13 says that Christ has redeemed us from "the curse of the law."

The Lord continues, "After that time (The Lord's day), I will put *My* laws in their minds, I will write them on their hearts, *I will be their God,* and *they will be My people.* Everyone will know me, from the least important to the most important, *all of them will know Me.*" This beautiful chapter of our Real Father's promises was all I needed. I knew I finally could rest in the arms of the *one* I was created by and loved by Abba, Father. And I know my big brother, Skip, could too.

The Psalms were telling when it came to the writers' gut-wrenching feelings. Wow! I could not say it any better. When he dealt with enemies, he asked God (not himself) to "break the bonds asunder, thou shalt dash them to pieces, thou hast smitten all my enemies upon the cheek bone, and broken their teeth, thou shall destroy those that speak leasing, the Lord will abhor the bloody and deceitful man." I honestly could understand these vindictive emotions. They are exactly what some of us want when we think of all the hurt others needlessly put us through. In my own life, I prayed this and got tremendous relief and release. Father, I need You to take the swords out of my soul, the daggers out of my back, the "darts out of my head," and the arrows out of my heart. God knew the depth of the hurt the psalmist endured and how badly he was hurting; the same way He knew my deep-rooted pain. Sometimes our enemy is *disease or illness,* and these same types of prayers would bring comfort, since I knew that God cared and was right there with me—whatever I was going through.

BOOK OF JAMES

Since the thief only comes to kill and destroy (John 10:10), I had to get cracking and outsmart him with the perfect weapon. When I got so very sick, I realized I needed God more than ever, and I got busy researching healing in the Bible. James had the conditions of the healing gospel, and the very first sentence puzzled me! What?! "Count it all joy when you fall into various trials."

Next, "have faith without doubt." Even the faith of a mustard seed will do the trick. Hmm, again, "I can overcome a mountain." Wow! My illness *was* a huge mountain. Then my mind started to question if I had confessed, prayed, studied, praised God, on and on. Enough to warrant healing? Ooh! The last sentence in James 1:7, "the person who questions or has doubts" gets zippo!

However, some little sensation in my soul said to just take things an hour at a time. I kept saying over and over as I laid in a pool of sweat, dehydrated, violent headaches, nausea, and flushing from head to toe, my heart skipping all over the place, "This too shall pass." All but one doctor gave up on me. Even Dr. B. did after several visits. He had a few vitamin/anti-inflammatory/protein powders but said he could do no more. At least he tried and prayed with me. The doctors were puzzled, but Joel Osteen's words kept running through my mind. Ignore the doctor's report. Focus on God, The Great Physician. I remember I kept asking Jesus, "Was one of those stripes for me? Is an abundant life too late?"

I can't blame doctors; every prescription they gave me made me so violently ill I could only depend on the one and only Great Physician. I went to Him first anyway. Somehow, I got focused on the supernatural healing of God. I read and listened to or watched all the things about how God heals. Of course, I had to be twenty-five feet from any TV to watch it. I allowed God to tell me in His words what he could do for me. I did not allow anything negative to come between God and me. I've always been a person who thinks out of the box, so I made myself think positive thoughts. Years prior, my thought processes were too toxic. Now, my blood stream and entire system became toxic. Down inside, a tiny voice said, "I'm not going to leave you."

I continued in James and came upon James 1:27. "Pure and undefiled religion before God" is this, "to visit or take care of orphans and widows." Hmm, well, I have adopted two children who needed love and a family, but the pureness of it is the kids, because they have taken any selfishness out of me, and I consider it the highest honor that they call me Mom.

The "widow" part is my aunt Dory. Oh, how I miss her. She was my mom's sister who told me and my dad that she wanted me to live with her. Her husband died, and Lance and I did our best to make her happy. We took her on drives, to the grocery, the bank, hairdresser, whenever we were in town. We had dogs, and she was the only relative that would allow us to have our dogs stay overnight with her as long as we wanted. She was generous and gave even her "good stuff" away to family. I would never say I really liked something of hers, because when I did, she would get tissue paper and wrap it to have it ready to go home with us!

The one thing I hated was that she collected dolls that looked like witches. Remember how my mom had the clowns? Well, I hated the ugly and horrible witches even worse than those clowns! What was it about my mother and her sister? Why did they like sinister stuff?

Aunt Dory had trouble sleeping, so I found out that when I called her before she fell asleep, she slept straight through the night. It was the least I could do for her. When she breathed her last and died, she was so loved by all around that thousands of people came to her funeral. The mold was broken when that woman was created. We all loved her!

Next in James 3:5, the Word says to "bridle the tongue." Ouch! Being a horsewoman, I know what a tight bridle and bit can do to the mouth. The tongue starts out as a spark of anger, and then it quickly turns into a forest fire. The Bible says, "It defiles the whole body and sets on fire the whole course of nature…and it is set on fire by hell." Woe! I made a vow to God not to hold onto anger and bitterness with this terrible illness. I also told God I would not start, carry forward, or listen to gossip! I vowed to forgive anyone I could think of who sinned against me or told lies about me.

Back to the book of James. The kids went to the youth group at the church my friend Charla and I were attending. The pastor that I mentioned previously told me of my frightening foreshadowing, then anointed me as did my missionary friend, Charla. One other pastor who attended to the homeless prayed the prayer of the sick over me. "Let the church elders pray over you and anoint you with oil." Then this prayer "will save the sick and the Lord will raise them up." It continued, "Confess your trespasses to one another that you may be healed." Okay, I met all of God's conditions. I held tightly to God's promises and thanked my Good Father for hearing me (James 5:13–16). I had to wait, trust, and have faith to know that Jesus will quench the fiery darts that were trying to kill me…but when?

My missionary friend handed me a very simple yet wonderful birthday card that had Jeremiah 29:11. Since she did that, the exact verse has popped up several other times. I claimed it and praised God for it I every time I saw it. I know it by heart. "I know the plans I have for you, not to harm you but to help you and give you a future and hope." I believe our Heavenly Father cares and will bless His children when we obey His word. I remind myself of it anytime I get discouraged or antsy about the length of my trial. It kept coming up that God Himself is long suffering. Yes, yes, I know, but… I really was having a hard time with this all. I had severe weight loss. The pain was so bad. Even my hair hurt!

Do you know what I honestly believe? Satan only hurts, destroys, and causes trials. Conversely, God "uses" what the enemy "causes" and makes it a test. Satan wants our flesh and soul… Our Father wants our spirit and soul. Just as I always want my children with me, our Father wants His children with Him. Not just here, but in the kingdom to come. We had *just* gotten to the middle of our Bible study. The book of Job explained a lot to me. I *just* didn't want to continue walking in his footsteps.

CHAPTER 20

By his stripes, we shall be healed.

—Isaiah 53:5

A Heart Can't Lie

*M*y dad had an angry heart for many years. Mom had a heart hungry for someone to love her. Father Quinton had a wild heart. Skip had a roaming heart. Myself? I had a gullible heart. This can cause lots of pain and desperation. Desperate people go to desperate measures. I was not going to let the enemy win as he did with Father Quinton and my brother. I was going to overcome my illness with God's Word, whatever it took. My first plan was going to get my Heavenly Father's attention. I do believe God had heard my prayers, but now, I needed His answer. Another book that helped me was *God's Pathway to Healing* by Dr. Reginald Cherry. In those pages, I learned to never get discouraged. God uses all kinds of other means, so His healing is rarely instant. I "just happened" to catch the name of his book while I was channel hopping one night on TBN, and I kept seeing the question, "What boulder had to be removed?" It was a sentence in Dr. Cherry's book.

With all this medical focus now on my heart, I again dove into the Word of God and other medical books about our hearts. Did you know that 250 times our hearts are more elaborated upon in the Bible? I also read scientific books about our meridian circadian rhythms and heart rhythms. Those must work together and stay in harmony with the rest of us. Since I had so much heartache and heartbreak, my heart had literally been weakened.

My heart was also greatly harmed. The things that can knock your heart off balance and even the things that give us normal harmony really fascinated me. It all boiled down to the fact that my heart had been overtaxed, undernourished, broken and, finally, harmed by high-voltage radio frequency and electromagnetic fields. Even my dental fillings were compounding my heart and health issues by drawing the current to my metal fillings and then to the organs these teeth lead to. Dr. B. said that our metal fillings touching one another can set off an electric charge.

With my heart, or any heart, things that happen in your life greatly affect this fascinating organ. God is known as the heart knower; He *only* can read hearts. Throughout the scripture, it is stated multiple times, that man knows the mind, but "God knows the heart." I love how our Heavenly Father is so powerful, but also loving at the same time. El Shaddai is the nurturing one. I found out how tender and gentle our Good Father can be during this scary time of my life. I still cried, but doctors warned not to-I was already dehydrated. This was frightening…our bodies are 80 percent water. Was I wasting away?

Divine Doses

Jonathan contracted the terrible swine flu while I was in the throes of my illness, and as he was ill too, he had moved to the lower level of our home and had a very nice "boy cave" going on downstairs. Lance could not assist me on waiting hand and foot on such a severely sick young man. So I had to be by Jonathan's bedside myself to help him get better.

In my weakened state, the stairs proved to be a challenge. I could barely catch my breath, and I was so weak my legs always shook, but Jonathan was sick, and he needed his mother...so I geared up, rolled up my sleeves, and got down to mom business.

One night, I had given Jonathan his prescription for his swine flu, "Tamiflu." Between his escalated fever and the Tamiflu, his reaction was unreal! He was talking about seeing frightening and satanic things one minute to seeing angels flying around with white wings and some without any wings. Jonathan spent the whole night talking in his sleep. His heartbeat had sped up so fast. It was truly awful to witness! I lay down next to him and kept cold compresses on him most of the night. I called the doctor, and the news was even worse the next day from the pediatrician. She said that since he had had such a bad reaction, I was going to have to get Jonathan through with only Tylenol and ibuprofen. Seriously? He had the swine flu, and I was only using the stuff for a headache?! Lord, help me! She'd informed us that all other flu medicine was basically the same thing as Tamiflu, so do not to use that again. Sheepishly, I asked her how long it takes to get someone over the swine flu without real flu medicine. She told me that it could be as long as thirty days.

Lance was not home, Jonathan was ill during most of Christmas break, and I was at the sickest I've ever been in my entire life. I definitely had my work cut out for me. I asked my daughter, Gloria, to help me keep up with the dishes and some of the light housework. So we were off. She and I geared up for the long haul. Mind you, I could not take any medication of any kind with my illness, I had just been tested for seventy-five different allergens because of my radiation and mercury poisoning, and I reacted to all but five of them! So what, in God's name, was I supposed to do? There was no way I could nurse Johnathan back to health every hour and not end up catching the flu. As my doctor had not given me much hope to begin with, I decided Jonathan was more important than my life, and I had to do all that I could to help him regardless. We moms must do what we have to do to ensure the health and safety of our children. With a new supply of items needed, again I crawled down to his lower level to help him.

So with a wet cold compress on the hour, every hour, and walking with him to and from the bathroom, we trudged on together. I took his temperature every four hours, and I swapped in and out the Tylenol and Ibuprofen as I was directed. On the fourth day, he had begun to have a reaction to the Ibuprofen! The Ibuprofen, by the way, caused him to have a measles-looking skin rash all over his belly! It was a miracle to both of us we got through. Now I knew it was up to God, Tylenol, and me. With all the little guy had to go through, he was very brave and cooperated wonderfully. Together, we stayed the course, and by the end of nineteen days, Jonathan was over the swine flu!

A giant relief was felt for getting us over that. I was beyond exhausted, and I had literally collapsed in bed. Every morning, afternoon, and night, I had made it a point to pray for my little family and especially for my son, Jonathan. "Oh, Father, Lance is gone, I am home alone with two children, and I'm afraid of my own lack of strength and stamina to get my son through this. Will you please fill in the gaps and not let me get the flu so I can try to take care of my children?" And by the grace of God, even though I was in the proximity of the virus bacteria every hour for nineteen days, I didn't get sick! Truly amazing! Even my husband, Lance, the scoffer he was sometimes, could not fathom that I did not get the swine flu!

UNSYMPATHETIC SYMPTOMS—A SUMMARY

The life-threatening storm was casting down bolts of lightning. In the same realm, a few weeks later, *the enemy* was not finished with me. Even though I escaped the bad flu, other symptoms and new things to avoid surfaced. I had dropped so much weight between diarrhea and dehydration that I was less than one hundred pounds. I also was losing my hair...and possibly my... Never mind, Lord.

It was three years, and Lance and I started seeing that we felt worse when we were close to this *radiating* modern-day technology. We also discovered we lived less than eight hundred feet from four cell phone towers which loomed on the high hill over our street. We had two when we moved there, but they added two more. My symptoms were *unbearable* when I was in the kitchen, living room, and dining room. Then a Doppler radar tower was added. Wait until you hear the diagnosis!

During the whole time, I dragged myself to doctors. Test after test was performed. I was CAT-scanned, x-rayed, MRI-ed, and I endured continual blood tests. I was dying, but I didn't know what was causing it. Dr. B. said that with the radiation and mercury in my system, again, I was a walking antenna! What? Who would really get this? Enduring more physical examinations, probably ten in all, I held on.

Many educated doctors came up with *nothing*. Finally, I went to two holistic doctors. One guessed a stress and hormone interruption of my entire system. I had gone through many traumatizing and excruciatingly painful events to be sure. But this was not to be the diagnosis I was to accept. It was a small part of it since my whole system *was* involved in breaking down, and it all broke all at the same time. I was in very bad condition. And for a few years, things would be touch and go, *if I made it at all.*

I presented all my x-rays and other doctor's reports to Dr. B. He was very kind and a naturalist-type doctor. After examining me and reading all my symptoms and medical reports, he said something that startled me. He said, "Thank goodness you came to my office this week, because you may not have made it to next week." Yikes! Deep down, I knew he was right; I was looking at the angel of death right in the eye and hoping against all hope it wasn't looking back at me. Again, in his office, I felt my life was surreal. Could this really be happening? Did all that equipment, cell towers, and radio stations cause Lance and me to be this bad? We were only there six months!

Dr. B. was the first and only doctor that was experienced with this out-of-the-blue, strange, debilitating illness. I had lost thirty-six pounds in the past four months, and it looked like I had aged ten years within two years. My system collapsed, inflammation was all through me, my skin was jaundiced and peeled. Dr. B.'s diagnosis was "overload of radiation *and* metal poisoning." I was told that I also have metal poisoning in my blood. I had eroded fillings that had bled into my whole bloodstream.

The diagnosis was made, and this time, I knew it was it. This health issue had grown into a full-blown crisis. No doctor would come up with anything to help me. Insurance would only pay for certain hospitals at this time, so I was all alone in this nauseating nightmare. My poor husband had to take over the role as mom, caregiver, chauffer, and cook and do the laundry for three years straight. Some have called it a train wreck crisis. I agree! Dr. B. did not trust the previous blood tests, so he ordered all of his own. Since he was more familiar with what to do with radiation, metal, and mercury-poisoned victims, he could give some relief with his prescription. Dr. B. and his nurses asked if it was okay to pray with me right there in the examining room? With tears, I nodded and bowed my head.

SYMBOLICALLY SYNCHRONIZED

I started reading everything I could *now* on electric frequency, magnetic, and vibrational fields. I was learning all about our amazing bodies and the way we were wired up (no pun intended).

I desperately tried to see something positive about this health crisis situation, so what I came up with was… I took it *spiritually and symbolically* and declared it would be my time to spend high quality time in prayer and a "frequent connection" to our heaven's high tower directly to me. I started with constant worship and praise music, intense Bible study, and I watched almost every Christian pastor on TV for months. I probably said the salvation prayer hundreds of times during that first year with each program. I really poured it on! I stirred up the fire within like I've never done before. Since

I already felt like a burning log in a bonfire, it was not a big step to accomplish. The embers were red hot.

About twenty years ago, I read my first self-help book. The title was *The Source of My Strength* by Dr. Charles Stanley. He is a pastor and a gentleman that really understands about abuse, forgiveness, and our Father's love. I'm working on another of his books, *When the Enemy Strikes,* now. I agree with Dr. Stanley that praying is essential, and he continues with, "To pray means to open a connection with God, just as if we were calling Him on the telephone...and then never breaking that connection or never hanging up. It means to have the line always open to speak to God or hear from God." Symbolically, what I was going through was my "disconnection from the world" as I knew it. I reconnected with my real Father and the whole Godhead. Jesus and His earthly ministry was what I studied. I assimilated as much of the miracles as I could. I was so scared! Is this an omen? My body constantly pouring out sweat? My panic buttons were pressed and held down. I was so worried. Could the body dehydrating be symbolic of my soul drying up? With my Bible in hand, I got on heaven's wavelength and was *determined* to overcome the devil's damage to me and Lance.

In *When the Enemy Strikes*, Dr. Stanley reports, "Behind every evil person and every evil act lurks the *real enemy* of our lives. He lives in the spirit realm and he is relentless in his pursuit of us." He frighteningly stated, "He (the enemy) is 100 percent evil," and he has a plan to destroy our lives. The EMF and RMF illness scrambled my flesh body system. My life frequency was in need of serious repair. I was holding together by but one frayed wire. I knew that my spiritual part was in desperate need of the living water.

My pastor says there will be victory because he read the end of the book. "This too shall pass," and though it seems like a never-ending war, Paula White says what I believe regarding my weight loss and overall health demise, "Even the most catastrophic loss is only for a season." Further, she concludes, "Compared to a lifetime and into eternity, it is a blip on a radar screen." I had to let it go, all of my anger and frustration. I let "my anger pass through me like a current of electricity." (T.D. Jakes) I was reading in some of my self-help books all the references to power, frequencies, radar and electric impulses that *matched* my physical energy crisis-It was amazing; the spiritual *connection* with the physical in a very real way.

FATHER I NEED YOU

Oh, Father, here I am again, in a medical mess this time. I'm so thirsty all the time. Have You got any mercy left for me? Any water from the pool of Bethesda? I really could use Your healing touch. Just one will do.

After many years of shuffling around priorities, keeping the Holy Trinity before all else, I started claiming God's promises. As Derek Prince so wisely explains, "When you have been through fifteen crises already and you remain unsteady and unmoved in the sixteenth, the believer is a manifestation of faith." So my life story testifies that God keeps His promises and His Word in every trial, storm, and turmoil. His mercy is so important at times when our health is laid on the line. I read His promises and held them in my heart. I'm sure there's something I'm missing. What is it? I honestly believe God's plans involve deep searching and connecting all the dots...but I'm so flustered. Lord do not leave me now. I need you more than ever.

Another promise that I recently claimed as a forgiving and believing daughter is, "So you shall *serve* the Lord, Your God, and He will bless your bread and water, and *He will take away sickness in the midst of you.*" Boy! I really needed that one. When fifty foods were being rejected by my body, this is where I have to say I have a really good idea of what the "wilderness" experience was like. However, when my doctor said, "Katia, your days seem to be numbered," I quickly claimed the rest of Exodus 24:26, God is speaking, "I will fulfill the number of your days." Is this for me, God? I need a positive response...badly.

It wasn't the pain of the symptoms so much as it was the *loss of my everyday freedoms* that I honestly took for granted. In my case, the places I automatically would jump in my car and go to accomplish errands were immediately curtailed. One day, I just could no longer get behind the wheel and safely drive. I could not attend church, take the teens to youth group, peruse garage sales, bookstores—it was so surreal I had to pinch myself to check my reality. I thought about the *Twilight Zone* marathons on holidays.

Was I stuck in a time warp in an unknown place? Me? I cannot drive?! I have driven across country several times. I've been to Europe, all the coasts and beaches, the mountains, canyons, and Redwood Forest. What was this?! *I am a female Job.* I don't think I'm going to make it through all of this! *Really...no! God, no! I didn't care* if I dried up from dehydration, like a prune. I sobbed. My kids and parents still needed me...didn't they, Lord? More sobbing.

After a few months of seeing that my situation was real, as my spouse of thirty years was going through similar obstacles and limitations, I started getting focused. What can I still do, and how do I survive this blow to my lifestyle? I still cried and prayed earnestly. Similarly, T.D. Jakes relayed how he felt after praying his mom would live and be healed. "After your cry, beg, become a wreck, bargain, and exhaust yourself with the abrupt change, you finally settle down." The inner hysteria must stop. Like him, I saw it too. "You realize and say it will take as long as it is going to take." It was so much easier to *say* this rather than latch onto it. Like Job, asked after twenty chapters of asking *why*, purging myself of every even inkling of a sin, and bearing down on the harsh reality that my ravaged system was in dire straits, I decided that, somehow, my Deliverer would take me through—come what may. The Psalms became my constant supplication, specifically Psalm 143:7 says it all. "Answer me speedily, God...lest I become like those who go down to the pit (grave)."

If I had even a 25 percent chance to have enough energy to survive this horrible assault, God had to do it all. I could hear Carrie Underwood's song, "Jesus Take the Wheel," played over and over in my mind. Since I've always loved the symbolism in the Bible, I started seeing harmony in what I was going through with my spiritual eyes. Don't ask me *how*...it *just* happened.

Pleasing God had become my very number one priority, and I really mean this. *I owe Him my life* and He has it in His loving hands. There, I am safe, and I know it. Inasmuch that this is true for me, there is a female pastor and gifted author whom I am in agreement with when it comes to everyday walking with Christ.

Rather than putting in my own words, may I pass on her words to you directly? They are clear and concise and very helpful. Paula White asks herself these things each day before bed. Is "my personal integrity intact?" Was I "true to my personal convictions?" Have I "done what God wanted done today?" Was I "authentic while pleasing God?" And am I "okay with everything I decided for this day?"

Paula White wrote several other books that were right where I was several times in my Christian journey. The last of my worldliness was ended. Like Paula, I believe that our tormenting might more come from a contrast between what we read in the Bible and what we end up really following through doing. We must become obedient and *active doers* of what it says and find "hearts that beat the same" in our spiritual growth.

Kind of like the verse whereby the seeds are planted in us at first but then the worldly pressures pull us in different directions. Many times, a fierce storm washes the seeds down the gutter. I highly recommend *You're All That* for any woman that has low self-esteem or lives with others who put her down or try to control her. It also goes through a process where we find our genuine selves.

Paula also is good friends with those two male PhD psychologists from Southern California, John Townsend and Henry Cloud. I have several of their books on boundaries and relationships. May I highly recommend all three of these authors whose many books occupy my shelves in my own home.

MAN CAN ONLY DO SO MUCH

Several of the Psalms let us know that man can disappoint and fall short more times than not. The Bible story that hit to the heart of my seemingly hopeless crisis is in Mark 5:25–28. In this fantastic account, Jesus exudes power without saying a word or lifting a finger!

Everybody knows this story with the woman who has an issue of blood. Nonetheless, this time, I caught the background of her sad tragedy. She not only had the blood that leaked out of her, but "she suffered" from many physicians; the woman exhausted all her money on those so-called doctors who could not help her and only used up her funds.

This victim of medical limitedness *heard* about Jesus and told others around her that she would finally be cured. "If only I may touch the hem of His garment." Can you imagine the healing power behind that cloth? Well, I did more than think on it... I went for it! I took my medical case to the throne of the Creator...and fell at His feet. It was up to Him to take on "the ruler of darkness" where the doctors and I were no match! (Ephesians 6:11–12).

Sometimes, God uses a man, such as a doctor, or suggests just talking with the right people, going to a website, or reading the right book. These are ways God helps pave our *path to healing*. According to Dr. Cherry, *scripture study is a must*. I wholeheartedly agree. When and since I went deep into The Word of God, my soul was healing, but the fire breathing dragon was *hot* on my trail. There was no let-up of the symptoms for four years.

THE ENEMY WITHIN...HIS MO (JOHN 10:10)

Wow! Talk about deception, subterfuge, and the insidious invisible attacks! The enemy, Satan, is always going to cause us trouble until we are all changed in a twinkling of an eye. Further, my pastor said something that made me sigh, Oh no, not again! Dr. Murray relayed to all of his church audience that the more you strive for spiritual connection, the more vicious Satan's attacks become. Oh terrific! The fire-breathing dragon was torturing my flesh with extreme sensations of heat all over.

So here I was, in another battle—a war against Satan for my flesh. The problem was my flesh wanted to just quietly go to sleep and be out of the symptoms, pain, and isolation (even from my loved ones packing cell phones all the time). My children did not know what was happening to their mom and dad. They were frightened! My old friends and some neighbors did not understand. Lance and I were whispered about many times. As I said, no one understood. I felt the darkness of depression pulling me down just like it did the family in *Poltergeist*.

Thank goodness, within four years, Lance started to improve. His symptoms were not as bad; he was back and forth around Christmas taking care of my mother and father. Keeping two teenagers away from their electronics was next to impossible! I don't blame them; all their friends were letting them know how strange it all was. Yeah, right, tell me something I don't know, but I had no choice if I did not want to experience ungodly symptoms again. It seemed like I cried for three years! How could this happen? As sick as I was, that old government accusation popped up. To make things worse, the enemy would not let go, and my marriage was shaken. He hit from all sides. It felt like I was in the atmosphere of hell!

In Charles Spurgeon's book, *Power over Satan*, he states that those of us who live in Christ "*hate the serpant with a perfect hatred.*" I do, and I know the devil knows it. During my time warring with him over this sickness, I felt his evil presence many times with his *fiery* darts of hatred. What kept me going was realizing and reminding myself over and over that the reason Jesus came to this earth was to heal, forgive, and *destroy the works of the devil* and overcome death. The oppressive ancient serpent had one fang sunk in my flesh, but I couldn't let him take my soul! "For the enemy has pursued and persecuted my soul, he has crushed my life to the ground. He has made me to dwell in dark places" (Psalm 143:3). Since Lance was getting well, the two kids and he went everywhere together while I cried alone at home.

Thus, if I ever needed Jesus, it was now. I don't know if it was a comfort or not when Charles Spurgeon stated, "The serpent's seed hates Christ in me!" and, "This truth exalts the sufferings of persecution to a position far above common affliction." Well, this radiation phenomenon is certainly not common. Nevertheless, the enemy always *loses* when Jesus takes over! He came to tear down Satan's theater of operation for us.

FEARLESS

For far too many years, I had internalized fear. Habitually, I was terrorized; even when I forgave my abusers, the residue of fear lingered. May I share with you what I've learned over my lifetime about fear? It is a choice. Again, do I choose to believe that God is with me in every situation? Can you get mightier than our Heavenly Creator? I think not. In the Bible, we are told to *"fear not"* over three hundred times!

Christos, the Anointed One; He alone is sinless even in His human role.

As the Lamb of God, He is blemish free, the only perfect Sacrifice whose blood is pure.

Greater love has no man than that He lay down His life for His friends.

We are the friends and adopted family of our Father.

The Perfect Lover washes away even the worst of sins by His blood.

The Perfect Lover is the Great Physician. "By His stripes, we are healed"

The Perfect Lover is the Wonderful Counselor who heals our minds. The pointed thorns were dug into His head.

The Perfect Lover, our acceptable Sacrifice, was pierced for our transgressions. We walk spot free and reconciled to God Almighty.

The True Body of Christ (His Church), claims all these and hundreds more to be in health and secure in our flesh bodies. With these gifts, we *can* say Lord cast out all my fears and He will. Our faith in Him activates what we need. As God's own, we can have full assurance that there is no fear of life/no fear of death. *Perfect!*

CHAPTER 21

Nevertheless not my will, but thy will be done.
—Luke 22:42

LORD, SHE HAS AN EVIL SPIRIT

*M*y mother Jezebella's gossip always led to turmoil. Her words, as false as they were, undermined my marriage… again.

This felt like my life and death battle of my entire existence! There is nothing more frightening than losing to the adversary. The Bible story goes that a mother had one daughter. Somehow, the daughter had become possessed by the devil. The mother was totally distraught but wanted to help. She was prepared to do whatever was necessary to get the help for her daughter, so she approached Jesus and his disciples. The mother was a Phoenician woman, and they were looked down upon by others for their pagan beliefs. She was desperate and had walked twenty-five miles also to speak to Jesus. She pleaded with him, saying her daughter was "vexed." However, Jesus was told by God to not help or save anyone from a pagan descent, *so* Jesus's disciples wanted to leave, and Jesus stayed silent. The mother begged again and dropped to her knees to worship.

Jesus reminded her, "It is not right to take the children's bread and cast it to the dogs."

The mother humbly and beautifully replied, "Yes, I know what Jesus said is true 'but even dogs eat crumbs that fall from their *master's* table."

Then Jesus admits to those around Him and says, "O woman, great is your faith, be it done unto you as you have asked." Her daughter was healed and made whole from that very moment. When I read this rescuing mission account, I pleaded with God to remove anything evil in my path—all the faith I could muster went up in that plea and thanked Him. At that, Jesus marvels at this Phoenician woman's faith and lovingly heals her daughter by driving out the demons. As this Phoenician mother knew, just the "crumbs" would do the miracle she needed. I asked Jesus for crumbs of His healing for me to get well so I could take care of my children and parents.

Someone once said that philosophy is like trying to find a black cat in a pitch dark room.

A relative of mine loves and respects many philosophers and offered me an ancient philosophy book to "see things clearly." I asked if the author was a Christian, and he said, "No." He still pushed more for the book, saying, "The writer was well respected for his thinking." My answer was simple and direct; I told him that when the writer performs miracles and is raised from death, then I'll read it.

The good thing is that I believe the stories of healing in the New Testament are true. But I had the hardest time thinking these miracles would happen to me. It took me many years to recognize my worth. I had to throw out all the lies from my past. So just a crumb or being able to touch the hem of God's Son's robe could heal all aliments, I was strangely filled with hope. I needed all the help I could get. I was desperate for healing. I turned to the *one* who held our abundant life in the palms of his blood-stained hands. I was determined to hold on tight with breathless loyalty.

BREATH OF LIFE

Frail, sickly, weak, and on fire, I dragged my eighty-eight-pound body into the bathroom, pulled off my clothes, and turned on the shower. I crawled under the gentle cool spray and immediately got down on my knees. Crying my heart out, I collapsed to the shower floor. With the cold water cascading all over me now, I looked up and whispered, "Lord, may I baptize myself here and now again? If you want me now, take me now, I'm yours." Then I asked my Father to "cleanse me of any sin, forgive me for hurting others and bless my spouse and my children's lives," so with the water still pouring over me, I stopped crying and got ready for whatever He wanted. I knew I was clean. I dried off, put my flannel PJs on and, with my hair wrapped in a towel, crawled under the covers. I wasn't scared at all. I felt relief and resolve as I prayed softly, "Father, stay with me." I prepared for my Father to take me with Him.

I remember clasping my hands around my pillow, squeezing tight, and whispering again. "Oh, my Father, my very breath of life, thank you for never giving up on me. If you want me, I'm yours. I love you so much, you've always been there for me, so right here and now, not my will but Yours be done. If I awake tomorrow, I'll know." I closed my eyes, clung tightly to my pillow, and must have drifted off, whispering, "Oh, my Father, into Your hands I give my spirit." Suddenly, yet calmly, in the wee hours, something woke me. I remember I looked up at the ceiling and all around me and tried to take a breath. I always had a night light in both ends of the bedroom, so I could see pretty clearly. I was not in a dream state at all. Again, I tried to catch my breath, and as always lately, it was labored. Almost like in slow motion, I felt my mouth open up, and I could not breathe out to exhale. I did not panic though, because strangely, I was feeling fresh air flowing in my mouth, throat, and lungs. It was almost like an oxygen mask was placed over my nose and mouth. The rest of me couldn't move. I was not inhaling or exhaling, but something way beyond me was doing it for me! The fresh flow blew for just a few seconds, I got a little light-headed, but the amazing thing was, after four and a half years of not getting a deep breath, I was breathing perfectly normal! I felt so relaxed and safe for those seconds and time stood still. I felt all over warmth and very loved. Ezekiel 37 came to my mind instantly. "Come from the four winds, Oh breath, and breathe on the flame that she comes to life." Wow! My Father does love me for real.

I was still very tired, but I stood up and, with a burst of energy, started crying out, "Thank you, Father!" Then I put on my praise music and, looking up with my hands spread over my head, danced on my bed. I thanked and worshipped my God. Ten minutes or so later, I laid back down and, as if lightly sedated, drifted off to sleep so peacefully and joy filled—thankful! After that mercy-filled, loving, incredible encounter, I've never been the same. A new feeling swept over me. I told my Father that I was His to do with what He wanted. What I deeply desired was what He said He wanted too—to bring the hearts of His children back to the Father. It felt so fantastic to finally know what He wanted and what I wanted were in agreement! Alleluia! I wanted to point others toward God.

The famous Bible verse in 1 Corinthians 10:13 was going to be my promise fulfilled. His mercy endures forever, Praise the Lord! Our Father was leading me out of my trials! Job declares God is our breath of life (Job 35:5).

A little while after having my strange yet wonderful encounter with heavenly air, I happened to run across something in my reading. In fact, even the "why" I dug into an old plastic book filled tote was puzzling. Nonetheless, the precious book at almost the bottom of the container was *The Ultimate Prescription* by Dr. James L. Marcum, MD. Still following my instincts to search, what I discovered as soon as I opened it almost halfway through blew me away! I opened up to chapter 7, "From Darkness to Light," and soaked in the profound part about transformation. The next page, chapter 8. Oh my God! There it was: "Breathing Lessons!" My eyes widened and my brows went up. "Oh my goodness!" If I ever wondered what really happened that fantastic and awe-striking night, it was spot on under "Life and Breath," chapter 8. Genesis 2:7 told me what our Father did with and for me that night. This is where God created Adam and "breathed life into the man's nostrils and the man became a living person." *Wow!* Then, as a medical doctor and a professional, Dr. Marcum states, "The effect of oxygen in us is profound. Our tissues need oxygen for survival." That night, the air I was allowed to breathe in was not only fresh, crisp, and pure, but it was life giving! "You have delivered me from the depths, from the realm of death." Praise the Father, Son, and Holy Spirit. Thank you, Lord, for Your breath of life (Psalm 86:12-13).

Just like the miracle performed for the Phoenician woman's daughter, one long loving puff from our Father whirled and brought me back from my near-death experience. I could breathe normally! I had an open sense of calm.

Paula White described it as a "heaven-breathed moment." Since that time, I have continued religiously to study my Bible daily, listen to praise music, and pray continuously with thanksgiving and love back to the Godhead. I have learned that I despise all evil, sin, and that God's enemies are my enemies. Yes, Satan does attack us physically as well as spiritually. I plead the blood of Jesus over my family and friends each week, even over my home and pets.

Do you know something I've noticed? The marvelous night the Holy Spirit breathed His life back into me, I had a touch from the Master! I believe it happened for all of us to discover something remarkable about God's closeness to His hurting and sick children. Perhaps, since it was the notion of "breath," *pneuma* (air) was flowing into me; this represented how we as Christians should handle situations daily. In other words, we take in (breathing) God's promise of life, and we breathe out (exhale) all the world's lies. We not only renew our minds, but we filter in good and filter out bad.

I found a very old prayer I wrote in my daily journal.

> Father, you are my vindicator. Help me Lord, to breathe in Your peace and healing power. Make me to breathe out all the hurtful words and painful symptoms." Then I added, "Father, just keep me breathing…and keep a tight hold on me please.

My dear friend Dinah told me something her adorable two-year-old granddaughter said. This little doll has an Italian father, and she is just precious. When Dinah sees her, of course she grabs little Casey up. However, instead of Casey saying, "Hold me," she turns it around and asks, "Hold you?" *Wow*, from the lips of a child! So profound. Isn't that what we all want to do with Jesus—hold onto Him?

I know I needed to cling tight to Him. No one else has the answers. His pure and perfect Spirit came to an almost dead female one night after she washed herself of the world. I know my God lives. I am living proof! He walked on this very earth... We will be with Him but, this time, as the benevolent King. I believed that was why I was saved, but now, I was one with my Heavenly Father. I surrendered all... and I did not hesitate to let go. It was marvelous! The Word "breath" was popping up everywhere—in the Bible, in my books, with TV pastors, and more. Our Father transmits to His Son, Jesus transmits to the Holy Spirit, and the Holy Spirit breathes life into us per Joyce Myer.

The final verification that the breath that came into me was divine; these Scriptures declared it. I believe Joel Osteen expanded upon this. I was meant to hear it that night on his program. In Ezekiel 37:4–6, the Lord is speaking dead dry bones to "come to life again."

He spoke in Ezekiel 37:5, "Thus says the Lord to these bones: Surely I *will* cause *breath* to enter into you, and you shall live." Further, regarding the flesh and the spirit, our Father continued with Ezekiel 37:6. "I will put sinews (tendons) in you and bring flesh upon you, cover you with skin and put Breath in you; and you shall live. Then you shall know that I am the Lord." From that divine epiphany, I have implored daily...and trusted.

Just recently, Dinah had to have a difficult surgery. Of all things, it involved sports medicine and her leg muscles and tendons. This verse was perfect for calling on our Heavenly Physician to help and heal her. He cares about every cell and atom in us. After all, He created them and loves to make us all better when we're suffering and infirmed. Satan wants to destroy us; God wants to heal us (John 10:10). This wisdom is paramount…to me…to us all.

FRIENDLY FIRE—*EMBRACING IT*

Jesus came to this earth to deliver us from evil and die for our sins; He came to destroy death and our fatal diseases. I believed this, and I started believing it for me. I claimed it as my own promise and reminded God of this many times as I prayed. His gentle touch was warm, sweet yet energizing!

Someone, I think my minister, once said that our Heavenly Father loves to have His own words prayed back to Him. I looked up all the Bible verses where the word "fire" had been. I was surprised that there were almost as many positive correlations as there were negative i.e. hellfire. On the good side, we are supposed to be "on fire for God" because of having the Holy Spirit in us. In Exodus 22, the fire is kindled to make restitution. Revelation 4, the lamps on fire; Deuteronomy, a burnt sacrifice to God in the fire. Nonetheless, the famous "chariots of fire" were our Father's soldiers coming to Elijah to protect him and Elisha straight from the heavens. In Numbers, a daytime cloud and a night-time pillar of fire guarded and guided the Israelites through the wilderness heading to the Promised Land.

Further, in reading one of my self-help books, *Knowing God Intimately* by Joyce Meyer, I came across something she states. God is a consuming fire (Hebrews 12:28); as such, he wants to remove anything in our lives that does not bring Him glory. Meanwhile, He puts us through the refiner's fire. "Those of us who go through the fire instead of running from it are the ones who will bring glory to God" (Malachi 3:2). While pondering this, I thought of John the Baptist. He baptized many in the Jordan River (where Jesus was later known to be the baptizer also.) John said, "I baptized with water unto repentance," but he continued, "A mightier *one* is coming who will baptize with water and fire." I believe I was being baptized with fire in going through my life daily. I am still going through the fire. I would be honored if this book brought Him some glory. Anything good that can come out of this, like Joyce says, has to be God.

As Peter 1:6–22 states, we can be tested through fire to produce faith and be purified coming out with a pure heart. I believe wholeheartedly that I've been tested in "the furnace of affliction." When I get in a dither of what I have gone through, I stop, and my thoughts go back to the Bible, where our Heavenly Father tried His own Son in the furnace of affliction. Instantly, I'd bow my head and obediently utter, "Okay, Father, your grace is sufficient."

Before my fiery trial, I thought I loved God. I know I depended on him all throughout my tumultuous years. Nonetheless, during my bedridden time in the stillness when I was at my weakest, I felt His strength flowing through me which kept me hanging on.

However, all in all, trying to glean something positive out of being flat on my back for almost one year and very sick for three more years now, what I didn't do for God kept coming up. While I laid there rehearsing the "why me?" mentality, my spiritual self was becoming more apparent to me. I made a promise late one afternoon, while standing up long enough to change my sweat-drenched clothes…that if my Father, in His role as the Great Physician, made me well, I would do so much more for others in His name and for His glory. I asked Him to show me what I need to do through reading His Word.

I told God, "I have nothing left to give You but me. If You can use my life in some way, will You do it?" *This was a defining moment, and I started to write my story.*

Contained in two of my very favorite books by pastors are some profound scriptural treasures. In my "on fire" condition, I just had to find clues in the Bible whereby I could make some sense of it all. Charles Spurgeon, in his book, *Power over Satan*, believes that the Lord, in His mercy, "drops the divine life into our souls and this becomes a 'spark of celestial fire.'" I love all of Tozer's books. He goes deep into the holiness, omnificence, and perfection of our Heavenly Father. One fantastic work in two volumes is *The Attributes of God*. In Exodus, God Appears to Moses inside of a burning bush and explains that the bush was on fire, but it did not burn up! This hit close to home.

Yes, I cannot help but use electricity, power source fields. They fit so well with my science-fiction-like transition. Thanks to my antenna-like focus on the Holy Spirit throughout my life, it sometimes led me to something very significant. Many times, it parallels with where I am currently in my life. I honestly felt like I was ignited when I read all this stuff on the *good* side of fire. My spiritual sense (I tease and refer to it as a seventh sense) became very alert to all the references to fire, burning, sacrifices, burnt offerings, and even into the eternal realm. Just as the two hundred fifty Levi priests had fiery censors to worship the Almighty in the scripture with Moses.

Both Spurgeon and Tozer pull out all the inferno words. Fire is all through in the books of Isaiah and Ezekiel. Sometimes it represents God's glory, the sun, the moon, etc. Again, in the book of Exodus, with Moses and the Israelites,

God stays with His people (watching over them) as "a pillar of fire by night." All of them journeying to the Promised Land—it is God's "incandescent brightness in the fire." To me, this appears to be a foreshadowing of the New Testament Holy Spirit.

Moses could not even look upon the GREAT I AM with his eyes. The brightness was so dazzling that he had to shade his face, which was so tanned that Moses wore a veil so as not to frighten the multitude down below. In Isaiah, the Seraphim around the heavenly throne are called "fiery burners," and in Genesis, when Adam and Eve are cast out of paradise, a fiery sword blocks and protects the entrance from all directions.

Moving forward to the New Testament, Paul, who was formerly Saul, was struck down by a light from heaven. He was struck blind. He was on his way to gather up Christians (like a bounty hunter) so they could be executed. Jesus Christ himself spoke out in the blinding light and scared him straight onto the right path. When the scales fell from his eyes, perhaps it was because he was burned by the fire of Jesus.

After Paul became seasoned and mature in Christ, he mentored young Timothy and, in one of his encouraging lectures, stated he was to "fan into the flames the gifts God gave" him (2 Timothy 1:6). This, to me, is saying, "Keep your light bright in the dark world, Timothy."

In other words, Paul wanted his young protégé to keep stirring himself up. We need to keep our faith fired up, and the healing power of the Holy Spirit will manifest itself. "God's fire purges all the junk and evil out of us. The darkness is chased out by His intense glow and all that remains is pure," per Joyce Meyer.

Then in the form of tongues of fire, the Holy Spirit glowed on the tops of the Apostles' heads on Pentecost. After, they were to go out into the world and teach all nations.

At the transfiguration, Jesus was so brilliantly radiant that the disciples scrambled to build an altar. The end times, could come sooner than most think. The fire and burning will only be of the wicked and evil rudiments. The world will not burn up and blow away. After the Antichrist's short reign, Jesus will come and do what He does better than any; He will clean up the whole mess *in the twinkling of an eye*. In new spiritual bodies, some will be ministers of fire forever (Psalm 104). Those who stay illuminated and ignited will prevail and serve into eternity.

The Book of Ezekiel declares that we will be awestruck from the Shekanah glory *radiating* from the Godhead's throne. Maybe it wasn't an accident that I have been set on fire. Now, I love that our Father is a *firestarter*. He is so bright that we will not even need a sun or moon; the whole new city will be glowing with His immense glow! It is described here as a "celestial fire" surrounding us. The creatures protecting the throne are described as holding "fiery swords."

Charles Spurgeon aptly describes fire and iron. He says you can keep iron in a fire, and it can learn to live with the fire by absorbing it and begin to "glow in the incandescent brightness of the fire." Moreover, in the Bible, the young Hebrew children, under the pagan king, were thrown into the furnace that was raised ten times hotter than its usual heat.

Remember how the *three* of them went into the flames, but when the king peeped in, he saw *four* men standing, and one of those was "the Son of God?" The three came out not even singed. I know that had to shine among the scoffers! Maybe we will be fire retardant in the heavenly city. I just want to be on the right side of the flames. Satan's fiery tongues could not penetrate when Jesus was with the teens in the furnace.

TRUST

With my next illuminating experience, as I constantly looked for God in every step, not only did my spirit become electrified (no pun intended); moreover, my flesh body started becoming rejuvenated. Again, Dr. Cherry's book kept running through my cleared mind. Sometimes, God has a *pathway* to healing. Either way, instantaneous or a process, I knew God Himself was the first and last part of my becoming well again. Period.

An article by Father Roher that I read in my favorite magazine, *Homecoming*, contained a good story by Gloria Gaither, who is a fantastic songwriter and super talented woman. She interviewed a monk who has written a couple of books. One of these books was on transformation and what it means to him. Richard Rohr is this Catholic Franciscan Monk, and in his book, *The Trinity and the Transformation*, he intelligently states, "A deeper conception of the Father, Son, and Holy Spirit will transform our relationship with God, touches me and resurrects my desire to live." As Father Richard says, "I *needed* our relational God." What was so marvelous was when I knew God wanted me to live, my spirit rose up again to help my flesh. I can identify with Richard's statement regarding transformation. He states, "Transformation implies an actual change of sub consciousness and, therefore, a new set of *eyes* by which you look out at the world." I had this! I now cared more about my fellow man than I had ever dreamed possible. I understood how some could go to third-world countries to help the poor, sick, and starving. I wanted family and friends to find Jesus. I even started to pray for my former enemies, not merely forgive them.

Like the flash cards of yesteryear, that Old Testament scripture in Jeremiah kept appearing and reappearing in front of me—in books, on a birthday card, plus two ministers fore-telling it to me as they prayed over me! It was mine, it was My Father's Word, and down deep in my soul, He wanted me to trust Him for it. For once, I did not ask all kinds of questions like, "Lord, did You send the Word for me?" My *spiritual neurosis* was fading, and this time, I repeated the verse from my kid's Bible. "I know the plans I have for you, announces the Lord, I want you to enjoy success, I do not plan to harm you, I will give you hope for years to come. Then you will call out to me. You will come and pray to Me and I *will listen to you*, when you look for Me with all your heart, you will *find* Me" (Jeremiah 29:11–14). This was another defining moment. After I prayed back God's own Words, I bowed my head and whispered, "Loving Father, I'm so sorry that I took so long to trust You completely. I am Yours. Thank You that I'm still of some use to You right where I am. I want to please. I love You, Father." Like Father Richard, a good monk, said, it's not just a private knowing, and we can be "known through." I felt a union with my Real Father as I had *never* had with any other human being before. I want to please You, the King who sits on the throne. I love You, Father. I want to work for You. In essence, Dr. Richard Rohr says we can never go back; the transformation is divine and changes us completely.

After discovering the two sides of Heaven in the book of Luke, I wanted all my relatives to be on the right side. Psalm 7 was a biggie that I'd prayed when I got so sick for it not to not to ruin my spirit. I prayed, "Oh Lord, my God,

in You I put my trust, save me from all that persecute me…
Deliver me…lest (my malady) tear me and my soul like a
lion, rending me in pieces…while there is none to deliver."
You must deliver me O Lord because "there is no soundness
in my flesh." And "my loins are filled with a loathsome disease. I am feeble and sore broken, my heart pants and my
strength fail me, and the light of my eyes is gone from me."
Lord, "forsake me not. Be not far from me…and make haste
to help me, O Lord my salvation" (Psalm 38:3–21).

My breathing was good, but I still had the other symptoms. I've prayed for God to raise me up because I was "weary
and heavy laden." I cried out when the radiation was cours-
ing through my veins and made me feel as if I was *on fire!*
Psalm 39. "My heart was hot within me, while I was musing
the fire burned." (Literally I did burn). Yet and still, there was
no temperature reading to support the hot flushes (nothing
to do with menopause). "The Lord will strengthen me on
my bed of languishing and take away my sickness." I trusted
every word and claimed it all. I told the Father that "whatever
my body is or isn't, it belonged to Him to do with what He
chose." I've *never* trusted any person that much…*ever.*

Scientist believe now that the human body emits defi-
nite rays of energy; somehow, my husband and my human
energy field got overloaded in the electromagnetic field of
high-voltage equipment. We were in the wrong place at the
wrong time. There are so many unsuspecting souls admitted
to the Environmental Health Clinic in Dallas, Texas. The
enemy of God, Satan, is so cunning and sneaky and goes
around roaring like a lion to devour any he can (1 Peter:5). *I
never blamed my Heavenly Father…ever. I knew who and what
the culprit was.*

MORE ABOUT LANCE

Lance was well, and my parents asked for help again. My husband stayed up with Mom and Dad to take care of them. He got them food, their medication, and any other misc. items they needed. Some family members were helping themselves to my parent's bank accounts. I had a horrible feeling for Mom and Dad; I was worried they were going to be left penniless. I was too sick to do anything though, so I stayed home with the two kids. He had to be gone four weeks at a time for six months to get to the bottom of things.

I prayed to God for the answers, and then it dawned on me. Duh! *Aha! Lance's experience!* Honestly, I did not have the nerve by myself, but I mustered up the courage to ask Lance to do whatever had to be done to insure that Mom and Dad would have enough funds remaining. They had to be taken care of comfortably in an assisted living facility… That was their only wish. We wanted to help. My problem was, will God be supportive of this? What about where it says somewhere in the Scriptures that, if a person takes your garment, give him your coat also? Is this it? Oh, how I prayed. I really didn't want to be left as ill as I was…but even so, Lance *had* to leave me and go to Mom and Dad's side. Somehow, I'd manage. Honestly, I was very afraid, with all my symptoms, to be alone with the kids…but I had no choice. My breathing was good, so I felt I could hold down the fort while my husband rescued Mom and Dad.

A firestorm was beginning to blaze. Do you recall that story about Esther and Haman? The last talk Ester was to have with the God of Israel before she told the king of Persia about how evil and wanting Haman was. "If I perish, I perish." I copied that prayer as Lance said goodbye to me at our front door to go rescue my parents. If I was asked many years ago after my dad bashed my head against the refrigerator or Mom saying that I was "rotten and no good," I probably would have said, "What will be will be. "Although both parents, in the flesh world, had abandoned and neglected Skip and me. Nevertheless, I held within my "spirit self" something more compassionate than I could even begin to describe, and as a result, I told Lance to go and leave it to God. I had achieved love for my parents, both without condition. Lance went to take care of business. "'Vengeance is Mine, I will repay,' says the Lord," but I added, "Father, please be merciful." I loved all these relatives at one time. Everything turned out fine. Lance was successful, and their future was secured.

Mom and Dad had peace of mind now, and I asked them to come to our town and give up on where they were. We got them in a lovely assisted-living building, and Mom grew to love where we lived. I had forgiven them so many years ago.

I'M SO THANKFUL

It's been three more years up to date. God has helped to heal many of my symptoms. Yet I still cannot be around *powerful* electronics. Notwithstanding, I lived close to my wonderful children. My son had been blessed with a four-year scholarship to a wonderful university and comes home every weekend to grocery shop for us and visit. During breaks, he spends time in the house he grew up in a few miles away. My daughter Gloria attends a university like MIT. She too comes home on the weekends to do our errands and visit. I have three beautiful Siamese cats—two girls that are sisters and one baby Mai Tai. They are so precious to us all. I am still recuperating, but I'm back to a normal, healthy weight. I have a gas stove, and I never use the microwave because I know what to avoid. I still cannot drive or go out in the public yet, but I believe I will in the future with my Heavenly Father's help. He never fails his own. I've learned a lot of patience and I know that I can wait on Him and depend on Him for all of my needs. He is totally trustworthy (Jerimiah 33:6, Proverbs 4:20.) Waiting is not a word we like, but endurance, diligence, and long suffering are expected sometimes of us.

I grabbed on the Scripture where it clearly states, "God is no respecter of *persons*." In other words, God did not care that I've messed up, not measured up, or wasn't perfect. He cares for me because he made me. He was willing to become my all in all. That was much needed (Acts 10:34). I ran into my Heavenly Father's arms like I used to my dad's.

In summary, regarding my health, I feel *much* stronger with each week. I added back foods that I was very sensitive to four years ago. I'm up to about thirty-eight different foods. I'm even eating pancakes, salads, chicken, and potatoes. Yum! With the mercury poisoning, I really have to watch fish (iodine), especially ones from the sea. But I'll be trying salmon soon as it is a freshwater fish and full of nutrients. I don't touch scavengers!

Speaking of sea creatures, I don't know where the picture and poem regarding "Footprints" originated, but it is very significant. There had been many times where I needed to climb up on the Good Shepherd's back and let Him carry me. He and I know that He has. This five-year period of misery had been scary. I've been the neediest I have ever been, but I know He's with me. I believe 1 Corinthians 10:13 when it states, "This is a terrible trial, but *He will take me through the other side*." God will use those experiences for good somehow. I trust my real Father. Perhaps my story will help someone who has been *waiting* on *God* to *forgive* them. Maybe some will come out of *denial* about a shameful incident. Perhaps this story will help people find it in their hearts to forgive those who have wronged them. I know God the Father loves all of his children and is good to us; I'm so honored to be a daughter of the King of kings (Romans 8:28, Revelation 19:16).

CHAPTER 22

The king's daughter is all glorious within.

—Psalm 45:13

DIANE (HER WORDS)

*M*y life has changed a lot since meeting my friend Katia. I had recently lost my mother whom I had been especially close to about the last twenty years. She was ninety-two when she passed—a true Southern lady and respected matriarch of the family. We have a large family, and we had taken shifts each day the last three years of her life when she was so ill, but she and I had a special relationship; she called us "a unit" because we were always together. Before she flew over the cattle guard that last time, she surprised herself and quit driving. We were best friends, it seemed, but I never lost the great respect a daughter has for their mother. We went everywhere together.

I love elderly people, and I have always been close and more comfortable with them than with younger folks. I love their stories and the things they have seen and know. When Katia called my church looking for someone to help with her elderly mother who was becoming ill, my pastor immediately thought of me. I called the phone number, went to meet Katia and her mother, and I felt I like I already knew these people! We had such a strong unspoken connection. Her mother has dementia, but I enjoy just spending time and listening to the same old stories, exaggerated or not, over and over. I think it is important all people know they still matter. We all need that, and I try to treat people the way I want to be treated.

Katia and I hit it off right away, like I said. She said, "You can call me Kitt." There was a comfort there and a deep sense of knowing each other almost intimately immediately. We had similar views, and our lives were a lot alike. We even discussed religion, which I try to stay away from in conversation; it can cause major arguments. Our views and opinions were so similar it was uncanny. We really clicked. I hadn't realized how much I missed my best friend. I don't now know what I did with my time since before Mama. I started helping with her mom and running errands, but we became best friends very soon. We talked about everything, and I was at her home every day.

Katia has brought the best out of me; love is supposed to do that. She helped me trust my inner voice again. I had been pushing it back and lost some confidence since Mama died. That true love and confidence a person has when they are completely accepted. We know everything about each other and do not judge each other or others. We discuss everything in the world, and it always comes back to a spiritual theme. I know God has changed her life and He is in control, but she has taught me to trust Him as a true friend with daily tasks and thank Him always. I've never felt such a personal relationship with God—it is real, and she taught me that it could be that way. God brought us together for so many reasons, and I am so thankful to have a true sister in Christ in my life. I love her and her family very much—truly and deeply love them. I am so thankful. I needed this in my life. I was drifting badly with no direction. God has done some wonderful things in my life since meeting Katia. It is almost magical. It is a wonderful relationship—they both are. I look forward to the future with childlike excitement.

DEBORAH

What I think of Katia…other than being about the finest person I've ever had the pleasure to know? She, in spite of a troubled childhood, abuse, etc., "God" blessed her with her brother, "Skip!" They loved and encouraged each other in a fun brother-sisterly way!

Life looked like it was over for her way too young. "God" knew she would be "His child" and a shining beacon in the dark. Believe me, she certainly can outshine the sunshine.

Intelligent, educated, yet humbly "down to earth." Funny, still a tomboy, yet a lady! A wonderful mother to her children and a loyal, loving, and honest friend for life! *I know!*

Katia always sees the good and the positive in negative and sad situations. Generosity is one of her many gifts. She goes the extra mile for people and makes every day like a blessing just to have another day! She can't lose. I try to keep negative things from her, but her eyes look into my soul. There is *no* fooling her! Her life story up to this point should be shared with everyone who feels, "I just can't go on anymore." She makes me happy to just talk to, and we have a great, natural friendship—sisterhood, which is rare. She also has a beautiful sweet daughter who is inspired by her mother's wonderful, loving fighting spirit, and her handsome son compliments his mom for being a hard-driving, successful woman. As such, God has plunked her in a powerful position as an owner of almost twenty apartments. Astonishingly, she handled it all—repairs and perspective tenants of the properties. She did this business by landline telephone to another state. This is my good friend, and I love her.

SHELLA

Named after her aunt some seventy years ago, my good friend Shella shines. I first had the pleasure of meeting her and her good husband when they visited with my mother and other elderly people at her new nursing home; this was just before Mom came to live with me on my five acres in a bungalow.

Shella is an active member of her church, and she works with the women's legion as a Eucharist minister among other duties. Her good works include taking meals to needy people for "meals on wheels" every Friday for many years. For Mom and so many others, Shella goes to where people cannot drive to administer Holy Communion and offer other services such as shopping, doctor and hair appointments, and anything else the elderly may need.

In fact, on Christmas, while I was still recuperating from radiation/mercury poisoning, Shella and her husband, who she affectionately called "the saint in the family," did a wonderful thing for Mom and myself. I could not drive, so the loving couple got my mother ready and picked her up, wheelchair and all, at the nursing home, put her in the back of a brand new station wagon, and brought her to our family's home for a wonderful Christmas together!

When all the festivities were over, both came back, took Mom to the nursing home, and put away her leftovers and packages! There is a really neat part to this; the family, children and all, own and manage one of the most successful businesses in our area.

Even in business, they give God the credit by calling it a miracle. I know how much Shella loves our Heavenly Father because, since the time she first came to my home to bring communion, we had wonderful conversations on the goodness of God. In fact, in talking, Shella humbly let it slip that in over sixty years, she has not missed going to church every morning unless she was sick. My daughter Gloria, Shella, and I have a pact. "Whomsoever gets to paradise first will pull the other up!"

Shella makes me feel normal and loved every time she comes, even though she has to turn off her cell phone while she is with Mom and me. She sweetly says, "Katia, it's okay. I like the peace of coming here on your five acres." One day, in our religious discussions, I asked her to describe in a few words what God means to her. In her quick-witted and kindly way, she looked at me and said, "Oh, that's easy. One word will do it. 'Perfection.'" Then she sweetly added, "Katia, I cannot imagine my life without God in it."

Shella and her husband Jim have been married and in love for over fifty-five years! They are great examples of how even people in powerful, successful, and progressive positions can fulfill God's will to show charity and do good works for the less fortunate.

In other words, status is trumped by compassion for the elderly and underprivileged. If many more would do their parts and serve the Lord in this Biblical way, this sad, sick world would become a "miracle" planet.

P.S. Apparently, some of the kids and in-laws in Shella's family are in the missions and help with the less fortunate. I'm sure God smiles when others mention this family's name.

PAT AND MARY ANN

I know, as I am becoming a mature Christian, two things. Those things are that our Heavenly Father intervenes in our lives and He brings good people into our path. Two of those good people are Pat and Mary Ann.

Again, through church connections and my good friend Shella, Pat came as a substitute Eucharist minister to give Holy Communion to Mom and myself at our home. Shella prepared us for her visit by saying, "I can't come tomorrow, but I'm sending Pat. You will really like her!" Well, that, with her coming over the past two years to intermittently bring communion, has become an understatement. I personally have grown to be enlightened about church, God, and our community with every visit from Pat. Her full and glowing cheeks bring joy.

When you look at Pat, she may remind you of an elementary school principal on a field day excursion. She always dresses for the weather. In camp-like style, with her cute, short, and naturally gray Buster Brown hair, she carries herself into our home with a sweet smile and big hugs every time. She exudes warmth and a true love.

However, like all my very close women-in-Christ friends, she has a terrific personality, and we laugh sometimes to joyful tears. In simpler terms, "she cracks me up!"

Honestly, I thought Pat was a cut up character. Well, Mary Ann was no slacker and with "personality plus!" At very close to eighty, this adorable, pretty, petite, and casually dressed woman walked into my living room and sat in my only hard straight-backed chair. The one hour with her and Pat was one of the most enjoyable and funny times I've ever had with anyone! My husband Lance was home that day and agreed that both Pat and Mary Ann were downright hysterically funny and intelligent and just plain fun to be around.

Furthermore, Mary Ann "happened to be" from an old-town area. We talked about the shops, stores, amenities, and town people. It was like old home day talking about the good times and familiar sights—amusement rides like the Wild Hatter, Potato chips, Root Beer, Orange Crush soft drinks, Germantown restaurants, baseball games, football teams, and much more. It was a divinely appointed day!

God really showed me how far He had taken me with my memory healing, and all I could really talk about was the enjoyable times twenty years ago. All the ugly, painful, and crazy recollections were gone. *Poof*, vanished as only our Father can accomplish, so tenderly, yet it took some years.

Needless to say, I love when Pat comes. And anyone who thinks that becoming or living the Christian life isn't exciting and chock-full of delightful days is sadly mistaken. In fact, invite Pat, Shella, and Mary Ann into your homes and you'll see what fun Christians can have!

What about Tamara

A little while ago, deciding to move on with my story, something peculiar kept happening. I still couldn't drive or get out, and I interviewed many women for Mom and Dad's caregiving. With my back being weak and getting sciatica, I could not care for Mom the way I wanted to. Thus, I needed help and I wanted to really be choosy on who I'd pick to help her.

To my surprise, we had quite a turnover of caregivers. Nonetheless, during the hiring process, I discovered some familiar themes with several of the women. Some of the ladies, after learning a bit about my past, identified with similar mishaps and even crimes against them—specifically committed upon them by the opposite sex. It turns out we became a *support group* for one another. Tamara was in a dark tunnel with nasty turbulent wind.

She was shy. I had two or three talks with her, as I believe the Holy Spirit was leading. Tamara too had a strong conviction and felt she must talk to someone. She was in so much pain about something. I could tell. She needed someone to understand and not judge her; she chose me.

With her tiny, frail body, she shook as she opened up about her misery. She almost whispered as her big beautiful eyes, resembling a baby deer, welled up with tears. Tam, as she asked me to call her, explained in graphic detail what happened five years ago.

Tamara had just been to her doctor, and he told her some very frightening news. As an outlet for her fears and worries, she called a friend of hers, and the two girls decided to forget their troubles, go out to hear a band, and then go to a restaurant/ pub in a pretty decent part of town. So off Sheila and Tamara went to paint the town pink and have a good time. They were both in their late twenties, no husbands, no kids, footloose and fancy free.

Well, several hours later, they ended up at a quaint pub and both were drinking Bloody Mary's. Only one each because they knew somebody had to drive. Sheila got a call, and an old boyfriend said he was coming to pick her up, so graciously, she left her car with Tamara to drive home to her apartment until the next morning.

Tamara stayed alone to nurse her hurt. Within a few minutes, some grungy looking men came in the bar area and sat at one of the bigger tables. There were three of them, and they "noticed" the very well built, pretty woman. Tamara, sitting alone, got up to use the restroom. She was crying, and all of a sudden, she rose up and started to bolt out. What happened was horrific! She said she felt uneasy and a bit dizzy, but she managed to exit the building by the side door. She started slowly and carefully taking steps to the car. With me, Tam was a nervous wreck retelling this and pulling at her sweater sleeves and turtleneck top. Obviously frightened and shame filled, her body language accompanied every word. She nervously laid it out. She kept saying over and over how "weird she felt, and she couldn't see or focus" that night. The men took her to some old unused river park. There, she relayed that they took turns with her sexually. She hesitantly and tearfully cried out the details of how "they sexually tortured her. Apparently, the three men didn't leave the bar, but they had drugged her and followed her. They must have put her in the trunk of a car and carried her to a park. There, she relayed that they took turns with her throughout the whole night. She hesitantly told me details of how they did painful and embarrassing things. By now, she had pulled her turtleneck over her face, and she was hiding her shame. I assured her as I held her like a mother holds a scared lost child. She broke down and slithered to the floor slowly and collapsed in a fetal ball.

She tried to contain herself, but she started crying again when she disclosed to me the doctor's report from earlier that day. The doctor had told her that she had cervical cancer. Oh my gosh! "No!" I exclaimed in horror.

Wow! That was too much. My heart broke for her. I lost it and started crying with her. I held her longer and we prayed. She pulled away and said angrily, "Where was God that night?" with that same lost child look.

What can I say when things so traumatic and violent happen to our women friends or any young girl anywhere at any time? Sometimes, it is only strong medicine that can keep a person from committing suicide, but that is only temporary relief. The morning after the tragic night, she woke up in a pool of her own blood and in terrific pain. Realizing what had happened, she said, "I wish they had let me die-right there."

In my twenty-five years studying the Bible regarding the commandments, I'd like to share a few with you, and you decide for yourself what these could possibly mean. The enemy reared his ugly head far too many times. Just like with me, all these women and their stories were evidence that the beast (poltergeist) still invaded and tried to destroy lives.

The verses that lay out what to do about a rapist or murderer who do these things by plan (premeditated), not passion, are as follows:

UNDER THE DEATH PENALTY

> If a man finds a woman and forces her to lay with him, the man who lays with her shall die. (Deuteronomy 22:25)

> You should take no ransom for the life of a murderer who is guilty of death, but he shall surely be put to death. (Numbers 35:31)

Another important scripture that I found a bit scary was about curses. No, we don't come under a curse for what our parents or ancestors do unless they hated God, however:

There are some curses, if even Christians choose to disobey God, these still stand. What Jesus took to His cross were the blood sacrifices and ordinances of worship from the Old Testament.

Jesus says, "I have not come to change one jot or tittle of the law...but to *fulfill* it." He is the one and all time Lamb sacrifice, but all else is still in full force with our Heavenly Father and the kingdom godhead.

Deuteronomy 28:15–68. Read them please and see what you think.

Sometimes, the Holy Spirit evaluates us where we know it. In the Sanfords' all-encompassing books, their idea of transformation is the past that we have lived and been "redeemed" from is where God has taken us "out of the ashes of what we have been and have done and has grown the ministry we are." Thereby, "nothing in our lives is ever wasted." Further, the Sanfords say that God "has turned every aspect of our (seemingly) defeated lives to glory" for Him. I *cannot* imagine where I would be without God in every area of my life. The key is we must invite Him in each area; although He is *almighty*, He is gentle about an invitation.

Our Heavenly Father transforms our very nature to conform to His plan. We are changed "for the equipping of the saints for the work of service to the building up of the body of Christ" (Ephesians4:12–14).

The Holy Spirit, by transforming my life, though being painstaking at times, has taken me from miserably lost to enthusiastically helping others.

A GRATEFUL DAUGHTER

Do you remember throughout the years, the thread of false accusations that had been alluded to in this life story? I'm now prepared to disclose a summary of the situation.

Unbeknownst to me, for at least ten long and miserable years, Lance kept a secret from me. This hidden accusation could have been dealt with much sooner had he calmly confronted me about it. Sadly, he chose not to; the rumor/ lie festered within him. Without going into the disgusting details that were used back, let me disclose what is necessary to get to the point.

Years ago, in the government working era, Lance's agency had a Tom Selleck lookalike agent named Gage. He was Lance's boss but only did enough training and cases to "get by." My husband eagerly moved up the work ladder and even passed Gage up in a matter of a few short years. This older agent thought he was "God's gift to women" and that he could get any woman on his good looks. His pride was a demon, and he bragged about his female "conquests." That was none of my business *until* he included me in that scenario and told a terrible lie about myself and him! You see, over the years, as Lance moved up, Gage got more and more jealous to the point that he wanted my husband's career and personal life to crash. I was good friends with Gage's wife, and I could *never* hurt her. The problem was a few of the other agents believed Gage, and the rumors spread like wildfire. Luckily, I did not know that this was circulating until a few years ago (Lance kept it from me, for at least ten years). Sadly, all those years my husband wondered, "Could it be true?" This broke my heart.

To add insult to injury, most of the other agents who were almost keeping advanced pace with Lance liked him very much. Several of them became like brothers. Even to this day, over twenty years later, they all contact and visit one another. Each one of these guys knew how much I hated that Gage was a hunter, but we all tried to keep peace when we gathered for recreation. It took time, but I forgave Gage for lying about me. A year ago, we discovered that Gage fell very ill.

Just a few weeks ago, I fell asleep on the living room couch and I had a dream. The agents from that time period, looking like they did back then, all sat on the couch across from me. Lance also was sitting in his usual chair. All of a sudden, from behind, I felt a hand on my shoulder; the voice that spoke was familiar, and I turned to see who it was. I was in shock! It was Gage (older now). He spoke softly but loud enough for all the guys to hear. "Katia, I am sorry that I hurt your reputation. Will you forgive me?" When I glanced back over my shoulder, he was gone! As much as I had hurt over the years, I was now free from the burden of the lie, and God allowed all of us to hear it! I never tried to get revenge. I just said prayers that our Father would handle it all. Guess what? That is exactly what He did. The part that was amazing but sad was that Gage passed away on the very night I had my dream about him and the doubters. Father Divine always takes care of His children, even if it takes time. Love of God, patience, and trust are the keys. "It is God that avenges me" (Psalm 18:47) and set the record straight.

CHAPTER 23

MY FATHER'S GIRL

*S*o sadly, my dad suffered from heart-related illnesses, but he was ninety years old at the time. I had written several letters to him over the years, but his eyesight was too bad to read them all. Mom tried to read them to him, but it was Lance who got a hold of them when he went to take care of them both. Tyler possibly had gotten over half of the real estate Father Quinton gave to Mom before we realized what was going on. He didn't care if Mom and Dad had enough left to even take care of them! My philosophy here—Tyler did us a favor and got rid of the possible ill-gotten stuff.

After many good visits with Dad, he and I became close once again. As a child, I thought Dad could fix anything. In the end, it was/is our Heavenly Father who "fixed" our relationship. The last days of my dad's life, like Father Quinton with me, ended very well. Dad, after analyzing all my positive letters to him, got so nice. He wanted to see me again and talk; he didn't come out and apologize to all of us, but he did give me his family's land. The *timely* prediction Lydia made came true. Dad said, "I want you to get a home with your mother and take care of her, *Wildflower*." Before he passed on, he told me he wanted me to take whatever was left, buy myself a home, and put Mom in it with me. That, I did do. That's my home on five acres now. It is very private, and it's a brick dollhouse. Dad and I called it "my bungalow." The fantastic thing about it is that, from the street, I'm four hundred feet up a gradual hill, and the *miraculous* part is that no one can get a cell phone signal from my yard and house, so no powerful electronics! When you pray for a wall of protection, God keeps His Word!

Lance got with Dad every night to read my letters to him. I kept all my stuff very positive, loving, and caring, never saying anything about the dark past. The Holy Spirit took me past all of that, and God healed the wounds. I loved both of my parents, even when they were not acting loving toward me. Now, they both were very loving toward me since Lance told them how sick I was. Dad actually was more worried than my mother; he had that caring side when he did not drink. Dad said, "I love you, my Wildflower," before he went to be with God. Joyful tears fell.

Lance did manage to help my parents secure enough money for them to not only live but to live comfortably. Dad lived another two years but then passed away. Mom, as you know, moved in with me, and we have had some wonderful times. She still loves to play cards and Scrabble. Mom also was a fantastic artist and still is at eighty-eight. The elderly need to know that they are still important, and residing in an assisted living home doesn't always provide that sense of worth. They need to be with their loved ones if at all possible.

With Dad's passing, they both wanted us to also have enough so Lance, the kids, and I could have our own business where we could work at home. With God's timing, we invested their money and ours into several small apartment buildings. I love being a landlady and have been told that I do honest, fair, and progressive work. But I pale in comparison to how my big brother would be. My family and Lance told me I was always good at getting along with others. I have a system to match my tenants up with those like themselves to avoid domestic conflict within the buildings. For example, one whole building is with singles over fifty, another with single moms. They all seem very happy and get along quite well. Thank you, God, Dad, and thanks, Lance, for your real estate knowledge.

I loved all of Hayley Mills's movies. Even now, I have her whole DVD collection. I have three Siamese cats, and two look just like the one in *That Darn Cat*. My daughter has our big baby boy Siamese; she keeps him at her house. He's handsome and a whopper! I love how beautiful, intelligent, and inquisitive they are. They're talkative but very independent and brave. I'm glad, in Isiah 11:1, animals will be with us in heaven. My own Siamese have actually warned me of insects like spiders, wasps, and centipedes. On three occasions, my blue Siamese woke me up when spiders got near my bed in my room. The sister gets right up in my face, and she'll lie on my chest to comfort me when I'm crying. She senses my hurt and lies on my heart.

CATS ARE SO COOL AND HISTORY

The history of cats, of course, has fascinated me and my cat-fancying friends. Many scientists believe that the domestic cat originated from the African Wildcat. The Egyptians brought them in to train to go after mice and smaller rodents that would otherwise eat up and destroy their grains their foods. Because these graceful and beautiful animals protected the farmers' food and grain storehouses, they were honored with paintings and sculptures from 3,500 BC until they actually made sacred idols out of them.

A fertility goddess of love was graced on top of her body with a cat head when she was sculptured.

As cats populated to Asia and the Far East in China and Japan, they (the Siamese especially) were used to protect palaces and guard stores by perching on the shelves, ready to pounce and attack any would-be robber.

Cats protected valuable manuscripts and writings from mice and other rodents who badgered authors by tearing and chewing their scrolls. Cat's highly intelligent minds and exotic bodies, to me, place them in the category of "God's best creations." I love their feistiness and enthusiastic yet loving and independent nature. Nothing gets past a cat.

I'll bet, in the garden of paradise, since God loves all things big and beautiful, there will be tigers, lions, cougars, leopards, panthers, and more. Probably Adam and Eve had a few as their pets. In the future "New Jerusalem," these gorgeous creatures will be with us (Isaiah declares this), but they will not be flesh eating—there is no flesh eating in the new paradise.

Cats are such a comfort, cuddling close and loving. My five cats that sleep, eat, and play are a coming attraction of what lies ahead. The newest addition, Ariel, had all the spunk and entertainment value any cat person could want.

P.S. Another positive trait of cats—they even clean up after themselves. Do you know many other creatures of God that do that?

FELINES AND FEMALES

So much of what I loved from being a kid resurfaced in the past ten years—for example, my extreme affection for cats and gathering with more women friends to talk snack and have a good time. Thankfully, my female kindred companions also seem to love cats!

Dinah, my dear friend I've mentioned, has truly been a marvelous blessing, as has my twenty-something daughter, Gloria. Both simply are crazy over their cats. We all think their quick actions and intelligent maneuvers rate them far higher than most of God's creatures. We all love dogs too, but to us, cats are so independent and fastidious that, for our crazy schedules, these felines fit into our lives perfectly.

Remember back when I took care of the Nature's Barn at Merryland? "No Hunting" signs are posted like stick-ums all over my property! My friends and I also feed skunks, squirrels, rabbits—anything that wanders by, even adorable, curious, and finger-nibbling raccoon families. All of these hungry critters know that they can safely mosey over and find something tasty on our feeding trays.

While speaking about "our girls," I was giving God credit for bringing me through so much in my life. I've had so many close calls and near fatal situations. I commented to Dinah that "the Lord must have wired me up with a nine lives switch when he created me."

She laughed with her cute and enthusiastic chuckle. She came back with, "God put some kind of feline survivor mechanism in me too." I told you she was quick on her feet and very witty. Paula White declares that our hearts beat the same. Dinah's my bud.

Like me, Dinah is so grateful that our Father pulls us out of the "miry clay" when needed and has many times.

My passion for cats makes me think God probably has a couple of *big* cats, like lion and tigers, as pets. He probably walks with them in the cool of the evening. Isaiah 11:.

In the company of so many dark souls for much of my life, I felt out of place. Since I've made it out of my "furnace of affliction" for the first time, I see I am okay. I confronted and dealt with the darkness. In the dark lion's den, Daniel called over the big cats and got mercy from above and said, "Here, kitty, kitty."

WOMEN IN SERVICE... YOU DECIDE

Talk about dysfunctional...

Ah, Mother Eve. I always had a big problem with her listening to a snake rather than God. Forgive me spoofing with this stuff, but *really?!* Then Sarah, what a strange personality she had. One minute she's setting up her maid to sleep with her husband, Abraham, and have her child, and the next minute, she is beating on the same maid and running her away because of her baby!

Then there was Rebecca... Wow! She was a wife to Isaac and mother to a set of twins. She showed favoritism so much to the younger that she committed fraud to ensure his future while not caring what happened to the other son.

Next, there was Leah. What a piece of work she was. Of course, with her slick, wily, sleight-of-hand father, how could she turn out normal? Then there was her crybaby sister, Rachael! Get over yourself and adopt!

Way to go, Jael, bedding down and giving hot totties to the leader of the enemy. Then, while he got all cozy under the covers, she quite methodically grabbed a hammer and tent spike and drove it through his dozing skull.

Then there's Tamar, the daughter-in-law of Judah, one of Jacob's sons. After her husbands are laid to rest, pushing up mandrakes, she hatches a plan. While Judah is seeking solace, comfort, and a little one-night stand, Tamar disguises herself as a prostitute and sleeps with him and conceives Judah's child.

Now, Deborah floats like a butterfly and sting s like a bee. The name Deborah means "Queen Bee." She earned this stinging reputation by leading the army of Israel into battle. No man was up to it… Perhaps they were too "buzzy." I do not mean to be caustic with these ladies of scripture, but do you see that the dysfunction was back then as it is now! However, each one of these messed-up malcontents were usable by God in a remarkable way.

In the New Testament, how many discontented and sinful Mary's can there be? Excluding our precious mother of God, who was holy, the others all had such serious desperate situations that all five of them met with Jesus Himself in some fashion and received a much-needed miracle.

On the other side, there is one thing that several of the Bible scholars now believe. Mary Magdalene was *not* a prostitute. The scriptures declared that Christ cast out seven spirits. It does not have to mean sexual sin. The secular world who keeps trying to paint her and the sinless Jesus together… that is sacrilegious! How can you be sinless, perfect, blemish free, and have sexual affairs or relationships? Plus being God?! Moreover, Mary of Bethany and Mary Magdalene turned out to be heroes in the end. Their complete devotion to our Lord was wonderful and, I believe, Holy Spirit led. I'm sure He picked them because they exuded compassion and loyalty. What a gutsy lady Mary Magdalene was to stay by His side even during the entire Calvary conclusion. Again, except for John, who was to care for Jesus's mother, there were no men to be with Jesus until it was finished… but Mary Magdalene stayed with Him until the bitter end. Jesus made Mary Magdalene *pure*. Wouldn't we all be loyal to Jesus after he cast out seven demons?

Even more amazing is that after Jesus was put in His uncle Joseph of Arimathea's, tomb, Mary Magdalene was there too. So as a reward, she got to be the very first person to see Jesus after His resurrection from the sealed and guarded tomb! What an Alleluia moment!

It all just goes to show us that Almighty God choses who He wants to do whatever He wants. He can change the unchangeable, create the uncreated, fix the unfixable, and raise up the departed—He could light up the world!

BLOWN AWAY!

Every so often, throughout my life, a pastor (speaker) has given such a dynamic lecture that it catches my attention. Case in point occurred just recently. The name of the church program was "Leading the Way," with the minister on Sunday mornings and repeated on Sunday nights. I watched *both* times. Wow! Being from a similar country as the Samaritan woman at the well, this sermon was so provocative… I must spread the Word to all you ladies. Even if you have never done or been involved with anything shameful, maybe someone you know really could use encouragement. The title of the sermon was "Freedom from Bondage." The internet entry is LTW.org. It is so interesting and informative once you know the distance that Jesus walked to get to this woman at the well of Jacob. I pray it will be a blessing to hundreds of hurting women who feel that they are "unworthy". Jesus brings her and all of us the *truth* that sets her free and gives her a purpose for her whole life after just one meeting. One encounter with Christ, she changed her lifestyle and went back to her town and preached the Word! Victoria Osteen's sermon on "the woman at the well" was *just* on TBN. She also told the story in a dynamic fashion. Joel and she take evangelicalism to a higher level.

MY MOM—QUEENIE

She's living the golden years.

What a huge difference time and God's transformation makes. If you would have told me twenty-five years ago the way Mom and I live now, I'd say, "Really?" We live together out on my five acres, and our roles have completely reversed. Due to her diabetes and dementia, I have been put in charge of everything with and about her. I just had her caregiver roll her out in her wheelchair to our screened-in porch. Our wonderful caregiver, Mary, has been a true blessing with my high-maintenance mother. Our home overlooks a beautiful, lush, green lawn, and a momma and baby deer just pranced across the whole yard, stopped suddenly, and both, with their big brown Bambi-eyes, looked at all three of us. What sight!

In the Bible, God constantly refers to us being compared to the swiftness, agility, and thirst of deer. With all the places where horses, cattle, deer, goats, sheep, and many more are, we see God loves his creatures. Remember, I had all these and more under my care from age eleven to sixteen when I worked at the nature barn at Merryland. Now, I'm out in the country and loving it!

Standing by the door, staring out, I see that young mother deer grazing while her tiny baby bounces and kicks with new life. She's brimming with "here I am, world!" As I glance over at my mom, now eighty-eight years old, another reversal. Once so full of life, she just wants to rest and have peace. Mom is all worn out…

Her once shapely, voluptuous figure sags all over. Her bright blue eyes have dimmed due to cataracts and eye surgeries. Her teeth, once TV commercial dazzling, have discoloration because of many years of coffee and antibiotics. But in a very sweet way, nature has been kind to her. She's pretty in another way. Lance, Jonathan, and Gloria noticed it too. They are around her all the time now.

Her once pushy, belligerent attitude has simmered down to a cute "what can we do about anything anyway" notion. She says this with a shrug of her shoulders that cause her pain due to arthritis.

Mom's one-time gorgeous, thick, shining hair, auburn and wavy as it used to be, was raised up on her head like a bronze crown. Now, it is almost white, cropped shorter, and very thin. Her Elizabeth Taylor look, including lots of layered jewelry (neck, wrists, ears, and ankles) has been replaced to nothing but her rosary. She holds it tightly as she mumbles prayers… So lovely to me to see her natural beauty and her worshipping our God.

Strangely, after all we've been through together, Mom has weathered the storms of life quite nobly. As I stare at her with her grey-white hair neatly pulled up on the top of her head with some combs holding it up, she looks stately and royal. With the sun hitting her hair, it glistens in the brightness. She looks like a sage-like queen!

Mom's all-time favorite games are Scrabble and Rummy. Lance taught her his family game that they all played called simply "Casino." She can hardly see, but she beams with energy on Scrabble night. When it comes to playing Scrabble, all of a sudden, her 5.0 reading glasses seem to do the trick; she wins all the time. So she "takes on" Gloria, Dinah, her granddaughter Jess, and me a bit aggressively in Scrabble quite often. Dinah lives just on the other side of my country road, and she has helped me care for my mom throughout the whole time she has been here. What a blessing! Mom and I have become so very close; she won't sleep until I climb up and hug her in her special bed, and we say we love each other and pray.

Being with Mom, and her being with all of us, has really made heaven's light shine for my little family and friends... Momma with me? I wouldn't have it any other way!

CURRENT COVENANT

In the beginning, our Creator with His supernatural power force, made everything.

God created day and night—the sun by day, the moon by night.

And He said all that He created, which included the *dark* sky, "was good." Night is darkness. Without some light, it would be completely black.

But God still made it. Satan, fallen angels, and sin-laden man is what made the dark...evil. I actually love looking at the dots that speckle the dark sky with lighted stars. Against that dark background, it is a sight to behold! So here, darkness is fine for night, and the contrast of light is awesome. God controls all His creatures unless free-will man takes the path and turns down the road of pure evil. However, the darkness is only bad when a soul chooses to remain unsaved. So I say we must *harness the darkness*, and with God's power, we rescue those who might otherwise perish.

As Louie Giglio states about sin, "Concealed problems find power in the darkness." This is so true. The power of evil diminishes as we come clean. We enter the light of the Divine.

Just recently, during the holidays, I went hunting for Christmas decorations. I found a couple of big tubs in the closet, but the first one I opened was packed full of bags with only one set of tree lights on top. While rummaging through, I happened to notice one small paperback squished on the side, being smashed and pages bent. Carefully, I pulled it loose so as not to tear it in any way.

The small paperback was visibly old and unfamiliar to me...at first glance. I must have bought it at a yard sale along with others years ago. It still had its fifty cents pink tag on it. My extreme curiosity kicked in. I aborted my Christmas ornament search and opted instead to read some stuff in this bright yellow book first written in the 1940s by Agnes Sanford. This tiny treasure is entitled, *The Healing Light* by Agnes Sanford

Unlike all my other books, this one had nothing under-lined or pinpointed with rainbow markers. It seemed unread, at least by me. Surprisingly though, the timing for what I started to read could not have been more perfect. Again, the uncanny parallels to exactly the season I was living in spiritu-ally... "connected" exactly.

The author's comments throughout the entire book were focused on God's "power" as an "energy" source flows through believers who are desperate for it! It is amazing that this good soul was in touch with the future technology from the 1940s! No computers, no cell phones!

Agnes visited with many sick children and adults throughout her life. She bears witness through several tes-timonies of healing that the power of God is awesome and continuous. Our Creator's "power" and super energy flows through patients, family, and friends like "electric current flows" through home wiring to lights. Further, she relayed that the Holy Spirit uses some as "transmitters" with their interceding on behalf of a sister or brother in need of a miracle. The faith-filled intercessor can be God's channel that transports the love signal needed by the lonely and unloved. In the simple acts of touching and patting hands or hugging the hurt, one can release an energetic "charge" that reacts from the transmitter to "the receiver" (the patient). In the Bible, it is known as "laying on of hands." A chosen vessel can be a conductor through which the Holy Spirit's energy flows. Agnes revealed to me personally: Jesus, by His stepping down from the high voltage of God's Divinity, got on a wavelength that we, as humans, could handle.

As so many pastors and ministers agree, the best way to keep God's mercy, love, and power flowing is to stay "plugged in" to our source. The Bible is our guide and roadmap to spiritual and earthly success by allowing the Holy Spirit to recreate us into *ministers of fire* for Him.

Forgiveness is the breaker switch that activates the Divine and releases to us who are believers in God's love and *power*. Perhaps we could all agree to say one prayer a day for a person sick or hurting. Even better would be to open up the "connection" of love full throttle by visiting and comforting the infirmed and lonely. This is what my good friend Dinah does all the time. So like Agnes, let's tap into power and stay on the right frequency with heaven's wavelength. It promises to be an awesome ride!

When God created everything, He used six days to do so. Our pastor reminds us that one day with the Lord is one thousand years. Thus, the Lord's Day, the millennium, will last one thousand years. It took twenty-five years to really dig and study, but the Bible makes so much sense to me now. I remove or add to my situation *what I need...by what He says.* It always turns out fine.

Further, God Himself declares what He created was "good;" even darkness can be good. Just think how hard it would be to get sleep only in the daytime. What about fireworks? Would they be so spectacular with the sun out? And how would we be without potatoes, tomatoes, eggplant, bell pepper, or red chili? Then those gorgeous petunias and flowers, they only grow in dark. I can't imagine not gazing upon a good garden and not seeing a group of these. So in essence, some darkness is "good," but we must discern and harness it and resist what is bad in it. When dark spirits come to our spiritual lives, we must *harness and divert* them, just as power plants harness and redirect electricity for usage every day and night.

Finally, for cat lovers who know about these marvelous pets, nighttime is playtime. I've got the great personalities of the Siamese and Persian. The Siamese are just like having monkeys. There is nothing off limits to cats. Their reign and range is limitless.

CHAPTER 24

Come boldly to the throne...that we might find mercy.
—Hebrews 4:16

BALANCING THE SCALES

$\mathcal{Y}$ears ago, my husband teased me about my overly religious ways. He kiddingly called it "conversion by contusion" unbalanced. I'm a Libra. I do not put much weight in that, but I do like balance if possible. All my childhood and into married life, my mother shared her and dad's financial gains with her Italian family. Mom always said this was because "my mother always helped the two young boys more than us girls."

In a way, I guess our Heavenly Father "restored what the locusts had eaten." His way is fair and balanced, you can be sure. He has taken my tortured heart and made it into a loving circumcised heart. I no longer convert by contusion... I take a deep breath and speak the truth in love (Ephesians 4:15).

Another thing that has balanced out is my everyday thinking process. Again, the Biblical self-help books have assisted me tremendously. This is where we see that most humans share a commonality in one way or another. With stress, hurt, pain, dysfunction, persecution, abuse and more, we join one another and unite to *overcome* all the wickedness life throws at us. In a sense, telling all of you and reliving my life story, I have written my own self-help book!! *Wow!* Thank You, God, for my mission script.

In His life on earth, Jesus Christ was blessed in all ways. He could converse one on one plus speak in a crowd with great authority yet natural balance.

P.S. Do you know what is not balanced and way-over-the-top but tipped our way? The Lamb of God. His dying for us. Like Louis Giglio aptly states, "What God did for us is greater than what anyone could do against us."

NOTHING WASTED

I never thought that I could *ever* find anything good from my fatal illness seven years ago; I *was wrong*! I have had one epiphany after another since that *destiny-filled* and miraculous night. I now believe the extreme heat combined with the radiation pulses purged out any evil or sin that could have remained in my soul. For three years, I prayed while in the furnace of affliction. My thirst was and will be quenched by the Living Water. Since *Jesus had harnessed the darkness*, now I listen with antenna connected to anything our real Father has to say. I have empathy for my sisters and brothers in Christ and those in the world. My compassion for the lost, the hurting, the poor, the afflicted, and the twisted has increased 100 percent. No waffling, no wondering. I'm sold out to Christ, moving ahead toward spiritual intellect while "redeeming the time" (Ephesians 5:16). Less time for bewitching busy-ness.

I learned what it means now when I see the Sacred Heart picture from my childhood holding onto His burning heart. Instead of my heart on fire from radiation, now my heart is on fire for the Trinity. As His constant radiating love draws me. I say without fear, "Lord, send me." A very favorite scripture, Psalms 139, has been my prayer throughout my prayers throughout my life. We are all fearfully and wonderfully made.

My inner man or self feels full because, every day, I study God's Word. The Holy Spirit's touch is sometimes evident, and I feel it when I read or hear Bible verses. My years of rejection, abandonment, and abuse are history—old news. I'm completely focused and enthralled in what the Good News says about me and those God put in my life—go lead the lost and hurt. As of late, I have purposely and immediately turned any controversies with life and home over to God. The trust I have, I don't have to worry, because He's on the throne of our life, and it is amazing! I never believed we could let go of literally everything and believe that God will give us all the help we need—the correct answer, put the right people exactly where we need them, and courage and strength to overcome any sickness or problem!

When the "worldliness" in us departs, a whole new Kingdom comes in. We seek, we knock, and keep knocking. The beast definitely tried to destroy me like Quinton and Skip, but Father God lifted me and harnessed the darkness every time!

We can't give up. Our Father lines up and calls on his army of angels to move heaven and earth for us... Why are we so impatient? I have learned so much! One sad thing that I did discover is that we have turned into a "modern-day, technology-addicted world." The sweet relationships where teen groups would meet at an outdoor restaurant and talk are long gone. Video games, gossip, and websites have become the daily routine. Face-to-face conversations have been replaced with "here's a selfie for you" and "who's on Facebook?"

Dates and walking hand in hand watching a movie at the cinema are almost obsolete. Instead, people open up their computers and watch a DVD while waiting for their car to be repaired while their three-year-old is playing on his iPad.

Even in our houses of worship, there are so many "performers." They are shown on twenty-foot screens in five different places, singing for praise rather than praising God while singing. The pastors seem more interested in popularity and church finances than revealing what God has to say in His Scriptures. *None of us would even be here if He had not created the world and put us here.*

Consequently, I have again gleaned out what's important and not wasted, I have learned that *God is calling back His children from darkness all over the world and into the light.* Similarly, the hero in Poltergeist said to Carrie Ann and the lost souls imprisoned in the house, "Come into the Light…" There is safety and love waiting.

I know my kids are both under God's canopy of protection, and I even anoint my cats if they become ill or in some danger. My life is Christ centered and never been more enjoyable! I want this for you too. There are no coincidences. *You* are reading this for a reason. *Everything that God has created good needs to stay good.* Mankind that harm His pets and wildlife will have a "special" consequence to be suffered.

FOR HIS GLORY

Over twenty-five years ago, my psychologist sister, Lydia, let me go with the statement, "*God will be with you,*

Katia." Since then, leaning on and trusting in the Holy Spirit has been amazingly rewarding. To glorify His Father, Jesus healed ten lepers in the Bible, and only *one* returned to give Him thanks. "Were there not others found who returned to give glory to God." I do, praise Him! Thus, this life for me now—excellent. I've found my authentic self only through the Spirit's processing and a life-transforming love. I have no enemies except Satan's crew. I've forgiven everyone every trespass and keep repenting along the way if needed. I've dove deep for the pearl of great price.

Searching for and holding to God's best for me and those around me, I have found something very important over these many years of overcoming—that is the "mysterious" and "elusive" *voice of God* is simply taking Him at His Word. I get direction and all the gifts of the Holy Spirit most times I read and respond to quotes of Scripture as they jump out from my books.

I no longer have a faulty belief system or a short-circuited life view. Because of God's constant gentle instruction, I am moving on and basically very happy and fulfilled—in Merryland…in the home and property He gave me. Simply put, what He says in His word should be our compass and GPS to avoid evil and choose good.

Seven years ago, the *Poltergeist beast* reared his ugly head, and his demon claws dug deep into my normal going life one more time. Like Job, he just about did me in. "Nevertheless"(I love that word), God, with saving and delivering power, pulled me up from the death grip the enemy tried to hold on me. The imposter of the True Christ may try again and again, but with the *armor of Gospels*, Jesus defeats the prince of darkness every time.

Satan *tried* his best to mess with my mind, and I could feel his strength jerking me inch by inch. However, in *that night of destiny*, whereby the gentle *breath of life* let me know who's going to win this frightening battle, the Holy Spirit literally *blew* the enemy away from my bedside!

Remember again how much God wants to draw us to Him? I love this tender side. Every day, I now know He is pleased when you and I read and study His love letter to us. It's the only one He's written, and He's made it very thorough. I now think this is extreme, urgent, and of vital importance, because when we hold up and walk day by day under the banner of Christ, *we win*. I believe my breathing, heartbeat, and sound mind are here to magnify and glorify Him. What an awesome purpose!

At the final call, descending down, the "New Jerusalem" will be "the City of our God." Merryland of the new *rejuvenated* earth (Revelation 21:2).

Our Father is the source of an everlasting *extraordinary* life. Our God *is* the Mighty God.

The Wedding of the Century... A Celestial Celebration! Wanna Attend?

First you must "crossover" and "come into the light" (Poltergeist).

T.D. Jakes, one of the most spiritually enlightened, humble, and enthusiastic pastors of all time, described Princess Diana and Prince Charles's palatial wedding in gorgeous detail. I have to pass this on to you. "Diana had a stately grace that was once revered and respected by all people. She represented what little girls once held sacred." He continued, "Diana exploded onto our television screens as the bride of the century. She, with lace-clad hands and silky smooth, satin-soft trains of buoyancy, had sashayed across the camera lens. It was a royal fairy tale come true!" Wow! Every girl's dream!

There is a wedding coming for all Christians who accept and follow the True Christ also. The Lamb's ceremony will far surpass the wedding feast at Cana. Jesus turned water into the best wine there. Can you only imagine what the menu will be like for the celestial extravaganza? It will be supernaturally awesome when Jesus Christ, The King of Kings, will take, for His bride, His Church.

I don't know about you, but I guarantee you this is one OCD moment that I'll follow through to the end. I will be there "come hades or tsunami!" Translated, "I will be there come hell or high water!"

If this sounds fantastic and you'd love to be the bride of Christ, may we pray this prayer together.

> Holy and loving Father, You sent Your Son to be our Savior. Through Jesus, our sins are forgiven, and we are redeemed, You have said in Your word. Forgive me all my sins and I forgive any who have hurt me and sinned against me. I also receive now healing that Jesus gives because of His stripes. Thank You that I am now saved. Show me the way to the Lamb's wedding whereby I marry Your Son. In Jesus's name, Amen.

Stay the course. Now John 14:1–4 can come into play whereby we who believe will spend forever with our Real Father right here in the new heaven, the new Jerusalem. Our

God will be our King, and we'll share an unending life of royalty.

Lead on, Spirit. You light up our life

PERSEVERANCE

May I let you in on something from my own life experience regarding healing? Many of us are tempted to give up and, as Douglas Pessoni admits in his book, *With Healing in His Wings*, abandon their faith. He pulls out Hebrews 11:6 as a reminder of how important it is to keep our faith, especially during sickness. Sometimes the enemy besieges us tirelessly and we want to give up.

"But without faith it is impossible to please Him, for he who comes to God must believe that He is, and that He is the rewarder of those who diligently seek Him" (Hebrew11:6). Keep persevering.

Another very important reminder of *how* important it is that we get in and remain in faith without wavering is in Matthew 7:7–8.

SCRIPTURE VERSES AND HEALING SCRIPTURE

In summary, I have chosen a few of my favorite Bible quotes that could help you all also. Proverbs 4:13, "Take firm instruction; do not let her go, keep her for she is your life."

Our Father in Heaven is called Rapha. Rapha means "the miracle healer." God says, in Exodus 15:26, "I am the Lord that heals thee." "Bless the Lord, Oh, my soul and forget not all His benefits: who forgives all thy inquiries, who heals all thy diseases... Being dead to sin (now) should live for righteousness, by whose stripes are healed" (1 Peter 2:24).

More healing words: "You are the God who heals all our diseases" (Psalm 103:3).

In the New Testament, Jesus goes among the multitude and states, "Many followed Jesus, and He healed them all" (Matthew 12:15) and that Jesus "came to heal the broken-hearted" (Luke 4:18).

EMF AND RMF BOOKS

It was not surprising to me that some of our acquaintances and friends wanted to know more about the strange and frightening illness. This disabled my husband and totally caused me to be housebound and bedridden for close to five years. Some were interested because they too were worried since they all constantly used top-of-the-line technology day and night. We educated them on the electromagnetic and radio frequency fields and the dangers of becoming sensitized to them. What follows are the books that I can recommend for anyone wanting further information on the possibly perilous signals. Let me tell you about these dangerous *silent* fields. Let me say that I knew nothing about this before becoming so ill.

Dirty Electricity by Donna Fisher
Backyard Secret Exposed by Beth Sturdivant
Healing Severe Chemical and EMF Sensitivity by Gary Petra
Zapped by Ann Louise Gittleman

God, in his infinite mercy, showed me how to use my misery by harnessing the darkness. My story is for His glory!

The Old Testament is chock full of warriors, battles, and war strategies and so on. As my pastor declares, "The Old Testament is the school we use to instruct us as much as the New Testament." Revelation lets us know the truth and how it all will end. Being victorious for God's fired up children. *We will not desert Him!*

MANY WILL BE DECEIVED. THE WHOLE WORLD WILL FOLLOW THE ANTICHRIST (REVELATION). DO NOT BE SWEPT UP AND AWAY.

The same cautioning concept by Jesus to His disciples (us) in Mark 13:4–27.

Read Luke's account in Luke 21:5–36.

Finally, in the Book of Revelation, where Jesus wants to *reveal* to us all that heaven will be on earth *after* the devil becomes His footstool, and we who have the Lamb and want to be in His book of Life will stand with Him. In Revelation 3:12," He who overcomes I will make a pillar in the temple of my God." Also, "I will write on Him the Name of My God and the name of the city of My God, The New Jerusalem, *which comes down from heaven* from my God."

The devil's demise—Revelation 19:20–21. "And I saw the beast, the kings of the earth and their armies… Then the beast was captured and the false prophet who worked signs by which he *deceived* many."

In these end times, there appears in the Bible a warning. *Do not be deceived.* After much research and listening to and reading interpretations for myself of this cautioning concept, may I relay what I have found?

Jesus Christ first warned His disciples, when they asked when the end would come (the signs). And Jesus answered them and said, "Take heed that no man deceives you, for many will come in my name. (They will declare), 'I am the Christ,' and will deceive many" (Matthew 24:4).

Verse 11: "Many false prophets will rise up and deceive many."

Then in verse 24: "False prophets and false Christ will rise and show great signs and wonders to deceive if possible, even the elect."

Further, just before Christ, our True Christ, comes back to earth, verse 29: "After the tribulation of those days the sun will be darkened, nor the moon give it's light (because the antichrist is here on earth sitting on God's throne). The Sixth Trump. Revelation 13:18. Number 666, the sixth trumpet call, the sixth seal, the sixth vial.

It appears to always be referring to Satan and his many roles. Further, the warning involves the coming of him as the antichrist, son of perdition, the old dragon, the false prophet, and so on. My message to all of you is *don't be ensnared.* The false prophet will set his kingdom up first here on earth. Then our True Christ returns with a shout at the seventh trump.

REGARDING HIS COMING AND THE END

Then in verse 30, then after the first tribulation of the son of perdition, dragon, destroyer is over—our True Christ, the Real Christ, will clean up as He always does. "The Son of Man will appear with a great sound of the trumpet" (the seventh trump) Remember, Jesus's number is 777, and gather His elect (on earth) from one end to the other. The seventh trump is the last one, "the furthermost out."

Did you know that many scholars of scripture could not find anything about rapture until the 1830s? If you're curious, read the story of Margaret MacDonald. The doctrine became published then, and mostly because of her. She had bad dreams. The Bible, on the other hand declares, "The (devil, son of perdition) was cast into the lake of fire" (with his fallen angels, [Jude]). Others to go in the lake of hell with them are the cowardly, unbelieving, the sorcerers (drug dealers), murderers, idolaters, all liars" (Revelation). Plus, Revelation 22 calls these "dogs who will be outside of the city gates." If I recall, the garbage pit was there. These were too carnal to be deceived; the enemy *had them,* perhaps all along. But those of us who cling to the supreme sacrifice in Jesus's name, we are free to fully live life. In his words, author Thomas Dubay wrote:

> Those of us who *stop the world* and listen for that 'still small voice' often begin to sense a thirst to love with abandon, without limit, without end, without lingering after tastes of bitterness." When my world came to a halt... I discovered a better world...a Kingdom... "A King and His Dominion."

WORSHIP SCRIPTURE TO MEDITATE UPON

Psalm 46 is a good one to call for God's help and intervention. God is the Creator of everything good. He stands up for those who are beaten down. The Lord lifts up those who feel helpless. In 2 Corinthians 6, God said, "Let light shine out of darkness. He made His light shine in our hearts."

Remember, the Heart Knower. I came across a place in the Bible where God described Himself and His credentials. Read for yourself, Job 38–42, and get a load of our Father! After ingesting all of it, why would any person not want to be connected to such an awesome Father!

SCRIPTURE VERSES CONT.

Reading God's Word (The Bible) is most important to continue worshipping God.

Do not touch anything that is unclean, or not pure, then I (Your Heavenly Father) will receive you, I will be your Father and you will be my sons and daughters. (2 Corinthians 6:17.

I am the Lord who rules overall. (2 Corinthians 6:18)

So let us make ourselves pure from everything that pollutes our bodies and spirits. (2 Corinthians 7:1)

We have been set free because of what Christ has done. Through His blood, our sins have been forgiven. (Ephesians 1:7)

Do everything without fault-finding or arguing. Then you will be pure and without blame. You will be children of God without fault in a sinful and evil World...

Among people you will shine like stars in the heavens. You will shine as you show them "The Word" of life!" (Philippians 2:14)

Don't worry about anything, instead, tell God about everything. Ask and pray. Give thanks to God. Then God's peace will watch over your hearts and your minds because you belong to Christ. (Philippians 4:6)

Here are the things that you must get rid of. Put away anger, rage, hate, lies, and don't let dirty words come out of your mouth... You have started living a new life, so that what you do know has our Creator's likeness. Forgive the things you are holding against one another, Forgive just as The Lord forgives you. (Colossians 2:3)

FOR FATHERS

"Fathers don't make your children bitter, if you do, they will lose hope. Anyone who does wrong will be paid back for what he does. Vengeance is Mine (God) declares, I will repay" (Colossians 3:21). God treats everyone the same.

SERVING HIM—WORSHIPPING

In Romans 12:1, we are to "offer our bodies to God, while we are still alive." Our bodies are holy sacrifices that are pleasing to God.

I opted to lay down my life as an open book. I pray that you will use my life story to in some way and that you have gotten a tiny nugget of gold from it. If not, then please just use the Bible Scriptures as a reference guide. The Bible is more precious than gold or silver... It is a manuscript of divine love.

THE LORD KEEPS US...

Another one of my favorite verses in the Scriptures is in the book of Isaiah. There, in Isaiah 42:3, the Father speaks of His "Elect One" Son, Jesus, and His gentleness toward us. He reveals that "a bruised reed He will not break, and smoking flax He will not quench."

When the people around us can be cruel and uncaring, "a reed," as we know, grows mostly next to lakes, and they are very thin and frail and can blow as the wind blows. The winds and storms of life can bend completely over a reed (us). But what Jesus means is that He will not let the (reed) or person "break" from too much stress or trouble. He's there to keep us standing up even though we get bent back and forth with life's negativity. He is the sustainer of all life. My personal favorite verse I've gone to many times and prayed—Psalm 27:10. "When my Father and Mother forsaken me, the Lord will take me up," and He has.

WOE TO THE MEN OF GOD

Sadly, I do not think that Father Quinton knew what an honor he possessed being ordained a priest. I do not judge my parents or Father Quinton; God alone is the Judge. In the same vein, I did happen to find a chapter and verse in Jeremiah that is a bit frightening. May I give it to you so you can discern for yourself?

> The prophets (and priests) are leading sinful lives. They don't use their gifts (power) in the right way. Prophets and priests alike are ungodly, even in my temple (Church) I find them sinning, so their path will become slippery. They will be thrown into darkness. There they will fall. (Jeremiah 23:10–12)

> I know the plans I have for you, says the Lord, a plan not to harm you, and hope for years to come. (Jeremiah 29:11)

I took that gladly for my own as I have heard it twenty times. I don't believe it was a coincidence." Daughters" will be included as teachers in the end times.

THE VEIL WAS TORN FOR US

In the Old Testament, the veil or big curtain separated the priest from the people. He would go behind the huge, heavy curtain to offer his sacrifice for his sins first. Then, once he was cleansed, he would stay in there and atone for the congregation of the multitude. In Matthew 27: 1, Mark 15:38, and Luke 23:45, when Jesus was crucified and hung on the cross, not only was there "darkness that covered the land," but there was "an earthquake." The Father's action was to wake up the world even before He resurrected His son. The curtain torn in two signified that our Father was pleased with the Lamb's sacrifice. Come to the Father directly. You don't need a mediator or go between. Come in.

OUR REAL FATHER HAS A GREAT SENSE OF HUMOR...

One of the most important things to me about relationships is when my friends have a "good sense of humor." Something fantastic that I have discovered is that our Father has a terrific sense of humor! Here are just a few examples. These incidences mostly occurred when God was taking on the enemies of His children.

FROM THE OLD TESTAMENT

David (prior to becoming King David) had assistance from God. God decided to keep the Philistines at bay, gave the entire enemy army "emrods"—emrods are hemorrhoids. They couldn't come after David as they had to take care of business first, so in turn, David got away!

In Daniel's life, God took care of the young arrogant king on the throne who was drinking wine out the temple chalices. With his perverted staff, the king was involved in an orgy. So God let this half-drunk evil whippersnapper king, know his days as a kingdom leader were ending that night. God wrote this on the palace wall with nothing but an *appearing hand*. In front of his concubines, the king wet himself.

GOOD LUCK, PAGANS

In the Scripture, another story continues with King Ahab, the king of Israel. He was a rotten king. His famous wife, Jezebel, was far worse! She had to be the most wicked woman there ever was (just read her account in the book of Kings).

Continuing, on this particular day, the children of Israel were gathered with 450 prophets of Baal (he is the god of evil) and many pagan worshippers. In fact, even God's chosen people (the Israelites) had many who worshipped fertility goddesses, gods of fire, gods of prosperity, fish gods, etcetera.

Elijah was taking a stand for God and asked all the people. "How long will you falter between two opinions (two gods)?" Elijah was one man of God. Prophets of Baal totaled over 450! But what happened next was that God told Elijah to "accept" the challenge, which was: Whoever gets their god to light the fire under the bull sacrifice on the altar will (win over) the crowd. In essence, *the winning group's* god will be worshipped.

Thus, Elijah told the prophets of Baal to go ahead and start calling on their gods. So these 450 prophets stomped, yelled, tore their clothes, and cried out to Baal. They blessed him, but this brought no results. Elijah taunts, "Maybe your gods are on a break and cannot hear you, speak louder!" The pagans danced, sang, begged, and even cut themselves. Elijah *had a little fun* taunting the Baal worshippers Where are they? Your gods?! Are they taking a vacation somewhere? Why don't your gods help you? Where are they?

Now God told Elijah to build a trench around his altar and fill four pots full of water. Then God said to pour the water over the bull, the altar, the wood, the ground, and to *fill the ten-foot deep trench with water*, letting it spill over the sides. Then Elijah stepped back and prayed to our Father, privately first.

After night was approaching, at the time of the "evening sacrifice," Elijah boldly *prayed for the entire crowd to hear*, including the opponent side. Elijah then said to God, "Lord, God of Abraham, Isaac, and Israel, let it be known this day that You alone are the God of Israel, and I (Elijah) am your servant, and that all this I have done, I have done at your word. *Turn these people's darkened hearts back to You*. You are the only Lord and God." Then the *fire* of the Lord fell from above and consumed the burnt sacrifice, the wood, stones, dust, coal, and it *licked up* the water that was in the trench!

All the people fell on their faces and declared in one voice, "The Lord, He is God. The Lord, He is God!"

Didn't know that God even competes for His kids, huh?

REWARDS

I am fearfully and wonderfully made.

I am forgiven—victorious.

I bring honor to my God! More than a conqueror-ambassador for God.

I am an example—beloved of God.

I am "light" to others! Joint heir with Christ. Overtaken with blessings more powerful than enemies.

I am God's child. The enemy must not touch me!!—Complete "In Christ," I am grounded in love, strong in faith.

I have Jesus and power over evil! I am able to do all things triumphant in Christ!

He is Risen—King! Those who believe are heirs of royalty.

Time means nothing to God…but to us. We have hurry sickness. Over time, my spiritual outlook has grown as I renew my mind daily with Scripture. When someone offends me now, I can bring the matter to their attention and give them an opportunity to retract it. Usually, if I respond with a loving tone, the situation can return to a peaceful manner. I try to find people who are interested in advancing God's kingdom as well. I no longer base my decisions on what others may think. There will always be naysayers who say, "Where is your God?" "Why aren't you 100 percent yet?" Wholeness takes time. I've broken my sick cycles and codependent ways. As my mind and spirit grow, my body gets healthier too. Our Savior does all these things, we just need to believe, ask, and wait. Many of you may be beginning to believe. Some of you are in the middle of your walk of faith. Then others are where my mom Queenie was…in the *Poltergeist* syndrome.

I can easily grasp onto T.D. Jakes as he states this right now, even though I'm going through my own trials. He also goes on about how going through similar trials we can "reminisce over the many obstacles we had to overcome, look behind, watch, and move beyond our limitations, and leave them in the dust." Sounds good to me, but how about you? You know what? I care. I've been there and am, no matter what, in it for the long haul. No matter what a parent, spouse, friend, or church has done to you… Jesus Christ is our *resolution*.

HEALING TOOLS

As many authors have enlightened me, can I pass the same on to you, women of much worth? As one of the authors so aptly stated, as old memories (hurtful ones) soak in Christ's love, our physical healing usually deepens.

I Don't Get Wholeness, You're All That! and *Move On Move Up* by Paula White

The Emotionally Destructive Relationship by Leslie Vernick

Then I've read several by Joyce Meyer:

   a) *Approval Addiction*
   b) *Beauty for Ashes*
   c) *Secrets to Exceptional Living*
   d) *Never Give Up*

Fool Proofing Your Life by Jan Silvios

Return to Love by Marianne Williams

Next, I highly suggest:

When Love Hurts by Karla Downing

Another biggie for me was:

A Woman's Worth by Marianne Williamson. *A Return to Love* was her first book.

Beth Moore has some too:

Get Out of That Pit, A Woman and Her God and *Breaking Free* (really good). I'm reading *Audacious* now. Her writing is as charismatic as her speaking!

Oh, Paula Sanford really understands hurting women with her fantastic book, *Healing Victims of Sexual Abuse*. In fact, any books by the Sanfords go deep as needed in the scripture foundations for any circumstance. So much can be digested from both this couple's books.

For sexual sins' victims, combining Isaiah with Paula Sanford's thoughts, her *big* prayer is: "Thank you Lord that you love me and have longed to set me free. You grieved for me when I was molested, and you carried my pain and sorrow in your heart all these years. We invite you now, to go to the depths of my heart where the little one has felt so afraid, so unclean, so used and ashamed. Pour in your perfect love to cast out all my fear. Speak to my heart and let me know that you accept me just the way I am, and there is no way I can lose that love. Draw all the pain and shame to yourself and fill my wounds with healing balm." My deeper study in God's Word has revealed the many terms that Jesus used in His Healing Gospels.

Stormie Omartian also is a wonderful example of taking the junk that parents and others fling at us and letting God reconstruct our lives for the good. I feel encouraged after reading Stormie's own account of her life. Wow! I can't imagine being in the presence of devil worship! Talk about being transformed!

Lead Me Holy Spirit, *A Praying Wife*, *A Praying Mom*, and all of her books over the last twenty years are marvelous (like Beth, Joyce, and Leslie, my two Paulas, and many more). These are women warriors, and they are not afraid to let us now about their spotted pasts. I say, "Bravo," to them and so many more that truly care about their brothers and especially their *sisters* lost in this messed up world!

A couple of books that I also recommend are written by Cloud and Townsend. Their books about safe people, personal, and marriage boundaries are very informative and helpful.

Moreover, one of the best books that literally was put in my hand was entitled *With Healing in His Wings*. Douglas Pesonni was a guest speaker at our church one Sunday that Gloria, Jonathan, and I attended. This book is very helpful. It goes into the many ways that divine healing can be postponed. His research made a heavy impact on me because of the concise way that he abundantly spells out "glitches" of healing and wholeness. This makes sense. I personally have applied many of his Biblical principles to my health crisis; as a result of this and other pastors' advice, I am healing. My newest book, *A More Excellent Way to Be in Health*, by Henry W. Wright is my next project.

Most transforming: The King James Bible, of course (author: God), will round out and repair any problems. I go to it first, middle, and last.

So now, just as all these compassionate Christians have helped me, I hope and pray that they will do the same for you, but the last book is a must-read. Our journey together has only just begun once we say yes to Jesus. He has come as light into the world so "we no longer abide in darkness" (John 12:46).

Incomprehensible

The Lord Will Set His People Free
The desert and the dry ground will be
   glad.
The dry places will be full of joy.
Flowers will grow there.
Like the first crocus in the spring,
The desert will bloom with flowers.
It will be very glad and shout with joy.

The glorious beauty of Lebanon will be
    given to it.
It will be as beautiful as the rich lands
of Carmel and Sharon.
Everyone will see the glory of the Lord.
They will see the beauty of our God.
Strengthen the hands of those who are
    weak.
Help those whose knees give way.
Say to those whose hearts are afraid,
"Be strong. Do not fear.
Your God will come.
He will pay your enemies back.
He will come to save you"
Then the eyes of those who are blind will
    be opened
The ears of those who can't hear will be
    unplugged.
Those who can't walk will leap like a deer.
And those who can't speak will shout
    with joy
Water will pour out in dry places.
Streams will flow in the desert.
The burning sand will become a pool of
    water.
The thirsty ground will become bubbling
    springs
In the places where wild dogs once lay
    down,
tall grass and papyrus will grow.
A wide road will go through the land.
It will be called The Way of Holiness.

Only those who are pure and clean can
    travel on it.
Only those who lead a holy life can use it.
Evil and foolish people can't walk on it.
No lions will use it.
No wild animals will be on it.
None of them will be there (no flesh eat-
    ing carnivores).
Only people who have been set free will
    walk on it.
Those the Lord has saved will return to
    their land.
They will sing as they enter the city of
    Zion
Joy that lasts forever will be
Like beautiful crowns on their heads.
They will be filled with gladness and joy.
Sorrow and sighing will be gone.
(Isaiah 35)

ACKNOWLEDGEMENTS

*F*irst and always, I give the highest of thanks to my Heavenly Father. Without Your loving touch, there would be no story—no me. Also, thanks to the Holy Spirit that leads, guides, protects, and steadfastly teaches me all things. I need You. Thank You for never giving up on me.

Aside from all the pastors, authors, and composers of self-help books that I have dedicated a page to previously, here are other family and friends I owe thanks to:

My husband. You always encourage me and say I can do anything I put my mind to. I add "in Christ's name." Thank you. I will hold you in my heart.

You, my children, are the most wonderful blessing that a once forlorn and barren wife could ever dream of. My whole world lights up when you enter a room!

My daughter, I love you with an undying love. You've been right there with typing, challenging me, and editing; you've been with me in some of my most pain-filled and darkest storms. Lean on the Word; it keeps things sane. There is a godly intelligent husband in your destiny and even a baby, perhaps by adoption.

My son, for all that you've already been through in your young life, our Heavenly Godhead has something wonderful planned for you. I'm proud, so proud, of both you and your sister. Most of all, I'm deeply honored you call me Mom.

I'm so happy you have someone to share your dreams with. I think you'll have those four kids to raise. Make sure your children study the Bible.

I also want to thank family and friends from years ago, some gone but nonetheless so special to me.

I want to thank my mom for most of the material for this book. I'll take care of you, Mom. Don't worry.

Dad, oh, Dad. I can't know your pain really, but be good to your son now that you are with him in heaven.

My only brother, my partner in kid crimes; where you are, you are receiving all the love you so much deserve. Save me a seat on the grass at our Savior's feet.

Old friends, Edna A, Gaston, and Janell, you all first opened my eyes to the real Father. May God bless you wherever you've gone. "Lydia," you are my champion, my coach, my dearest friend. I'm forever in your debt for all you let me pour out to you and the caring manner you helped with God to set me free! Rhonda and Juanda, thanks for holding my hand and crying with me and just being with me there at such an incredible moment in my Christian walk. Chris, I'm keeping up with my Spanish. I'll always remember, "Got ez goot," (God is good). Bless you. Jane, I thank you for being such a nice neighbor and a good example to all of us in your Christ-like living. You kept telling me to allow God use my life to help others... I did it! Lisa S., even in your hustle bustle world, you are a shining influence to girls and women. Thank you for encouraging me to "use my life for Christ."

Now to my newer friends. Bless you all for your prayers, support, and help in keeping me on track with this writing project. Shella, your energy, friendship, and encouragement with this story has kept my old Olympia smoking! God is richly blessing all your compassionate good works. Diane, you are so valuable as a person and a true friend to me. When

I needed help with a very difficult mom, you were there. Family projects and jobs around the business, you were there; organizing this lifetime journal and helping put it together, you were there; keeping both of us encouraged and fun loving, you were there; editing with Mary Ellen and myself, you were there; and now, the final correcting and typing, you are there! Diane, I love you to pieces. You are so precious. Life's hills and valleys that we have in common are amazing! The moment at my home when we first sat down to meet, I felt a kindred warm spirit like none other. When I thought this project was so insurmountable and overwhelming and was in dire need of a typist and a shoulder to lean on, you were there, my bud. You are an angel and a friend for life eternal. Debby, I just broke out in a big smile when I wrote your name. God's personality was apparent when He created you. You are one of the most fun loving, hard-working, and big-hearted women at 5'1" I've ever had the pleasure of being around, and I love you. Thank you, Karye, for your honest and careful editing. Pat, thanks so much for prodding me along with my story. I'm sure Father thinks both Shella and you are good and faithful servants who please Him. Father Q., thank you for giving us our childhood at Merryland. My brother and I got a sure taste of heaven here on earth. I pray, wherever you are, that you know I did care about you. I was very confused and sometimes dismayed about just what to think about Mom and you together. On the other hand, separate from her, I'd like to thank you for all the good you did for all of us and the exciting world you opened up for my brother and me. Now you finally know more about the celestial world you always wondered about.

Special thanks to Rhett and Angela with the whole TBN family for adopting me into your hearts.

WORKS CITED

America. *Ventura Highway.*

Anderson, Neil T. *Beginners Guide to Spiritual Warfare.* Ventura, CA: Gospel Light Publishing, 2004.

Anderson, Neil T. *The Bondage Breaker.* Irvine, CA: Harvest House Publishing, 1990.

Avalon. *Faith: A Hymns Collection.*

Avalon. *Another Time Another Place*

Avalon. *Avalon: The Greatest Hits*

Avalon. *Number Ones*

Avalon. *In a Different Light*

Avalon. *Creed*

Baker, Paula-LaPorte, Erica Elliot, John Banta. *Prescription for a Healthy House (Third Edition).* Gabriola Island, BC, Canada: New Society Publishers, 2008.

The Booth Brothers. *The Booth Brothers.*

The Booth Brothers. *The Best of the Booth Brothers.*

The Booth Brothers. *Still.*

Brown, Brené. *Rising Strong.* New York. Spiegel & Graw Publishing, Penguin Random House, 2015.

Christiana, Katia. *"Anyone?"*

Daniel Iverson. *Spirit of the Living God.*

David Phelps. *Freedom.*

Downing, Karla. *When Love Hurts.* Kansas City: Beacon Hill Press, 2004.

Dr. Cloud, Henry and Dr. John Townsend. *Boundaries.* Grand Rapids, MI: Zondervan, 1992.

Dr. Cloud, Henry and Dr. John Townsend. *Safe People.* Grand Rapids, MI: Zondervan Publishing,1995.

Dr. Marcum, James L. *The Ultimate Prescription.* Carol Stream, IL: Tyndale House Publishing, 2010.

Dr. Reginald Cherry. *God's Pathway to Healing, The Doctor and the Word.* Lake Mary, FL: Creation

Duke, Daryl, director. *The Thorn Birds.* Season 1, episode 1-4, 27 Mar. 1983.

Evanescence. *Bring Me to Life.*

Gaither, Gloria. *Homecoming Magazine.*

Gambill, Charlotte. *The Miracle in the Middle.* Nashville, TN: W. Publishing Group, Thomas Nelson, 2015.

Giglio, Louie. *Goliath Must Fall.* Nashville, TN: W. Publishing Group/Thomas Nelson of Harper Collins, 2017.

Grant, Amy. *Behind the Eyes.*

Grant, Amy. *Heart in Motion.*

Grant, Amy. *House of Love.*

Hammerstein, Oscar. "*Cinderella* (1965)."

Hooper, Tobe, director. *Poltergeist.* MGM, 1982.

Hopkins, Stephen, director. *Lost in Space.* New Line Cinema, 1998.

House Publishing, 1996.

Houston, Bobbie. *Sisterhood.* Hodder & Stoughton Ltd, 2017.

Jakes, T.D. *Destiny.* New York, NY; Faith Words, Hachette Grays, 2015.

Jakes, T.D. *Maximize the Moment.* New York: G.P. Putnam's Sons, Penguin Putnam Inc, 1999.

Jewison, Norman, et al. *Agnes of God.* Columbia Pictures, 1985.

Kafka, Franz, Donna Freed (Translator) and Jason Baker (Introduction). *The Metamorphosis and Other Stories.* Barnes & Noble Publishing, 2003.

Kendall, R.T. *The Sensitivity of the Spirit.* Lake Mary, FL: Charisma House, 2002.

Kelly Clarkson. *Stronger* (What Doesn't Kill You).

King James Bible, Giant Print Red Letter Edition. Thomas Nelson Inc, 1992.

London, Jerry, director. *Shogun.* 1980.

Lowry, Mark. *"Mary Did You Know?"*

MacPherson, Dave. *The Rapture Plot.* Muskogee, OK: Artesian Publishing, 2010.

Mankiewicz, Joseph L., director. *Cleopatra.* Twentieth Century-Fox Film Corporation, 1963.

MercyMe. *I Can Only Imagine.*

Meyer, Joyce. *Battlefield of the Mind.* Tulsa, OK: Harrison House Publishing Inc, 1995.

Meyer, Joyce. *Knowing God Intimately.* Waterville, ME: Warner Books Inc. Large Print (Walker), 2003.

Meyer, Joyce. *Never Give Up.* New York, NY: Faith Words, Hachette Book Group, 2008.

Moore, Beth. *Breaking Free.* Nashville, TN: Broodman & Holman Publishing, 2000.

Moore, Beth. *Get Out of That Pit.* Nashville, TN; Integrity Publishing (Thomas Nelson), 2007.

Murray, Andrew. *Indwelling Spirit—the Work of the Holy Spirit in the Life of the Believer.* Baker Publishing Group, 2006.

Murray, Dr. Arnold and Dennis Murray. *"Shepherds' Chapel"* (Television broadcast). Gravette, AR. (Pastors & Teachers of the King James Bible.)

Osteen, Joel, and Victoria Osteen. *Wake up to Hope: Devotional.* Faith Words, 2017.

Pam Tillis. *Cleopatra, Queen of Denial.*

Pat Benatar. *Hit Me with Your Best Shot.*

Pessoni, Douglas H. *With Healing in His Wings.* Pittsburg, PA: Dorrance Publishing, Inc., 2001.

Phillips, Ron. *Everyone's Guide to Demons & Spiritual Warfare.* Lake Mary, FL: Charisma House, 2010.

Poltergeist (1982). Directed by Tobe Hooper. By Steven Spielberg. Performed by JoBeth Williams, Heather O'Rourke, Craig T. Nelson.

Prince, Derek. *God's Word Heals.* New Kingston, PA: Whitaker House, 2010.

Prince, Joseph. *Healing Promises.* Lake Mary, FL: Charisma House Publishing, 2012.

Prince, Joseph. *Live the Let Go Life.* New York, NY: Faith Words Hachette Book Group, 2017.

Robertson, Pat. *The Secret Kingdom.* Dallas, London, Vancouver, Melbourne: Word Publishing, 1992.

Rogers, Adrian. *The Incredible Power of Kingdom Authority.* Nashville, TN: B&H Publishing Group, 2002.

Sanford, Agnes. *Healing Light. Benediction Classics,* 2017.

Sandford, Paula. *Healing Victims of Sexual Abuse.* Lake Mary, FL: Charisma House, 2009.

Sanford, John & Paula. *Healing the Wounded Spirit.* Tulsa OK: Victory House Inc, 1985.

Sanford, John & Paula. *The Transformation of the Inner Man.* Tulsa, OK: Victoria House Inc, 1982.

Sandford, John, et al. *Awakening the Slumbering Spirit.* Charisma House, 2008.

Shoffstall, Veronica A. *"After a While."*

Silvious, Jan. *Fool Proofing Your Life.* Colorado Springs, CO: Water Brook Press, 1998.

Spurgeon, Charles. *Power Over Satan.* New Kensington, PA: Whitaker House Publishing, 1997.

Stanley, Charles. Sermons.

Stanley, Charles. *The Source of My Strength.* Nashville, TN: Harper Collins, Oliver Nelson Books, Thomas Nelson Publishing, 1994-2005.

Stanley, Charles. *When the Enemy Strikes.* Nashville, TN: Thomas Nelson Publishing, 2004.

Stevenson, Robert, director. *That Darn Cat!* Buena Vista Distribution, 1965.

Streisand, Barbra, director. *The Prince of Tides.* Columbia Pictures, 1991.

Strong, James. *The New Strong's Exhaustive Concordance of the Bible.* Nashville, TN: Thomas Nelson Inc., 2010.

Stuart Townend. *In Christ Alone.*

Swift, David, director. *Pollyanna.* Buena Vista Distribution, 1960.

Tenney, Tommy. *The God Chasers.* Thorndike Press, 2004.

Thoreau, David Waldon. *The American Tradition in Literature, Fifth Edition.* Toronto, Canada: 1956-1981.

Townsend, John. *Beyond Boundaries.* Grand Rapids, MI: Zondervan, 2011.

Tozer, A.W. *The Attributes of God (Volume 2).* Camp Hill, PA: Wing Spread Publishers, 2003.

Trinity Network Broadcast. Sermons.

Truman, Karol K. *Feelings Buried Alive Never Die.* Las Vegas, NV: Olympus Distributing, 1991.

Underwood, Carrie. *Jesus Take the Wheel.*

Webster's Concise Collegiate Dictionary. Springfield, MA:. Merriam Webster, 2001.

White, Paula. *You're All That.* New York, NY: Faith Words Publishing, Hachette Book Group, 2007.

The World Book Encyclopedia, Volume 3.

Wright, Henry W. *A More Excellent Way Be In Health Pathways of Wholeness Spiritual Roots of Disease.* Henry W. Wright, 2008.

Youssef, Michael. *"Freedom from Bondage." Leading The Way with Dr. Michael Yourself,* www.ltw.org/watch/teaching/freedom-from-bondage.

Zschech, Darlene. *Shout to the Lord.*

Zschech, Darlene. *Shout to the Lord 2.*

Zschech, Darlene. *Here I Am, Send Me.*

P.S. If I did not give anyone the proper credit, please pardon me.

About Microwave, Electric and Magnetic Dangers

Blank, Martin. *Overpowered.* New York, NY: Seven Stories Press, 2014.

Evans, Jerry. *Chemical and Electrical Hypersensitivity.* North Carolina: MacFarland & Co. Publishing, 2010.

Fisher, Donna. *Dirty Electricity and Electromagnetic Radiation.* Queensland, Australia: Joshua Books, 2011.

Gittleman, Ann Louise. *Zapped.* New York, NY: Harper Collins Publishing, 2010.

Sturdivant, Beth. *Backyard Secret Exposed.* Pineville, NC: ONENAMILLION LLC Publishing, 2013.

CPSIA information can be obtained
at www.ICGtesting.com
Printed in the USA
LVHW080105180120
643924LV00003B/4